PARLAY YOUR **IRA** INTO A FAMILY FORTUNE

PARLAY YOUR IRA INTO A FAMILY FORTUNE

3 Easy Steps for Creating a Lifetime Supply of Tax-Deferred, Even Tax-Free, Wealth for You and Your Family

ED SLOTT

VIKING

VIKING

Published by the Penguin Group
Penguin Group (USA) Inc., 375 Hudson Street,
New York, New York 10014, U.S.A.
Penguin Group (Canada), 10 Alcorn Avenue,
Toronto, Ontario, Canada M4V 3B2
(a division of Pearson Penguin Canada Inc.)
Penguin Books Ltd, 80 Strand, London WC2R 0RL, England
Penguin Ireland, 25 St. Stephen's Green, Dublin 2, Ireland
(a division of Penguin Books Ltd)
Penguin Books Australia Ltd, 250 Camberwell Road, Camberwell,
Victoria 3124, Australia
(a division of Pearson Australia Group Pty Ltd)
Penguin Books India Pvt Ltd, 11 Community Centre, Panchsheel Park,
New Delhi – 110 017, India
Penguin Group (NZ), Cnr Airborne and Rosedale Roads, Albany,
Auckland 1310, New Zealand
(a division of Pearson New Zealand Ltd)
Penguin Books (South Africa) (Pty) Ltd, 24 Sturdee Avenue,
Rosebank, Johannesburg 2196, South Africa

Penguin Books Ltd, Registered Offices: 80 Strand, London WC2R 0RL, England

First published in 2005 by Viking Penguin, a member of Penguin Group (USA) Inc.

10   9   8   7   6   5   4   3   2   1

Publisher's Note: This publication is designed to provide accurate and authoritative information in regard to the subject matter covered. It is sold with the understanding that the publisher is not engaged in rendering legal, accounting or other professional services. If you require legal advice or the other expert assistance, you should seek the services of a competent professional.

LIBRARY OF CONGRESS CATALOGING IN PUBLICATION DATA

Slott, Ed.
Parlay your IRA into a family fortune: 3 easy steps for creating a lifetime supply of tax-deferred, even tax-free, wealth for you and your family / Ed Slott.
    p.   cm.
ISBN 0-670-03396-0
1. Slott, Ed.   2. Individual retirement accounts—United States.   3. Retirement income—United States.   4. Estate planning—United States.   5. Tax planning—United States.
HG1660.U5 S56 2005
332.024'0145'0973—dc22   2004043121

This book is printed on acid-free paper. ∞

Printed in the United States of America   Set in Sabon

*To my wife, Linda, my children, Ilana, Rachel, and Jennifer,
and our granddaughter, Victoria*

CONTENTS

Appendices

What Comes After a Trillion?[1]

"If Willy Sutton were alive today, he wouldn't be very interested in banks—because that's not where the money is. To be specific, Willy would find about $4.5 trillion in total deposits at U.S. depository institutions, according to the Federal Reserve. But far greater assets are accumulating in retirement plans, where Americans now hold an estimated $11 trillion of wealth. For frame of reference, that's about $2 trillion more than the total market value of all publicly traded U.S. stocks."

—Judy Diamond, *Journal of Financial Service Professionals,*
    July 2003

The Perfect Storm

This book is based on one simple, but powerful, premise: The longer your IRA is sheltered from taxes, the more it will grow in accumulated wealth. The key to sustaining that shelter and achieving such growth is to milk the tax laws for all they are worth!

IRA exposure to taxation is unavoidable. The tax rules generally require that sheltered retirement money begin to leave its nest when the owner turns 70½ or dies, whichever comes first. It is when IRAs are exposed to taxes during a period of transition, such as inheritance, that they become vulnerable to the most complex tax rules known (or *unknown*) to man.

---

[1] By the way, it's a "quadrillion," but even Bill Gates hasn't gotten there yet.

Since exposing IRAs (including Roth IRAs) to taxation at inheritance time cannot be avoided, it is critical for IRA owners to plan for that eventuality. It is equally important that those who will be inheriting IRAs know what to do when the time arrives. If not, the consequences could be disastrous.

On the flip side, it is also when IRAs are in transition during inheritance that the opportunity presents itself to parlay them into a fortune! I call this combination of risk and opportunity the "perfect storm," because either way the result can be a potential windfall. The question is: For whom—you, your family, or Uncle Sam?

Uncle Sam really doesn't have to do anything to cash in—except hope that you make a mistake setting up your IRA so that the opportunity for your beneficiaries to keep it growing will be lost. Of course, even if you make no mistakes, the government still gets a second bite at the apple when your beneficiaries actually inherit—if they expose the IRA to taxes, they will sacrifice the option for continued growth. On top of all this, the taxman gets a third swipe at your IRA—because even if *you* make no mistakes and your beneficiaries do everything as instructed, a slipup on the part of your financial advisor, or the financial institution (bank, broker, mutual fund company) holding your IRA, can kill the chance to grow the account into a fortune by making the IRS your biggest beneficiary. Slipups of this magnitude by financial advisors and financial institutions are not only quite common, but widespread.

These are the land mines that must be successfully sidestepped so as not to trigger an explosion of taxation that costs you and your family the opportunity to parlay your retirement nest egg, no matter how small, into an obscene amount of cash over time.

IRAs in Transition

Over the next decade, the greatest transfer of wealth in American history will take place—to the tune of approximately *$11 trillion* in *current* retirement savings! By the year 2013, most of the surviving members of the World War II generation (approximately

40 million aging Americans) will have passed into history, and that generation's accumulated life savings in IRAs and other retirement accounts will have passed to their children, the baby boomers (approximately 77.6 million Americans, according to the U.S. Census Bureau). Meanwhile, the number of baby boomers now retiring will swell to record numbers, all of them faced not only with managing the transition of their parents' IRAs to themselves, but also with setting up their own IRAs for transition to their children.

It is critical that you, your heirs, and the financial advisor handling your affairs start preparing for the perfect storm *now.* Whether you are married, single, or an unmarried domestic partner, this seismic event presents a chance to build a lifetime supply of tax-deferred, in some cases even tax-free, wealth for you and your family. Or risk losing that chance—perhaps for a generation.

No Weak Links

If you read my earlier book *The Retirement Savings Time Bomb . . . and How to Defuse It,* you've got a leg up, because you already know the moves necessary to keep your nest egg from being gobbled up by the confiscatory taxes levied on retirement accounts when you start taking money out to live on.

Now you are ready for the slam dunk—to parlay what you've protected into a fortune. So there are no weak links in the chain, several key elements must be addressed to achieve this slam dunk:

1. What you can do now to parlay your IRA into a windfall during your lifetime.
2. What you must do now to ensure that your beneficiary—spouse, domestic partner, or child—has all the options available for growing your IRA into an even greater fortune after you're gone.
3. What your beneficiary (or beneficiaries) must do at the time of inheritance to be able to take full advantage of these options.

4. How to pick a financial advisor who is an IRA *expert* to help you and your beneficiaries make all the right decisions.

How to Use This Book

Sidestepping just one or two land mines won't do. You need to hurdle *all of them*. That's why this book is divided into three parts, each devoted to what you must do to avoid that particular land mine. Under our current tax laws, an IRA can be turned into a windfall that will take care of you and your family for generations. This book shows you how.

My strategy for sidestepping all three land mines has evolved from more than 20 years of experience as a CPA consulting with clients on estate and tax planning, preparing tax returns, as well as being a keynote speaker, teacher, and coach to consumers and professional financial advisors. It shows you and/or your heirs how to:

- Convert your traditional IRA (or other plan) to a Roth IRA now, and achieve unlimited tax-free income when you retire.
- Name a beneficiary who can make the most of your retirement savings after you're gone.
- Pass more assets on to loved ones and other beneficiaries.
- Keep retirement assets in the family for decades, even generations, with minimal or no taxes.
- Expand your knowledge of passing on and inheriting retirement accounts—the largest single asset most people have—and make better, more cost-efficient use of financial advisors.
- Take advantage of the latest tax laws and inherited IRA rule changes.
- Integrate your IRA with your overall estate plan to create the ideal estate plan for you and your family.
- Avoid obscure tax traps if you inherit an IRA or other retirement account.
- Protect your retirement account from creditors, divorce, bankruptcy, lawsuits, or other problems that could expose it to loss.

- Keep track of key beneficiary and other vital instruction material.
- Keep track of key IRA deadlines (missing them could be devastating).
- Use a Roth IRA to build a tax-free fortune for your family.
- See that beneficiaries do not miss out on special tax benefits, deductions, and tax elections they may not know about (because their financial advisors don't know about them either).
- Evaluate whether an IRA trust is right for you and your family.
- Use IRA trusts to protect and grow savings for your family.
- Take advantage of the separate account rules governing IRAs when there are several beneficiaries, so that each one can independently parlay his or her share into a fortune.
- Set up your retirement account so that it allows your beneficiaries the greatest flexibility in seizing advantage of every possible post-death option available.
- And much more.

Assets for a Lifetime

This is a comprehensive, winning strategy for taking advantage of existing tax laws to parlay your IRA or other retirement account assets into a potentially tax-free fortune. No matter how large or small the account, no matter whether you are married, single, or among the millions of today's unmarried domestic partners, this goal is attainable.

If you have worked long and hard all your life to build a nest egg and want to see it keep going and growing, this is the plan for you. It's time to knock the ball out of the park—with a home run that takes care of you, your loved ones, and their loved ones *for generations*!

PART ONE

KEEP IT TOGETHER

Dear Ed,
I am age 73, have several IRAs, am currently taking minimum distri-
bution, and have my beneficiaries listed to receive equal shares, which
I do not think is the right thing to do. Or is it? The ages of my bene-
ficiaries are 78, 51, 49, and 42. I need some guidance as to what
would be the right way to go.
   —IRA owner

ONE

The Ninth Wonder of the World

The Devil Is in the Details

Bill and his two siblings had inherited a $270,000 IRA from their mother, a widow when she died in 2002. Their mom had bequeathed to them equal shares of her account. Bill informed the financial institution holding the account that he and his brother and sister wanted the proceeds split three ways so that each could manage his or her own share of the inherited IRA. This is normal, since most adult beneficiaries (Bill and his siblings were in their 30s) usually don't want the others knowing how they are investing or spending their share of the inheritance.

The advisor at the financial institution then cut three checks, one for each sibling, for $90,000 apiece. Simple as pie! Right?

Wrong!

Early in 2003, Bill went to have his 2002 taxes prepared and was told by his accountant that he owed tax on his $90,000 inheritance—*$30,000 in tax*, as a matter of fact!

Bill went into shock.

When he saw me quoted in a recent *Wall Street Journal* article on inheriting IRAs, he called me out of desperation, even though we didn't know each other from Adam. He related his woeful tale and asked if his accountant was right. Did he really owe $30,000 in tax? I told him yes.

"But it's worse than that," I added. He owed not only $30,000 in tax on the $90,000 inheritance, but also state tax on it, plus tax on all his regular income (wages, interest, etc.). The $90,000 he'd taken had pushed him into a higher tax bracket, which resulted in *all* of his income being taxed at a higher rate than it otherwise would have been. Furthermore, due to his increased income, he lost out on many tax benefits that he would have qualified for, such as the child tax credit, medical deductions, and work-related tax deductions. Bill's siblings were in the same boat.

Through weak links along the entire chain—their mom's not having set the IRA up correctly, their lack of awareness as beneficiaries as to how to inherit the account properly, and the professional ignorance of the financial advisor in managing the transition of the IRA—most of what their mom had worked for was wiped out instead of having a chance to blossom.

Now Bill was experiencing awe *and* shock. He asked, "Is there anything that can be done to correct this?"

"No," was my answer.

"Couldn't I get the financial institution to put the money back in Mom's IRA and start over the right way?"

Again my answer was no. Our tax laws do not allow that. Our tax laws are rigid, unforgiving, and draconian in this area. Once a mistake is made, it is often irreversible. In Bill's case, all the money was removed; therefore all of it was taxable in the year it was moved, and it could not be returned. The opportunity to parlay the inheritance into a fortune was lost to Bill and his siblings for all time. Game. Set. Match.[2]

---

[2]Bill's wife, Jennifer, a litigation attorney, asked me to run the numbers and see how much Bill and his siblings might eventually have been able to withdraw from the inherited $270,000 IRA had they known to take maximum advantage of the option for growing that money over each of their lives. Even at a modest rate of interest, the figure came to just over $2 million! As an addendum to this story, Bill and his siblings are suing the financial institution for that amount for giving them such bad advice. But I wouldn't hold my breath.

Astounding Growth Through Long-Term Compounding

With the blessing of the IRS (but don't expect any government press releases coming out and saying so anytime soon), a *scenario can be created where the value of any inherited IRA can grow into a fortune.* The reason most people don't create this scenario for themselves and their families is simple: *They don't know about it.*

Why not? The answer to that is simple too: The tax rules are so abstruse that many financial advisors and the institutions they represent who deal with retirement accounts don't know about it either—or shrink from offering any kind of tax advice.

If I were passing on an IRA to someone, I would want to know that I could choose that the money I had worked so long and hard for would go intact to my family, who could then parlay it into a fortune, instead of its being lost to taxes that might otherwise be avoided.

One would assume that most estate planners (as well as books on estate planning) address this issue. But they don't. Yes, they cover how to inherit a house, stocks, insurance, and so on, because these are *easy* to inherit. These types of assets are not loaded with their own set of obscure tax rules.

For example, there is no law that says that when you inherit a house, the first year you can take possession of the kitchen, the second year you can take possession of the bathroom, then the third year you can take possession of the roof, then the den, and so on. Then every time you take possession of one of these items, you must pay income tax and become subject to an entire set of separate tax rules that, if not followed correctly, could lead to stiff fines rather than growth and income. If the IRA rules applied to other property like your house, for example, then after your death Uncle Sam could end up moving in, since he would already own most of the home anyway. Maybe your kids could rent the basement.

Inherited IRAs *are* subject to such complex tax rules. And while those rules can work against you if you do things wrong, *they can also work to your benefit if you do things right—and make your family rich!* And the best part is, you don't have to start out with an IRA worth a fortune in order to achieve that goal. How so? Through the magic of the Ninth Wonder of the World—the phenomenon I call "compound interest on steroids," otherwise known as the "stretch IRA." Here's how it works.

If your beneficiary inherits a $100,000 IRA from you, the value of that IRA depends on how long it stays in the hands of your beneficiary and is protected from taxation. If it is taxed immediately after your death, the IRA will have little value to your beneficiary. But if your IRA is set up properly and your beneficiary handles this inherited IRA properly, it can be worth a fortune over his or her lifetime.

The tax rules allow any person you designate as your IRA beneficiary to stretch (extend the required distributions) that IRA over his or her lifetime. The term "designated beneficiary" for tax purposes means that you have named a *person* (as opposed to an estate, a trust, or a charity, for example) as heir to your IRA. This is like bestowing royalty upon someone, because an inherited IRA can *only be stretched* over the lifetime of your *designated* beneficiary, whom you name as such on an IRA beneficiary form (see Chapter Five).

There can be only one designated beneficiary to an IRA. So, if you have multiple IRAs, you need to designate a beneficiary for each of them to gain the stretch for all the accounts. If you have one IRA but multiple heirs (three kids, for example), you can split the IRA among your children (or they can split it among themselves after you're gone) so that each child can claim the title of designated beneficiary on his or her separate share of the inherited IRA and can thus stretch that share out over a long period of time. (For more on splitting IRAs, see Chapter Six.)

The stretch is based on the projected life expectancy of your designated beneficiary (or designated beneficiaries in the case of multiple IRAs) according to his or her age the year after you die. The younger the named beneficiary is, the longer the stretch. The IRS Single Life Expectancy table (see Table 1) is used to determine that period of time.

Table 1. Single Life Expectancy (for Inherited IRAs)
To be used for calculating post-death required
distributions to beneficiaries
(From the April 2002 Final Regulations)

Age of IRA or Plan Beneficiary	Life Expectancy (in years)	Age of IRA or Plan Beneficiary	Life Expectancy (in years)	Age of IRA or Plan Beneficiary	Life Expectancy (in years)
0	82.4				
1	81.6	41	42.7	81	9.7
2	80.6	42	41.7	82	9.1
3	79.7	43	40.7	83	8.6
4	78.7	44	39.8	84	8.1
5	77.7	45	38.8	85	7.6
6	76.7	46	37.9	86	7.1
7	75.8	47	37.0	87	6.7
8	74.8	48	36.0	88	6.3
9	73.8	49	35.1	89	5.9
10	72.8	50	34.2	90	5.5
11	71.8	51	33.3	91	5.2
12	70.8	52	32.3	92	4.9
13	69.9	53	31.4	93	4.6
14	68.9	54	30.5	94	4.3
15	67.9	55	29.6	95	4.1
16	66.9	56	28.7	96	3.8
17	66.0	57	27.9	97	3.6
18	65.0	58	27.0	98	3.4
19	64.0	59	26.1	99	3.1
20	63.0	60	25.2	100	2.9
21	62.1	61	24.4	101	2.7
22	61.1	62	23.5	102	2.5
23	60.1	63	22.7	103	2.3
24	59.1	64	21.8	104	2.1

Table 1. Single Life Expectancy (for Inherited IRAs) *(continued)*

Age of IRA or Plan Beneficiary	Life Expectancy (in years)	Age of IRA or Plan Beneficiary	Life Expectancy (in years)	Age of IRA or Plan Beneficiary	Life Expectancy (in years)
25	58.2	65	21.0	105	1.9
26	57.2	66	20.2	106	1.7
27	56.2	67	19.4	107	1.5
28	55.3	68	18.6	108	1.4
29	54.3	69	17.8	109	1.2
30	53.3	70	17.0	110	1.1
31	52.4	71	16.3	111+	1.0
32	51.4	72	15.5		
33	50.4	73	14.8		
34	49.4	74	14.1		
35	48.5	75	13.4		
36	47.5	76	12.7		
37	46.5	77	12.1		
38	45.6	78	11.4		
39	44.6	79	10.8		
40	43.6	80	10.2		

For example, if at your death your designated beneficiary is your 29-year-old daughter, she can stretch the inherited IRA over a projected life expectancy of 53.3 years, according to the Single Life Expectancy table. If you died in 2004 when she is age 29, she would then use her age in 2005 (age 30) to calculate her first required minimum distribution for that year.

She needs to use the life expectancy table only once. For each succeeding year, she just subtracts one year from the life expectancy figure. In this example, the required distribution for 2006 (her second distribution year) would be calculated using a 52.3-year life expectancy (53.3 years less 1 year = 52.3 years). For the third year the life expectancy would be 51.3 years, then 50.3 years, 49.3 years, and so on until the original 53.3-year term has expired, unless she completely withdraws the IRA before that time. She can always withdraw more than the required amount.

If she dies before the 53.3-year term has expired and there is still a balance in the IRA, then *her* beneficiary can continue to stretch the remaining years left on the original 53.3-year schedule. That's why it is so important for every beneficiary to name a successor beneficiary of his or her own as soon as he or she inherits so there will be someone named to keep the stretch going on schedule if the original beneficiary dies prematurely. (This will help to avoid probate and other will-related problems that might also endanger the stretch—see Chapter Two.) There will be more on naming successor beneficiaries in Part Two.

FAQ

Q. Ed, if I have no designated beneficiary, does this mean no one will inherit my IRA?

A. Someone will get it, and it may even be the person you would have wanted. It also may not be. Either way, the huge benefit of the stretch IRA is lost, and it cannot be reclaimed after you're gone.

The Power of the Stretch—Victoria's Millions

Let's see in real numbers what happens if we were to milk a stretch IRA for all it's worth. The power of the stretch IRA lies in its compounding over time. Therefore, the younger your IRA beneficiary, the longer the life expectancy, thus the longer he or she can spread out required withdrawals and compound the IRA in value. So, let's use a 1-year-old as an example. I'll call her Victoria.

Born in 2003, Victoria is named beneficiary of her grandfather's

IRA when he passes on later in 2003. Victoria's life expectancy begins at age 1, the year after her grandfather's death. According to IRS projections based on actuarial figures drawn from the Single Life Expectancy table for inherited IRAs (Table 1), the life expectancy of a 1-year-old is 81.6 years. That is her stretch period.

Let's say the December 31, 2003, value of the IRA Victoria inherits from her grandfather is $100,000. Based on her life expectancy of 81.6 years, Victoria is required to withdraw only $1,225 ($100,000 divided by 81.6 years = $1,225, or 1.225 percent) from the IRA in 2004. The balance can keep growing tax-deferred. Because her life expectancy factor will drop by one each year, in 2005 she will have to withdraw based on 80.6 years (divide the balance by 80.6 years), then by 79.6 years in 2006, 78.6 years in 2007, 77.6 years in 2008, and so on down the line. Therefore, by taking only the required minimum distribution each year, Victoria will not have to empty the account until she is 82 years old. If we assume an average growth rate of 8 percent over her life expectancy of 81.6 years, by the time she has to empty the account, that $100,000 IRA she inherited from her grandfather would have paid her an astonishing $8,167,629 (see Table 2)!

Table 2. Victoria's Millions
Watch 1-year-old Victoria's inherited IRA grow at an interest rate of just 8 percent!

Year	IRA Beneficiary's Age	Value of IRA	IRA Beneficiary's Life Expectancy Factor (in years)	IRA Required Minimum Distributions (RMDs)	Cumulative IRA Distributions
2004	1	$100,000	81.6	$1,225	$1,225
2005	2	$106,677	80.6	$1,324	$2,549
2006	3	$113,781	79.6	$1,429	$3,978

Table 2. Victoria's Millions *(continued)*

Year	IRA Beneficiary's Age	Value of IRA	IRA Beneficiary's Life Expectancy Factor (in years)	IRA Required Minimum Distributions (RMDs)	Cumulative IRA Distributions
2007	4	$121,340	78.6	$1,544	$5,522
2008	5	$129,380	77.6	$1,667	$7,189
2009	6	$137,930	76.6	$1,801	$8,990
2010	7	$147,019	75.6	$1,945	$10,935
2011	8	$156,680	74.6	$2,100	$13,035
2012	9	$166,946	73.6	$2,268	$15,303
2013	10	$177,852	72.6	$2,450	$17,753
2014	11	$189,434	71.6	$2,646	$20,399
2015	12	$201,731	70.6	$2,857	$23,256
2016	13	$214,784	69.6	$3,086	$26,342
2017	14	$228,634	68.6	$3,333	$29,675
2018	15	$243,325	67.6	$3,599	$33,274
2019	16	$258,904	66.6	$3,887	$37,161
2020	17	$275,418	65.6	$4,198	$41,359
2021	18	$292,918	64.6	$4,534	$45,893
2022	19	$311,455	63.6	$4,897	$50,790
2023	20	$331,083	62.6	$5,289	$56,079
2024	21	$351,858	61.6	$5,712	$61,791
2025	22	$373,838	60.6	$6,169	$67,960
2026	23	$397,083	59.6	$6,662	$74,622
2027	24	$421,655	58.6	$7,195	$81,817
2028	25	$447,617	57.6	$7,771	$89,588
2029	26	$475,034	56.6	$8,393	$97,981
2030	27	$503,972	55.6	$9,064	$107,045
2031	28	$534,501	54.6	$9,789	$116,834
2032	29	$566,689	53.6	$10,573	$127,407

Table 2. Victoria's Millions *(continued)*

Year	IRA Beneficiary's Age	Value of IRA	IRA Beneficiary's Life Expectancy Factor (in years)	IRA Required Minimum Distributions (RMDs)	Cumulative IRA Distributions
2033	30	$600,605	52.6	$11,418	$138,825
2034	31	$636,322	51.6	$12,332	$151,157
2035	32	$673,909	50.6	$13,318	$164,475
2036	33	$713,438	49.6	$14,384	$178,859
2037	34	$754,978	48.6	$15,535	$194,394
2038	35	$798,598	47.6	$16,777	$211,171
2039	36	$844,367	46.6	$18,119	$229,290
2040	37	$892,348	45.6	$19,569	$248,859
2041	38	$942,601	44.6	$21,135	$269,994
2042	39	$995,183	43.6	$22,825	$292,819
2043	40	$1,050,147	42.6	$24,651	$317,470
2044	41	$1,107,536	41.6	$26,623	$344,093
2045	42	$1,167,386	40.6	$28,753	$372,846
2046	43	$1,229,724	39.6	$31,054	$403,900
2047	44	$1,294,564	38.6	$33,538	$437,438
2048	45	$1,361,908	37.6	$36,221	$473,659
2049	46	$1,431,742	36.6	$39,119	$512,778
2050	47	$1,504,033	35.6	$42,248	$555,026
2051	48	$1,578,728	34.6	$45,628	$600,654
2052	49	$1,655,748	33.6	$49,278	$649,932
2053	50	$1,734,988	32.6	$53,220	$703,152
2054	51	$1,816,309	31.6	$57,478	$760,630
2055	52	$1,899,537	30.6	$62,076	$822,706
2056	53	$1,984,458	29.6	$67,043	$889,749
2057	54	$2,070,808	28.6	$72,406	$962,155
2058	55	$2,158,274	27.6	$78,198	$1,040,353
2059	56	$2,246,482	26.6	$84,454	$1,124,807

Table 2. Victoria's Millions *(continued)*

Year	IRA Beneficiary's Age	Value of IRA	IRA Beneficiary's Life Expectancy Factor (in years)	IRA Required Minimum Distributions (RMDs)	Cumulative IRA Distributions
2060	57	$2,334,990	25.6	$91,211	$1,216,018
2061	58	$2,423,281	24.6	$98,507	$1,314,525
2062	59	$2,510,756	23.6	$106,388	$1,420,913
2063	60	$2,596,717	22.6	$114,899	$1,535,812
2064	61	$2,680,363	21.6	$124,091	$1,659,903
2065	62	$2,760,774	20.6	$134,018	$1,793,921
2066	63	$2,836,896	19.6	$144,740	$1,938,661
2067	64	$2,907,528	18.6	$156,319	$2,094,980
2068	65	$2,971,306	17.6	$168,824	$2,263,804
2069	66	$3,026,681	16.6	$182,330	$2,446,134
2070	67	$3,071,899	15.6	$196,917	$2,643,051
2071	68	$3,104,981	14.6	$212,670	$2,855,721
2072	69	$3,123,696	13.6	$229,684	$3,085,405
2073	70	$3,125,533	12.6	$248,058	$3,333,463
2074	71	$3,107,673	11.6	$267,903	$3,601,366
2075	72	$3,066,952	10.6	$289,335	$3,890,701
2076	73	$2,999,826	9.6	$312,482	$4,203,183
2077	74	$2,902,332	8.6	$337,480	$4,540,663
2078	75	$2,770,040	7.6	$364,479	$4,905,142
2079	76	$2,598,006	6.6	$393,637	$5,298,779
2080	77	$2,380,719	5.6	$425,128	$5,723,907
2081	78	$2,112,038	4.6	$459,139	$6,183,046
2082	79	$1,785,131	3.6	$495,870	$6,678,916
2083	80	$1,392,402	2.6	$535,539	$7,214,455
2084	81	$925,412	1.6	$578,383	$7,792,838
2085	82	$374,791	0.6	$374,791	$8,167,629
2086	83	$0	0.0	$0	$8,167,629
Totals					**$8,167,629**

Many people have IRAs worth more than $100,000 when they pass on, so I can hear what you are thinking: "If little Victoria could parlay her $100,000 IRA into $8 million what could my family do with my $200,000 (or $250,000) IRA?"

Here's how it works, based on the bottom-line even figure of $100,000 I originally used. For a $200,000 IRA, simply multiply the $8,167,629 result by 2. For a $250,000 IRA, multiply the result by 2.5.

For example, if 1-year-old Victoria had inherited a $250,000 IRA from her grandfather in 2004, she would withdraw a total of $20,419,073 over her lifetime. How did I get that? $8,167,629 by 2.5 = $20,419,073. Think of it. If 1-year-old Victoria had inherited a $1 million IRA from her grandfather, she would receive an astounding $81,676,290 over her lifetime.

These are amazing numbers, which may not sound realistic to you, but consider this fact: *The amount little Victoria begins with in each example is very realistic, because it is not unusual for people these days to have accumulated $100,000 or much more in their IRA nest eggs.* By stretching withdrawals, a huge pile of cash is fully attainable for anyone with an IRA, even a modest one (see Table 3).

Table 3.

If you began with:	Then your 1-year-old beneficiary would end up with:
$3,000	$245,029
$4,000	$326,704
$10,000	$816,762
$20,000	$1,633,524
$30,000	$2,450,286
$40,000	$3,267,048
$50,000	$4,083,810

If you began with:	Then your 1-year-old beneficiary would end up with:
$60,000	$4,900,572
$70,000	$5,717,334
$80,000	$6,534,096
$90,000	$7,350,858
$100,000	$8,167,629
$200,000	$16,335,258
$250,000	$20,419,073
$300,000	$24,502,887
$400,000	$32,670,516
$500,000	$40,838,145
$1,000,000	$81,676,290
$1,500,000	$122,514,435

This is why the stretch IRA concept truly is the Ninth Wonder of the World.

The Heck with My Kids—
I Want to Enjoy the Money Myself!

"Ed, this is a great strategy you've come up with for turning my heirs into potential millionaires on my retirement money, but I want to eat filet mignon and lots and lots of carbs in the time I have left on this planet (my beneficiaries can eat cat food for all I care). What do I do now to parlay my IRA for me to enjoy?"

The starting figure I use in all my examples of what your family can parlay your IRA into when they inherit is *what's left over* in your IRA after you've gone to your great reward having had a high old time in your retirement. (Virtually everyone leaves some amount over. I think it may be in our genes not to deplete every last nickel.)

Of course I have taken your own retirement fund growth and spending into account. It's not your job to make your beneficiaries rich. Start with yourself.

But imagine a tax-free retirement for yourself *on top of* leaving a tax-free inheritance that pays tax-free money to your beneficiaries every month for the rest of their lives. It doesn't get better than that. You can achieve these goals if you begin now by parlaying your IRA first on your own behalf—and you don't have to start with much at all to reach some pretty amazing results.

If your main concern is your own retirement needs, then it makes even more sense to grow your IRA for as long as possible before it is absolutely needed and, when that day comes, to take only the minimum amounts that you must under the regular required minimum distribution (RMD) rules. This will leave more for you.

The best way to parlay your IRA for yourself first is to convert to a Roth IRA as soon as you qualify. Here's why:

With a Roth IRA, unlike a traditional IRA, you pay the tax up front when you contribute or convert to it, not at the back end when you start taking distributions. Why does this matter? Because after you pay the tax up front, you never pay it again; your money in the Roth keeps growing tax-free *forever*, and that's what boosts your exponential return over time.

To use a farm analogy, it's like paying tax on the seed so the crop can grow free. Remember our mantra: The longer you keep your IRA sheltered from taxes, the more money your family will accumulate. Well, that goes for you too. Don't buy into the argument that tax-deferred is always better than tax-free. YOU SIMPLY CANNOT BEAT A ZERO PERCENT TAX RATE ON IRA WITHDRAWALS! The Roth IRA is the way to get Uncle Sam out of your wealth-building potential *permanently*!

FAQ

Q. Ed, will the Roth IRA always be tax-free?

A. The only things sure are death and taxes (on a tax-deferred IRA), but personally I think the Roth IRA will keep its income-tax-free status for our lifetime, because our tax policy seems to be moving in that direction—that is to say, letting people who save for retirement with after-tax dollars keep those dollars growing tax-free for themselves and their families. The looming Social Security shortfall (if there really is one) is another reason our government is leaning toward offering programs like the Roth IRA, where if you want to take personal responsibility for your own retirement, the tax laws will provide an incentive—tax-free growth—to encourage you to save so that the government won't have to foot the bill for your retirement with money it may not have. I also believe that if Congress ever changes this and says Roth IRAs are taxable, it will grandfather in anyone already in the program, so it will still pay now to convert your IRA to a Roth to increase the long-term benefits of the stretch.

There are two ways to get money into a Roth IRA. One is by making annual contributions up to the amount limited by law (see Table 4) and the other is by conversions where you convert any part or all of your Traditional IRA to a Roth IRA. There is no limit to the amount you can convert to a Roth IRA once you qualify.

Roth IRA Contributions

All you have to do to be able to contribute to a Roth IRA is to have earned income from a job or self-employment. You can contribute to a Roth even if you are active in a company plan at work. Unlike a traditional IRA, this will not affect your Roth IRA contributing because Roth IRA contributions are not deductible. Age does not matter either. No matter how old you are, if you have earned income, and your income does not exceed certain limits (covered later on here), you are eligible to contribute to a Roth IRA. New opportunities to contribute greater amounts to your Roth IRA through increased annual contribution limits are available for you to take advantage of. Some of you can also make catch-up contributions. The maximum annual contribution to a Roth IRA is increasing gradually (see Table 4). For example, if you are age 50 or over by the end of 2005 and you earn at least $4,500, you can contribute up to $4,500 to your Roth IRA ($4,000 regular contribution plus the extra $500 catch-up contribution). So age and plan participation have no effect on your Roth IRA eligibility.

Table 4. Roth IRA Contributions

Roth IRA contributions can be made up to April 15 of the following year (for example, for a 2005 Roth IRA contribution, you have until April 15, 2006). There is no extension beyond that date, regardless of whether an extension is filed.

Year	Maximum Contribution	Additional Contribution (for those who turn age 50 by year-end)	Total Contribution
2005	$4,000	$500	$4,500
2006	$4,000	$1,000	$5,000
2007	$4,000	$1,000	$5,000
2008	$5,000	$1,000	$6,000

FAQ

Q. But, Ed, what if I'm too old to contribute?

A. Too old? Phooey! Nobody's too old to parlay a fortune for themselves and their family by contributing to a Roth IRA—as long as they have earnings to put in. Let's say your 75-year-old granny lives with you. If you're up north, hire her in the winter to remove snow from the driveway—hey, I'm not being cruel here; it can be great exercise, especially if you have a snowblower. (If you live in the South, substitute mowing the lawn on a rider.) Pay her $4,500 a season to be on call, which she can then contribute, as wages, to a Roth IRA, naming your son Bill—her grandson—as beneficiary. Even if she gets in just ten years of contributions before dying at age 85, that's $45,000. Assuming an 8 percent return over those ten years, at death she will have accumulated $70,405. Let's say grandson Bill is age ten the year after Granny dies. That means he can stretch over his life expectancy of 72.8 years, according to the Single Life Expectancy table. Again, at an average 8 percent growth rate, if he stretches that long withdrawing only the minimum each year, he will have withdrawn an astounding *$3,267,631* tax-free by the time he reaches his life expectancy. That's right, more than $3 million—just from Granny's ten years' worth of contributions with not one more cent ever being put in! Now that's what I call a legacy!

To qualify for tax-free treatment, your Roth IRA must generally be held for five years and until you are 59½ years old. Unlike a traditional IRA, you do not have to start taking minimum distributions beginning at age 70½ or any later year; in fact, you can keep contributing to a Roth IRA as long as you like, provided you are receiving earned income from a job or self-employment.

If you are eligible for a Roth IRA conversion, there is no limit to the amount of your traditional IRA you can convert. In any year your income exceeds certain limits, however, you can no longer contribute to a Roth IRA. To be eligible to convert, your MAGI (Modified Adjusted Gross Income) must not exceed $100,000 and you cannot file married-separate. That $100,000 limit is the same for both married-joint and single filers. The amount you convert is not included in your MAGI. It is taxable income, but it does not count as income for Roth IRA conversion eligibility purposes. Beginning in 2005, required minimum distributions from your traditional IRA also do not count as income for Roth IRA conversion eligibility purposes. The required distribution is still taxable for income tax purposes though.

2005 Rule Change for Roth IRA Conversions

For those who are over 70½ years old and subject to required minimum distributions on their traditional IRAs, the Roth conversion eligibility rules change beginning in 2005 allowing you more of an opportunity to convert to a Roth IRA. In 2005, your required minimum distribution will no longer count as income for Roth conversion eligibility. Make no mistake, your RMD is still income for income tax purposes but it is not added to your MAGI for determining if you are eligible to convert to a Roth IRA.

Example:

You are 75 years old and are subject to RMDs from your traditional IRA. You want to convert all your IRA funds to a Roth IRA in 2004. Your income is $80,000 and your 2004 RMD amount is $30,000. You must first withdraw the $30,000 before you can convert any funds to a Roth IRA. Under the old rules (before 2005), once you took your $30,000 RMD for 2004, your income for Roth IRA conversion eligibility would be $110,000, so you would not be able to convert any of your traditional IRA to a Roth IRA.

But in 2005, this problem is removed. Using the same example above, if we moved the dates up a year to 2005, taking your $30,000 RMD in 2005 would increase your taxable income, but you would still qualify for a Roth IRA conversion. The $30,000 would not throw your Roth eligibility income (MAGI) over the $100,000 limit as it would have in 2004.

To qualify to make annual Roth IRA contributions (as opposed to Roth IRA conversions discussed above) you not only need earned income, but your income must fall below certain limits. But our tax laws do not make this income limitation easy to figure out. The tax code creates what it calls "phase-out ranges." This is tax talk that means that the amount you can contribute to your Roth IRA gets less and less as your income rises—until your income rises to a point where you cannot contribute at all. For example, if you are single, your Roth IRA phase-out range is $95,000 to $110,000; for married couples filing jointly, the income phase-out range is $150,000 to $160,000; and for married couples filing separately, the income phase-out range is zero to $10,000.

These phase-out limits have not changed since the Roth IRA was first available in 1998. What these ranges mean is that if your annual income is under the range, you can contribute the full amount to your Roth IRA. If your income falls within the range, you can contribute a portion of the full amount. If your income exceeds the range, you cannot contribute anything. In other words, as your income rises within the phase-out range, the amount you can contribute decreases.

Roth IRA Conversions

The big money is in the Roth IRA conversions since the amount you can convert once you qualify (when your income does not exceed the $100,000 limit) is unlimited. As long as you can pay the tax, you can convert all you want. You should not convert to a Roth IRA, however, if you cannot afford to or if you do not have enough money outside of your IRA to pay the conversion tax. After all, you don't want to go broke converting. But you still do not have to convert all or nothing. You can convert part of your traditional IRA to a Roth over time.

Those who accumulate the most in their IRAs obviously stand to make the most of the stretch option. That's why a Roth IRA conversion works best. You can jump-start your Roth IRA buildup with big chunks of money no matter how old you are. But if you are young, contributing to a Roth IRA from the start is the perfect way also to build the accumulation in your retirement fund.

I've already shown you the power of compounding. When you see this kind of buildup and what it can amount to tax-free, you see why the Roth IRA is a key part of parlaying your IRA now into a fortune (and in the future for your beneficiaries to parlay it even bigger).

Obviously, I don't know for sure how much of your IRA you will spend during retirement. Given today's increased life expectancy, I anticipate it will be substantial, though. I'm simply pointing out the remarkable fortune you can start building now—and that can keep building in your family out of what you leave behind, however much or little the amount.

Even if you are not concerned with how much of your IRA is left for your beneficiaries, by letting your IRA money compound untouched for as long as possible, you'll have more to spend on yourself—but once you tap that money, it is no longer sheltered and you'll have less accumulation over the long haul.

Just Pennies a Day

I just want to make this final point before moving on. You do not have to be rich for you and your family to benefit from the stretch IRA. The compounding power of the stretch is that it works no matter what the size of your IRA.

While I often use $100,000 as an example of what a small IRA can achieve through the power of the stretch (and most people have IRAs many times that size), I want to emphasize that just pennies on the dollar can achieve big things and make a real difference in your own and your beneficiaries' lives.

For example, let's say you die leaving $50,000 in a Roth IRA to your grandson. At 8 percent compounding over the rest of his life, he can withdraw $334.59 every month for the next 70 years tax-free. That $334 may not sound like much, but it could be a car payment or help with the mortgage or other monthly bills. Can you imagine how your life might have changed when you were starting out if you had another $334 a month coming in tax-free every month for the rest of your life?

Here's another example illustrating the long-term value of making regular Roth IRA contributions each year. We'll start very small. You can contribute up to $4,000 per year to a Roth IRA. (That amount is increasing over the next few years, but let's stick with only the $4,000 per year for our example here.) Let's say you don't begin contributing until you are age 35, because with bills and a growing family you just didn't have the extra money until then. Putting away just $4,000 a year—provided you did this religiously for the next, say, 30 years until you reached age 65 and didn't touch it until then—would achieve remarkable growth. (In case $4,000 a year sounds like too much to be able to contribute each year, think of it this way: That's $333.33 per month or about $11 per day! Surely most people can sock that amount away without having to touch it.) By the end of that time, you would have contributed $120,000 ($4,000 per year for 30 years = $120,000). At an average 8 percent rate, which is a fair example over a long period of time, at age 65, your $120,000 of Roth IRA contributions would be worth $489,383! But it gets better. Because this is a Roth IRA, that $489,383 is all tax-free! Obviously you will use much of your IRA (let's say 90 percent) for your own retirement. But the 10 percent left over for your children, grandchildren, or other loved ones could still change their lives.

Now that you are amazed and enthused, you'll be motivated to do this for yourself. Just to give you that last hit of incentive, if in the above example you began 10 years earlier at age 25, this is how the numbers would work out. By the time you reached the same retirement age of 65, you would have contributed for 40 years (instead of 30 years), so you would have contributed $160,000 to your Roth IRA by age 65 ($4,000 per year for 40 years = $160,000). All you contributed is $40,000 more than you did if you began at age 35, but that extra 10 years will more than double your return. At age 65 (using the same 8 percent compounding rate, and contributing early in the year), that $160,000 would be worth a whopping $1,119,124—all tax-free! That's just you. If you are married and your spouse does the same thing—just contributing $4,000 per year until age 65, if you both begin at age 25—those amounts can double, and combined you will have accumulated over $2 million! Now you can see the advantage contributing or converting to a Roth IRA adds to the power of the stretch in building a family fortune. If you begin with lots more, your family will end up with lots more.

TWO

Your Incredibly Missing IRA Transition Strategy

Dear Ed,
I already have an estate plan. I just finished meeting with my attorney
and CPA. I'm sure this has all been addressed![3]
  —IRA owner

Here Comes the Sun

Think of your IRA as the center of your family's solar system, not as some distant planet; it's the sun, and should be accorded the importance of the sun in your estate plan. It should be given the respect it deserves in coordination with all your other assets.

It is unlikely, however, that your estate plan includes a transition strategy for your IRA or other retirement accounts. This is because most IRA owners and estate planning professionals neglect or omit such a strategy due to a lack of knowledge of the complex tax rules. "But I have a will," I can hear you say. "Wouldn't that cover my IRA, since it's the largest amount of money in my estate?" The answer is: probably not. Generally, retirement accounts don't pass through a will—and when they do, this often creates more tax problems.

[3]I'll bet not, and if I'm right (which I am), this chapter will prove it and open the door for your family to accumulate more in your IRA than you left them.

If the total value of your estate, including your IRA, does not exceed $1.5 million, or you do not expect it to grow to that amount during your lifetime, then federal estate taxes will probably not be an obstacle for you to overcome, and you can skip to Chapter Four. But before you do, keep in mind that beneficiaries will always need cash to pay after-death expenses—even if estate taxes aren't one of them. The last account you want your beneficiaries to have to dig into to cover those costs is your IRA, as this will kill, or at least greatly diminish, the compounding power of the stretch.

The information and advice here and in Chapter Three are geared to those of you who may be subject to estate taxes. That is why the stretch IRA strategies in these chapters are different from those I would otherwise recommend if estate taxes were *not* an issue. For example, if estate taxes are not an issue, then most IRA owners are better off leaving their IRA to their spouse, who will do a rollover and name the children as beneficiaries. When the spouse dies, the IRA will then pass to their children. That is how I structure all of the examples elsewhere in this book except for these two chapters. But if the IRA is large enough (over the current $1.5 million federal estate tax exemption), that strategy could create a larger estate tax bite when that spouse dies. To avoid that problem, you would leave your IRA to your children (or a trust for your children) instead of your spouse, to take advantage of the federal estate tax exemption and cut out as much of the estate tax as possible. That is why before you can proceed with my three-step plan for parlaying your IRA into a family fortune, you must first know whether estate tax needs to be addressed.

Use It or Lose It

The basic principle of IRA transition planning is to take advantage of the current $1.5 million estate tax exemption ($3 million for a married couple with proper planning), also called the "credit shelter amount." Under tax law, each person is entitled to have his or her assets protected by the estate exemption that is in effect at the time of his or her death. Married couples can double the exemption since each spouse is entitled to his or her own estate exemption. But the exemption for the first spouse's death is not automatic. Some planning must be done to make sure that each spouse's estate receives the *maximum* federal estate exemption of $1.5 million (or whatever the prevailing maximum may be at the time of death) so that the first exemption is not lost.

The reason many couples lose the first exemption is because they own most of their assets jointly or simply leave all their assets, including retirement accounts, to each other. An unlimited amount of retirement plan money or other assets can pass estate-tax-free to a spouse (provided he or she is a U.S. citizen). If everything goes directly to the spouse, the first exemption is lost as there is no taxable estate. This can be a hugely expensive mistake. It could cost your family *hundreds of thousands of dollars in unnecessary estate taxes*.

Therefore, one of the most powerful ways to make sure the first exemption is used is to pass a retirement account through the exemption, especially if there are not enough other assets to fund the exemption amount. In other words: Leave some or all of your IRA to someone other than your spouse.

How much of your IRA should you leave to a non-spouse beneficiary—for example, your 40-year-old child? The answer is: as much as possible. In other words, whatever your spouse does not need. If your spouse has other assets, or you can transfer or leave other assets to your spouse, you are better off doing that and leaving your IRA to your children. The power of the stretch rests in its compounding potential over time and the increasing estate exemption adds to the power of the stretch IRA as a long-term family wealth builder. So, if your retirement plan is under the exemption limit *and your spouse has sufficient funds to live on*, your family will end up with more money if you leave the retirement plan to your children or grandchildren and use the exemption against it. This way the child starts off with 100 percent of that retirement plan. It is not eroded by estate taxes. This may not happen if the retirement plan goes to the surviving spouse and the child gets it at the second death, as the estate may be much larger at that point.

For example, let's say in 2004 Bob leaves his $1.5 million IRA to his 39-year-old daughter Amy. Beginning in 2005, when she is age 40, Amy can stretch required distributions over her 43.6-year life expectancy according to IRS tables. Amy gets to keep every dime of this $1.5 million IRA as none of it is eroded by federal estate tax, as well as every compounding dime thereafter, simply by having been named beneficiary. By spreading distributions over her lifetime expectancy of 43.6 years, she can parlay that $1.5 million into $11,903,767—estate-tax-free—all because the IRA passed to her under her father's $1.5 million federal estate tax exemption! See Table 5 to see how this works.

Notice also in Table 5 the small amount of annual required distributions. Amy must start off by taking out only $34,404, which is not much relative to the $1.5 million account balance. The lower the annual required minimum distributions, the lower the income tax, and the more money that builds. Even when Amy reaches 70 years old in 2035, she still only has to withdraw $346,192, which sounds like a lot, but is less than 10 percent of the account balance of $4,708,212 at that point. As she gets older, more has to be withdrawn, but the amount she must withdraw will not exceed the annual growth in the account until 2037, when she is 72 years old. This means that, until that point, everything Amy must withdraw is being replaced (and more), and the account is growing income-tax-deferred. The full effect of the income tax will not materialize until the last few big distribution years, but by that time the account has had time to grow free of federal estate taxes and with relatively minimal income taxes.

Table 5. Value of $1.5 Million IRA Inherited by a
40-Year-Old, Estate-Tax-Free
(Assumed rate of interest is 8 percent over the 43.6-year term.)

Year	IRA Beneficiary's Age	Value of IRA	IRA Beneficiary's Life Expectancy Factor (in years)	IRA Required Minimum Distributions (RMDs)	Cumulative IRA Distributions
2005	40	$1,500,000	43.6	$34,404	$34,404
2006	41	$1,582,844	42.6	$37,156	$71,560
2007	42	$1,669,343	41.6	$40,128	$111,688
2008	43	$1,759,552	40.6	$43,339	$155,027
2009	44	$1,853,510	39.6	$46,806	$201,833
2010	45	$1,951,240	38.6	$50,550	$252,383
2011	46	$2,052,745	37.6	$54,594	$306,977
2012	47	$2,158,003	36.6	$58,962	$365,939
2013	48	$2,266,964	35.6	$63,679	$429,618
2014	49	$2,379,548	34.6	$68,773	$498,391
2015	50	$2,495,637	33.6	$74,275	$572,666
2016	51	$2,615,071	32.6	$80,217	$652,883
2017	52	$2,737,642	31.6	$86,634	$739,517
2018	53	$2,863,089	30.6	$93,565	$833,082
2019	54	$2,991,086	29.6	$101,050	$934,132
2020	55	$3,121,239	28.6	$109,134	$1,043,266
2021	56	$3,253,073	27.6	$117,865	$1,161,131
2022	57	$3,386,025	26.6	$127,294	$1,288,425
2023	58	$3,519,429	25.6	$137,478	$1,425,903
2024	59	$3,652,507	24.6	$148,476	$1,574,379
2025	60	$3,784,353	23.6	$160,354	$1,734,733
2026	61	$3,913,919	22.6	$173,182	$1,907,915
2027	62	$4,039,996	21.6	$187,037	$2,094,952
2028	63	$4,161,196	20.6	$202,000	$2,296,952

Table 5. Value of $1.5 Million IRA Inherited by a 40-Year-Old, Estate-Tax-Free *(continued)*

Year	IRA Beneficiary's Age	Value of IRA	IRA Beneficiary's Life Expectancy Factor (in years)	IRA Required Minimum Distributions (RMDs)	Cumulative IRA Distributions
2029	64	$4,275,932	19.6	$218,160	$2,515,112
2030	65	$4,382,394	18.6	$235,613	$2,750,725
2031	66	$4,478,523	17.6	$254,462	$3,005,187
2032	67	$4,561,986	16.6	$274,818	$3,280,005
2033	68	$4,630,141	15.6	$296,804	$3,576,809
2034	69	$4,680,004	14.6	$320,548	$3,897,357
2035	70	$4,708,212	13.6	$346,192	$4,243,549
2036	71	$4,710,982	12.6	$373,887	$4,617,436
2037	72	$4,684,063	11.6	$403,799	$5,021,235
2038	73	$4,622,685	10.6	$436,102	$5,457,337
2039	74	$4,521,510	9.6	$470,991	$5,928,328
2040	75	$4,374,561	8.6	$508,670	$6,436,998
2041	76	$4,175,162	7.6	$549,363	$6,986,361
2042	77	$3,915,863	6.6	$593,313	$7,579,674
2043	78	$3,588,354	5.6	$640,778	$8,220,452
2044	79	$3,183,382	4.6	$692,040	$8,912,492
2045	80	$2,690,649	3.6	$747,403	$9,659,895
2046	81	$2,098,706	2.6	$807,195	$10,467,090
2047	82	$1,394,832	1.6	$871,770	$11,338,860
2048	83	$564,907	0.6	$564,907	$11,903,767
2049	84	$0	$0	$0	
Totals					**$11,903,767**

If instead of leaving his $1.5 million IRA to his daughter Amy, however, Bob had left it to his wife, Flo (who also has an IRA of her own worth $1.5 million), thus wasting the first exemption, what would happen? Let's take a look.

Flo rolls the $1.5 million IRA she inherited from her husband over into her own IRA. She does not have to begin taking required minimum distributions from the combined $3 million IRA (her own plus the inherited IRA) until her required beginning date after attaining age 70½. To make things simple, let's assume Flo, who has named daughter Amy the beneficiary of all her assets, passes away *before* the required beginning date for taking distributions. Let's assume also that Flo dies in 2005, when the federal estate tax exemption is still at $1.5 million. As the father's exemption was lost, daughter Amy will now have to pay an estate tax of $695,000 when she inherits from her mother. If that money cannot be raised from other inherited assets, including life insurance (see Chapter Three), Amy must use the IRA to pay the estate tax. She will also have to pay income tax on what she withdraws. Roughly estimating the income tax on a $695,000 IRA withdrawal as $180,000 (after figuring in the IRD deduction—see Chapter Ten), this means Amy must remove approximately $875,000 ($695,000 plus $180,000) from the IRA to cover the combined taxes. This lowers the value of the IRA to $625,000 ($1,500,000 minus $875,000) and puts a real dent in the IRA's stretch potential. It would end up being worth $4,959,895—or nowhere near the potential value of $11,903,767 it might have been if Amy had been named beneficiary of her father's IRA initially and the first exemption had not been lost. As you can see in Table 6, that's almost a $7 million difference!

Table 6. Value of $625,000 IRA Inherited by a 40-Year-Old
(Assumed rate of interest is 8 percent over the 43.6-year term.)

Year	IRA Beneficiary's Age	Value of IRA	IRA Beneficiary's Life Expectancy Factor (in years)	IRA Required Minimum Distributions (RMDs)	Cumulative IRA Distributions
2005	40	$625,000	43.6	$14,335	$14,335
2006	41	$659,518	42.6	$15,482	$29,817
2007	42	$695,559	41.6	$16,720	$46,537
2008	43	$733,146	40.6	$18,058	$64,595
2009	44	$772,295	39.6	$19,502	$84,097
2010	45	$813,016	38.6	$21,063	$105,160
2011	46	$855,309	37.6	$22,748	$127,908
2012	47	$899,166	36.6	$24,567	$152,475
2013	48	$944,567	35.6	$26,533	$179,008
2014	49	$991,477	34.6	$28,655	$207,663
2015	50	$1,039,848	33.6	$30,948	$238,611
2016	51	$1,089,612	32.6	$33,424	$272,035
2017	52	$1,140,683	31.6	$36,098	$308,133
2018	53	$1,192,952	30.6	$38,985	$347,118
2019	54	$1,246,284	29.6	$42,104	$389,222
2020	55	$1,300,514	28.6	$45,473	$434,695
2021	56	$1,355,444	27.6	$49,110	$483,805
2022	57	$1,410,841	26.6	$53,039	$536,844
2023	58	$1,466,426	25.6	$57,282	$594,126
2024	59	$1,521,876	24.6	$61,865	$655,991
2025	60	$1,576,812	23.6	$66,814	$722,805
2026	61	$1,630,798	22.6	$72,159	$794,964
2027	62	$1,683,330	21.6	$77,932	$872,896
2028	63	$1,733,830	20.6	$84,167	$957,063
2029	64	$1,781,636	19.6	$90,900	$1,047,963

Table 6. Value of $625,000 IRA Inherited
by a 40-Year-Old *(continued)*

Year	IRA Beneficiary's Age	Value of IRA	IRA Beneficiary's Life Expectancy Factor (in years)	IRA Required Minimum Distributions (RMDs)	Cumulative IRA Distributions
2030	65	$1,825,995	18.6	$98,172	$1,146,135
2031	66	$1,866,049	17.6	$106,026	$1,252,161
2032	67	$1,900,825	16.6	$114,508	$1,366,669
2033	68	$1,929,222	15.6	$123,668	$1,490,337
2034	69	$1,949,998	14.6	$133,562	$1,623,899
2035	70	$1,961,751	13.6	$144,246	$1,768,145
2036	71	$1,962,905	12.6	$155,786	$1,923,931
2037	72	$1,951,689	11.6	$168,249	$2,092,180
2038	73	$1,926,115	10.6	$181,709	$2,273,889
2039	74	$1,883,958	9.6	$196,246	$2,470,135
2040	75	$1,822,729	8.6	$211,945	$2,682,080
2041	76	$1,739,647	7.6	$228,901	$2,910,981
2042	77	$1,631,606	6.6	$247,213	$3,158,194
2043	78	$1,495,144	5.6	$266,990	$3,425,184
2044	79	$1,326,406	4.6	$288,349	$3,713,533
2045	80	$1,121,102	3.6	$311,417	$4,024,950
2046	81	$874,460	2.6	$336,331	$4,361,281
2047	82	$581,179	1.6	$363,237	$4,724,518
2048	83	$235,377	0.6	$235,377	$4,959,895
2049	84	$0		$0	$4,959,895
Totals					**$4,959,895**

Slott's Tips

KEEP YOUR OPTIONS OPEN

All hope is not lost if Bob leaves his IRA to wife, Flo, instead of daughter Amy. Flo has time to decide whether she wants to inherit the IRA or not. This option is called an "IRA disclaimer plan." Known in legal parlance as a "renunciation," it is a written statement refusing a gift or inheritance. To be effective, it must be executed within nine months of the date of the decedent's passing, and there can be no strings attached. To be a valid disclaimer (what the tax law calls a "qualified disclaimer"), Flo cannot use or touch any of the IRA she disclaims. For example, she cannot take possession of the IRA, roll it over, and then decide to disclaim it. Once disclaimed, the IRA would go to the next beneficiary in line—provided Bob named one. Flo, the primary beneficiary, has no say in that matter. It's Bob's job to name a contingent beneficiary (see Chapter Five). If daughter Amy is the contingent beneficiary, then she gets the IRA and can use Bob's federal estate tax exemption, which would otherwise have been wasted if the IRA were left to her mom, Flo. Once Amy receives the IRA as a result of the disclaimer by her mom, as the designated beneficiary she can stretch the inherited IRA over her lifetime. That will add decades of tax-deferred compounding to the value of the inherited IRA. It's true that without the disclaimer Amy might have inherited the IRA later from her mother, but at that point an estate tax might have been triggered and Amy could end up receiving much less. With a disclaimer plan in place, the best of both worlds are available; Flo can be named primary beneficiary in the event she thinks she may *need* the IRA cash right away when Bob dies, then opt out of that decision after his death if she finds she doesn't need that cash after all. This is not an all-or-nothing choice for Flo. She can disclaim all or only part of the IRA.

Repeal of the Estate Tax

The 2001 tax act, also known as the Economic Growth and Tax Relief Reconciliation Act of 2001 (EGTRRA), nullifies the estate tax on January 1, 2010. But just like Jason in those *Friday the 13th* movies, the estate tax comes roaring back from the dead full force on January 1, 2011—unless the nullification is extended by future legislation. (This is a ridiculous system created by politics, but this is all we have to work with.)

Like the federal estate tax, the "generation skipping transfer" (GST) tax will also be repealed in 2010. But for now, EGTRRA has increased the generation skipping transfer tax exemption. In its simplest terms, the generation skipping transfer tax is an additional transfer tax imposed when you transfer property directly or through a trust to a person who is *more than one generation younger than yours*, such as a grandchild. The GST tax is imposed at the highest estate tax rate. If the tax applies (to GST transfers over the GST exemption amount), your estate gets hit with both the estate tax and the GST tax. Needless to say, the GST tax is really a penalty for trying to beat the government out of an estate tax by bypassing a generation. Assuming you had a taxable estate, if you had left the property to your children, the government would have received an estate tax on that transfer, plus a second estate tax when your children passed the same property on to your grandchildren. When you skip your children and give assets directly to the grandchildren, you cut the taxman out of the second estate tax. But take note: The GST tax was put in place to limit your ability to do that. In 2005, for example, you could leave up to $1.5 million of IRA funds to a grandchild without triggering the GST tax.

The "gift tax," however, continues in effect. The exemption is still $1 million and remains at that level even after the estate tax is repealed. The top gift tax rate will decrease the same as the estate tax rates through 2009. In 2010, the gift tax rate is 35 percent for transfers in excess of the $1 million gift tax exemption.

The annual gift tax exclusion amount remains at $11,000 per

person. Married donors can double that amount to $22,000 if the donor's spouse agrees to add his or her $11,000. These annual exclusion amounts do not cut into your $1 million gift tax exemption—they are in addition to that $1 million. These numbers may sound small, but over the years these tax-free gifts really add up. And any appreciation on the money or property given remains estate-tax-free to your beneficiaries. For example, every year you and your spouse can jointly give $66,000 tax-free to your three children ($22,000 to each child). The $66,000 is removed from your estate, along with any earnings on those funds. If you do not use these annual exclusion amounts, they are lost forever. You cannot add any unused exclusion amounts from prior years to the following year's $11,000 or $22,000 gifts.

FAQ

Q. Ed, what about basing IRA planning on the coming changes in the tax system?

A. As Yogi Berra once said, "I hate to make predictions, especially about the future." Who knows what the estate tax system will be in the next 30 to 50 years or more? If your IRA is growing to the point where it looks like it may trigger estate tax based on what the estate tax exemption and tax rates are *currently*, make that assumption, and address the issue in your estate and IRA transition plan *now*.

Plan for State Estate Taxes Too

Most married people set up their estate plans based solely on federal law and do not plan for a possible state estate tax. The state estate tax should be planned for as well. How bad can it get?

When states decide they do not want to go along with the federal estate tax rules (such as the exemption increase and the phase out of the state death tax credit)[4] because they will lose revenue, they "decouple" (break away from) the federal tax system and create their own system to make sure they continue to get a piece of the action. In a state that has fully decoupled from the federal estate tax changes, this will result in a state estate tax of $64,400 on a $1.5 million taxable estate in 2004 and 2005; $96,600 on a $2 million taxable estate from 2006 to 2008; and $229,200 on a $3.5 million taxable estate in 2009!

The bottom line here is that if you have, say, a $1.5 million estate, it is true that there will be no federal estate tax (if you die in 2005 while the exemption is currently $1.5 million), but in New York and other states that don't follow the federal system anymore, your estate would be hit with a state estate tax of $64,400. With large estates, the hit gets even worse. You don't want your family to have to withdraw from your IRA to cover unexpected state estate taxes, so plan for them as well. Life insurance (see Chapter Three) is the best way to do this.

Don't Forget Probate

Probate is not, as many believe, a tax. It is the judicial process by which a will is validated and the wishes of the deceased expressed in the will are carried out. Probate court (also called "surrogate's court") is where this process takes place, and a combination of court costs, legal fees, and other estate-related expenses are incurred.

The probate process covers property that is directed by your will.

---

[4]Under the old federal system (pre-EGTRRA), states would receive the state death tax credit individuals could claim on their federal estate tax return. EGTRRA removed that revenue from the states by eliminating the state tax credit in 2005. So as not to be "disinherited" from their share of the federal estate tax pie, many states have broken from the federal system to escape the new rules so they can collect on their own.

For example, if you state in your will that "I leave my house to my daughter," that house will go through probate to make sure it goes to your daughter, who is the beneficiary named in your will. However, there are certain items that pass *outside the will* and thus are not probate property, meaning you do not have to take special steps to avoid probate on these assets. They include:

- Jointly owned property with right of survivorship
- Life insurance with a named beneficiary
- Pensions, IRAs, 401(k)s, 403(b)s, Keoghs, annuities with a named beneficiary
- Property owned inside a revocable living trust

In other words, non-probate property is property that is spoken for. It already has a named beneficiary either through the law or through a beneficiary designation form (see Chapter Five). For example, joint property passes to the surviving joint owner by operation of law, thus bypassing the will. IRAs and life insurance benefits pass by beneficiary designation, also bypassing the will. These non-probate items, however, can easily become probate property if you are careless. For example, if you neglect to name a beneficiary for your IRA, it is likely you have just turned a non-probate asset into a probate asset. Now your IRA may have to pass through your will, and your beneficiaries may not receive the full advantage of the stretch. In addition, they may have to pay probate costs out of the IRA.

It is important to remember that some assets that are non-probate—for example, pensions, IRAs, joint property, and property placed in a revocable living trust—*are still subject to estate tax*. On the other hand, property may be subject to probate but not to estate tax, for example, if your estate is below the federal exemption amount (and is also not subject to any state estate tax). An inventory of your estate (see Chapter Three) should clearly show which assets will pass through probate and which assets will bypass it.

Transition Planning for Unmarried Domestic Partners

As noted, unmarried couples do not receive an unlimited marital deduction. Therefore, you cannot just leave (or even gift) unlimited amounts to your partner without tax having to be paid.

Even though you might want to provide for your partner the same way a legally married couple can, you cannot do this without incurring a tax. If you want to make a gift over the gift tax limit there is a gift tax (see Chapter Three for these limits). If you want to leave an IRA or property in excess of the federal estate exemption, then that will trigger an estate tax even though it is going to someone (your partner) whom you view as your spouse. As of this writing, however, the law does not see it this way, so you need to prepare for this by having cash available at your death to pay estate taxes and any expenses so that your partner can receive the full benefit of your IRA.

If your estate exceeds, or if you think it will exceed, the estate tax exemption, you should plan this out ahead of time so there will be money to pay the taxes. Again, life insurance (see Chapter Three) is a solution, since it provides cash to your partner upon your death, which can be used tax-free by your partner either to pay estate taxes and other post-death expenses or to pay living expenses.

THREE

Will Estate Tax and a Need for Cash Be an Issue for *You*?

Dear Ed,

I am widowed. My husband passed away four years ago. He left me an IRA and I rolled it over into my IRA. Four years later now, I am in desperate need of some money. I cannot wait until I am 59½. I am 55 now. I need to know if there are any ways in which I can access more money, even with taking some penalties. But, I have many concerns about it. I have consulted with my accountant, broker, and tax attorney, and none of them could help me.

—IRA owner

Inventory Your Assets

For most of you reading this book, estate tax will not be an issue because the value of your estate (IRAs plus *all other* assets) likely will not exceed the current $1.5 million federal estate tax exemption. But for those of you with an IRA and other assets worth more than $1.5 million, consider this a heads-up: Your heirs may have to pay federal and state estate taxes, and if they need to dip into your IRA to pay those taxes, both the IRA and the opportunity to parlay it into a fortune may be lost.

But here's the good news: *Federal and state estate taxes are impediments that can be easily removed by proper planning. First, though, you have to find out whether they're really in your way or not.*

How do you know if your overall estate is (or may grow) large enough to exceed the estate tax exemption when you're gone? You need to inventory your assets to find out. That means *all* your assets—everything from your big screen TV, baseball cards, stamp collection, official Les Paul guitars, and anything else of worth that can't grow legs and outrun the IRS when you pass on.

I find that most people grossly underestimate their net worth. Often, once you go through and list all your property, you will be amazed at how much you own. That's why it pays to do an inventory now in order to get a quick fix on whether or not your beneficiaries will be subject to estate tax so you know exactly what steps you have to take to avoid killing the stretch IRA option.

DON'T FORGET TO INCLUDE . . .

- Annuities (that have post-death value)
- Other real estate (list location of property, deeds, and insurance information)
- Rental real estate (list tenants and leases)
- Investment real estate
- Vacation home
- Boat/recreational vehicle/motor home
- Club memberships
- Ownership interests in a business (value of your own business or your interest in another business—you'll need a valuation/appraisal for this)
- Inheritances or gifts (it's not yours yet, but it should be figured into the mix)
- Valuables hidden or stored

Use a columnar pad (one of those green accounting pads—what else would a CPA suggest?) to list your assets and property down the margin on the left side, and across the top, list how they are owned.[5] For example, if the assets are in your name (John Smith) alone, then put the value of assets in the column under John's name. If they are in wife Mary Smith's name alone, then put the amount under Mary's column. If the asset is jointly held (John and Mary as joint owners), then put the value under the joint column. If the asset is jointly held by people other than John or Mary—for example, by Mary and daughter Susan—then enter the value under Mary's column. But mark on the left-hand-side column where you enter the asset, "joint with Susan."

Start with cash, since that is the easiest to put a value on and the most liquid of your assets. Then just work your way down through all the bank, stock, and funds accounts, and then on to IRAs and non-cash property. Keep IRA and other retirement accounts in a separate category. IRAs and the like are subject to different tax rules, and IRA cash is nowhere near as liquid as regular non-IRA accounts, because they are laden with tax. If you have cash in an IRA, for example, do not list that under cash. Instead list it under retirement accounts.

Some people have property titled in revocable living trusts. If that is the case, then enter the property under the column of the person whose trust it's in. For example, if a home is owned in John's revocable living trust, then enter the value of the home in John's column. When you are inventorying your assets, I recommend coding them at that time as either liquid or non-liquid so as to make this analysis easier.

It is important to separate the property by ownership—first to know who owns what, and then to determine how it will pass

---

[5]You can also do this on a computer, but it works just as well if you write your inventory down the old-fashioned way and keep it where you and your family can find it. (If you do store it on your computer, make sure to let someone know how to access the document you created.) You can also use a computer spreadsheet, like Excel, to list all your accounts and property and their values. The benefit to using a spreadsheet program is that you can update it with new account values, and all the totals update automatically. It's a great way to keep track of your estate. There are programs you can buy in the store that are set up for this. Whatever works best for you is fine.

when that person dies. You also want to know how much property is in each person's estate (for a married couple) so that you can possibly rearrange the property to take better advantage of the federal estate tax exemption. In 2005 everyone receives a federal estate tax exemption of $1.5 million. If property is arranged the right way, each spouse can receive an exemption of $1.5 million and double his or her protection from estate taxes to $3 million. Under our current tax law, which seems to change every year, that exemption is set to increase over the next few years as follows:

CURRENT FEDERAL ESTATE TAX AND GENERATION SKIPPING TRANSFER TAX EXEMPTIONS (THE 2001, 2002, AND 2003 AMOUNTS ARE ALSO INCLUDED FOR YOUR REFERENCE.)

Year	Estate Tax Exemption	Top Estate Tax (and GST Tax) Rate
2001	$675,000	55% (prior law)
2002	$1,000,000	50%
2003	$1,000,000	49%
2004	$1,500,000	48%
2005	$1,500,000	47%
2006	$2,000,000	46%
2007	$2,000,000	45%
2008	$2,000,000	45%
2009	$3,500,000	45%
2010	Estate tax is repealed	-0-%
2011	$1,000,000	55%

GST Exemption Amounts

Year	Amount
2001	$1,060,000
2002	$1,100,000
2003	$1,120,000
2004	$1,500,000

CURRENT FEDERAL ESTATE TAX AND GENERATION SKIPPING TRANSFER TAX EXEMPTIONS *(continued)*

2005	$1,500,000
2006	$2,000,000
2007	$2,000,000
2008	$2,000,000
2009	$3,500,000
2010	GST is repealed
2011	$1,000,000 (indexed for inflation)

It's best to round to the nearest thousand just to get an easy overview of what you have. This is for your planning purposes only, so you don't need to list items to the exact dollar and cent. Once you get to your home and other non-cash property, you will be using an estimate in the thousands anyway, so stick with that for now. You'll see that it will be easier for you and you'll still be pretty accurate.

Here's an example of what your inventory list might look like:

JOHN AND MARY SMITH
ESTATE INVENTORY
MAY 31, 2005

Ownership	John	Mary	Joint	Total
Assets				
Cash (non-IRAs)				
Citibank—savings account number 123456			$35,000	$35,000

Ownership	John	Mary	Joint	Total
Bank of America— checking account number abcdefgx	$56,000			$56,000
Mutual Fund Accounts (non-IRAs)				
Fidelity XYZ fund Account number		$5,000		$5,000
Vanguard XYZ fund Account number			$10,000	$10,000
Broker Accounts (non-IRAs)				
Merrill Lynch Account number			$65,000	$65,000
Schwab Account number	$12,000			$12,000
U.S. Treasury bills		$30,000		$30,000
Bonds				
Nassau County bond			$10,000	$10,000
Life Insurance				
Owned by John Beneficiary is spouse	$250,000			$250,000
Home—Residence				
123 Maple Lane Oceanside, NY Market value			$800,000	

Ownership	John	Mary	Joint	Total
Less: Mortgage (or home equity loan)			($100,000)	
Net value				$700,000
Land (Florida)			$35,000	$35,000
IRAs and Other Retirement Accounts				
Nationwide— traditional IRA Beneficiary is spouse	$740,000			$740,000
XYZ Company 401(k) plan Beneficiary is spouse		$520,000		$520,000
Personal Property				
Autos, home furnishings, collectibles, and misc. other property			$50,000	$50,000
Totals	**$1,058,000**	**$555,000**	**$905,000**	**$2,518,000**

Your estate inventory is a great starting point that will show you how much you are worth in overall assets, including your IRAs. If this is over $1 million, or you expect it to exceed that amount during your lifetime, you'll need to take estate taxes into consideration.

If you have projected that there is no way, no how estate taxes will be an issue for your beneficiaries, you can move right to Chapter Four and start setting up the stretch so your beneficiaries parlay whatever size IRA you leave them into a windfall. On the other hand, if you have a huge estate and estate tax will be an issue, you will need to remove this obstacle now so as to avoid compromising the stretch option for your beneficiaries.

Estate Tax Elimination Planning

Do a Liquidity Analysis

Show me the money!

If your inventory indicates a potential estate tax problem, determine which assets in your estate can be turned into cash *quickly*—i.e., are the most "liquid." Obviously cash is the most liquid asset because it can be spent immediately. It's true that most IRAs can be cashed just as quickly, but you should not consider your IRA a "liquid asset," as tapping it to pay estate taxes (or any other expenses) is what you are planning to help your beneficiaries to avoid. Furthermore, the minute your beneficiaries withdraw from the inherited IRA, they will owe income tax, which reduces the value of that cash. They will, of course, have to withdraw the minimum required distribution each year prescribed by Uncle Sam, but that's OK, since the stretch concept is predicated upon building the most wealth possible by withdrawing no more than the minimum required so as to keep the rest of the inherited IRA growing tax-deferred for as long as legally possible.

List assets in the order of liquidity—that is, all cash accounts (again, excluding IRAs) first, then money market accounts, mutual funds accounts, and so on. Non-liquid assets would include your home or other real estate—these take time to sell, and while estate taxes are due nine months after death, other bills and legal fees may have to be paid sooner. A family business may take even longer to sell and is probably one of the most illiquid assets. List IRAs and other retirement accounts as non-liquid assets for the reasons I've explained.

Once you've done your analysis, you may find there's not a lot of ready cash in your large estate—or assets that can be turned into ready cash—for your beneficiaries to pay those pesky taxes, plus other post-death expenses. It is not unlikely that an IRA owner may have a multimillion dollar IRA but few other assets besides a home, thereby triggering an estate tax and liquidity problem. What can you do before you die to avoid this problem?

The Best Source of Post-Death Cash

The best and most cost-effective way to provide money to cover estate taxes and other post-death expenses when there are few other liquid assets in the estate is through gifting and life insurance.

While you cannot make a gift of your IRA, you can withdraw funds from it to buy life insurance, which will provide tax-free money to your heirs. It's better financially to tap your IRA and pay the income tax on the withdrawal now, using the net after-tax proceeds to invest in insurance premiums, rather than for Uncle Sam. Every time you pay an insurance premium, you will have removed that money from your estate. If you will be in the top estate tax bracket, which many owners of large IRAs will be, this means the government is paying almost half of the premiums. This is because had you not purchased the insurance and left the money to grow in your estate, the IRS would have taken almost half of it anyway.

To avoid the estate tax on life insurance, all you have to do is not own it yourself. Your children can own it, or you can set up a trust to own it, and make annual gifts to the children or trustee, respectively, to be used to pay the premiums.

For pennies on the dollar, life insurance is the best leverage you can get from your assets. It's also a way for people of modest means to invest a relatively small sum now and provide their family with an estate much larger than they ever had. The fact that life insurance money received in an estate can be totally estate- and income-tax-free is one of the biggest benefits in our tax code and should be taken advantage of by everyone who owns anything, large estate or small. (Just so you know, I *do not* sell life insurance. I just believe in it.)

Let's look at a liquidity analysis of the estate of John and Mary Smith to see how this plays out:

LIQUIDITY ANALYSIS: THE ESTATE
OF JOHN AND MARY SMITH

Liquid assets

Cash	$91,000
Mutual funds	$15,000
Broker accounts	$77,000
T-bills and bonds	$40,000
Life insurance	$250,000[6]
Total liquid assets	**$473,000**

Non-Liquid assets

Home	$700,000
Land	$35,000
IRAs, 401(k)s	$1,260,000
Personal property	$50,000
Total Non-Liquid assets	**$2,045,000**
Total estate	**$2,518,000**

[6]You'll notice that $250,000 in life insurance is included in the estate total of their inventory. That's because it is owned by John, so the proceeds will remain in the estate for his wife, Mary, to inherit, but this estate may be small enough that even when Mary dies, there will probably be no estate tax (though there could be state estate tax—in which case it may pay to remove the life insurance from the estate).

This analysis shows that 81 percent of the estate is non-liquid ($2,045,000 divided by $2,518,000 = 81 percent). That means only 19 percent is liquid. Depending upon post-death needs for cash, this could be dangerous; while there is life insurance in place, there may not be enough to keep the IRA from having to be spent down soon after death. If this couple had no life insurance, 90 percent of the estate assets ($2,518,000 less the $250,000 of life insurance = a total estate of $2,268,000, and $2,045,000—the non-liquid assets—divided by $2,268,000 = 90 percent) would be non-liquid, a recipe for disaster, which shows the difference even a modest amount of life insurance can make.

If you have (or project) a large estate, liquidity planning is the first step in eliminating the estate tax issue, and one you can—and should—take care of now in order to move ahead and set up your IRA to be parlayed into a fortune by your beneficiaries. If non-liquid assets are more than 70 percent (50 percent if estate tax is due), and no other cash is available to pay for post-death expenses, beneficiaries may be forced to use your IRA for cash, endangering the IRA's compounding ability. In such circumstances, especially those where most non-liquid assets are IRAs or property such as a home (as is the case for many people), buying life insurance for your estate can be just the ticket your beneficiaries need to keep your IRA and its growth potential off the endangered list.

Slott's Tips

Note also in your estate analysis the retirement accounts that are not IRAs. For example, in the case of John and Mary Smith, John still has a 401(k). If he is retired he might consider rolling that 401(k) over to an IRA where his family will have better distribution and investment options. If he wished to leave his 401(k) to his children, they would probably not be able to take advantage of the stretch IRA concept, because they are not inheriting an IRA. They are inheriting a 401(k), and that is very different. The tax rules also allow a beneficiary the stretch on an inherited 401(k), but most 401(k) plans do not allow the stretch. They do not have to and they generally will not, because they do not want the paperwork nightmare of keeping track of their deceased ex-employees' beneficiaries as they travel around the world distributing annual amounts to themselves over a span of 50 years or so. The companies just won't do that. Instead they will pay the full amount out to your child and it will all be taxable at once. *No* stretch. That's because once plan or IRA funds are paid out to a non-spouse beneficiary—say, your child—your child cannot then roll the 401(k) funds to an IRA. The tax law prohibits this. A non-spouse beneficiary cannot do a rollover. All 401(k) funds become taxable. If instead you had rolled that 401(k) over to your IRA your child could inherit your IRA, and stretch that over his lifetime.

FOUR

Setting Up Your IRA for the Stretch

Dear Ed,
If I name my grandkids (ages 6, 4, and 3) as beneficiaries on my IRA,
will my minimum required distribution at age 70½ be the same as if
I named my wife, who is the same age as me?
    —IRA owner

The Stretch IRA Means You Get to Be the Bank

Do you remember when you first applied for a home mortgage and had to figure out whether to take a 15-year loan or a 30-year one? Remember becoming aware of the huge difference in interest you would have to pay the bank the longer it took you to pay off the loan—and thus, how much more money the bank makes on you since you are paying more interest?

The stretch IRA works the same way—only in reverse. It works to *your* benefit—not Uncle Sam's—because the longer you take to withdraw from your IRA and pay tax on it, the greater the interest compounding, all of which grows tax-deferred (or tax-free in a Roth IRA) in *your* name!

How do you set up your IRA to take advantage of this sweet deal? That depends on what you want to accomplish. To find out, ask yourself the following questions:

Is your objective to build an estate for your beneficiaries? Or to spend all you can on yourself—in other words, how much do you care about what happens to your IRA after you're gone? Some people don't care—a widow, a widower, or a single person, for example, who may have no kids or grandkids, just distant relatives. Others may not care because they want to take care of Number One first; after that, let the chips fall where they may. That's fine, but you still want to make the most of the money in your IRA while you are alive—and make it available for *you*, not Uncle Sam!

What keeps you up at night? Do you worry about: Running out of money before running out of time? Making sure your spouse is taken care of for the rest of his or her life? Making sure your children get the most benefit out of your IRA? Making sure everything is clear to your family and everyone gets his or her fair share? Whether you have considered beneficiaries from prior marriages (and do you want to)? Having liability concerns such as alimony payments and child support as a result of divorce, or lawsuits, malpractice claims, and bankruptcy issues?

Do you want post-death control? In other words, what good is the stretch if a beneficiary won't take advantage of it? Maybe he or she wants all the money now instead of in installments taken out over time for growth purposes, because that new Ferrari is calling, and it can't wait. Or maybe there are special circumstances, such as disability, incompetence, lack of knowledge and/or interest in financial matters on the part of the beneficiaries, or lack of maturity and sophistication in the case of minor children. If it's likely your child or other beneficiary will not exercise the stretch, then it is something you need not plan for—you can simply designate the child (or other person) you named beneficiary and let the child do as he or she pleases; this will at least guarantee that the stretch option exists for the child in the event he or she eventually sees the light. If you have more than one child, only one of whom is the responsible type who will maximize the stretch, it might be better to leave other assets (a non-IRA bank account or fund, a piece of the family business, or a home) to the child who probably wouldn't stretch, and bequeath your IRA to the child who will; this way, you can leave both children the inheritance that works best for them according to their aims. And if you really want to exercise post-death control by making sure your beneficiaries have no other choice but to take full advantage of the stretch according to your direct guidance, you can name a trust (see Chapter Seven) as your IRA beneficiary for their benefit and state in it the degree of post-death control you wish.

Do you have charitable intentions? Leaving an IRA to charity in whole or in part renders the stretch option moot. Besides, charities just want the cash all at once so they can put it to good use immediately.

Some additional questions you will need to ask yourself include:

- *How old are the beneficiaries you are considering (when will lifetime distributions begin)?*
- *Are those beneficiaries still working?*
- *Will your beneficiaries need to tap into your IRA for living expenses?*
- *Should you leave a Roth stretch IRA instead of a traditional stretch IRA if you are a candidate for a Roth?*

Your answers to these questions will tell you a lot about yourself and your options, as well as your short- and long-term goals for your retirement nest egg. What you find out will guide you in making the right beneficiary and other choices to achieve those goals.

Can *Your* IRA Be Stretched?

You'd certainly hate to go through this whole book salivating over the incredible amounts of cash your IRA can be parlayed into for your family, only to find out that *your retirement fund cannot be stretched*, wouldn't you? Well, relax. In just about all cases, an IRA *can* be stretched—provided you set it up properly (I'll get to that in a moment). The reason I hedge and say in "just about all" cases is that, believe it or not, some banks and other financial institutions are ignorant of the stretch IRA—the option for your IRA beneficiaries to extend distributions on inherited IRAs over the rest of their lives—or so unclear about the tax laws that they do not allow it.

If your retirement account cannot be stretched, your beneficiaries will have to withdraw the funds soon after death and in some cases in a lump sum. That means all taxes are due right away and the long-term value of your tax-deferred retirement account will vanish. That completely defeats the benefits of the stretch and the fundamental concept of this book, which is to keep your IRA away from the IRS for as long as possible. Even though the stretch IRA is permitted and actually encouraged by the tax law, it is not automatic if your retirement plan is not set up properly to take advantage of it.

So, let's ask again: Can *your* IRA be stretched?

Yes, if you do three things (and they are all easy). Skip or backslide on any one of these points and you'll be sick at the millions of dollars you will have cost yourself and your family in potential wealth:

1. Name an IRA beneficiary NOW—by filling out an IRA beneficiary form for each IRA you own, designating a person (or persons)—as opposed to an entity—as your named beneficiary. Inform beneficiaries where each is kept, and regularly update each form to stay current.
2. Make sure your IRA custodial agreement allows the stretch. Not all do.
3. Roll company plan funds, such as a 401(k) fund, into an IRA as soon as you can—usually right after you change jobs or retire.

Only *you* (not your heirs) can do these three things, and they are *all* you can do to ensure the stretch for your beneficiaries. (It's still possible, of course, for your beneficiaries to screw up the stretch when they inherit by not inheriting properly. That's where Part Two comes in. It tells your beneficiaries what *they* must do—and how to do it—to capitalize on the potential bonanza you've served up on a silver platter.) Let's dig into each of them:

1. Name an IRA Beneficiary NOW!

Even if the required beginning date (after age 70½) for taking required minimum distributions (RMDs) is a long way off for you yet, name a beneficiary for your IRA now. You could die prematurely; then there'll be hell to pay!

As noted in Chapter One, to get the stretch, you must name a living, breathing person as your beneficiary on an IRA beneficiary form, because only the person named to inherit on that form is the *designated beneficiary* and thus gets to extend required distributions over his or her life expectancy and parlay the IRA into a fortune.

Ask your IRA custodian (the bank, broker, or mutual fund company holding the account) to supply you with the IRA beneficiary forms you need, and fill out one for each IRA you own, making sure to name both a primary and a contingent beneficiary—just in case your first named beneficiary predeceases you. This will also allow you to take advantage of post-death estate planning and disclaimer opportunities under IRA rules.

Make sure when there are multiple beneficiaries that you clearly state on the form the name of each beneficiary and his or her share, using a fraction, a percentage, or the word "equally" if that is applicable. Otherwise some beneficiaries may be left out or it may be unclear what their portion is. There should be no question as to who gets what. This includes contingent beneficiaries as well.

If you neglect to name a beneficiary for your IRA, your estate will most likely be named the beneficiary, although the IRA custodial agreement could bail you out here, depending on the default provision that kicks in. But hoping the default provision will save your beneficiaries is no way to plan. Whether by negligence or by design, naming the estate as beneficiary of your IRA is the same as leaving the IRA to pass through your will. If the IRA does pass through the will, it becomes a probate asset subject to estate claims and probate costs. The stretch is lost and your beneficiaries will not be able to reclaim it.

Review and Update IRA Beneficiary Forms Regularly

The IRA beneficiary form trumps a will as far as who will receive your IRA. If you name a beneficiary on your IRA beneficiary form and a different person in your will, the person named on your IRA beneficiary form will inherit your IRA. This is why it is important not only to designate a beneficiary by filling out a beneficiary form for each IRA, but also to keep each form updated regularly as events (a death, a birth, a marriage, a divorce) in your life unfold, or things may not turn out as you want them to.

For example, people often name their mom, dad, or siblings as IRA beneficiary when they are single. After they get married they might want it to go to their spouse or children instead, but if they neglect to change or update the form, it won't reflect this wish. Imagine being a widow and finding out that your mother-in-law has just inherited your deceased husband's IRA! Even if you are named beneficiary in an updated will, if the IRA beneficiary form hasn't been updated too, your mother-in-law would prevail since her name is on the outdated form, and the IRA beneficiary form trumps the will.

If that kind of IRA beneficiary form mistake isn't bad enough, imagine what would happen if you are divorced but you never updated your IRA beneficiary form because it fell through the cracks after the heat of battle. Most likely, you named your spouse (now your ex-spouse) originally. Well, guess what? Even if you've remarried, your ex-spouse still inherits your IRA after you're gone! I'm sure your new wife or husband will be delighted—fortunately you won't be around to hear just how delighted. (Even Barbie and Ken have split after 40-some years—I never knew they were married—and there's a new doll now: "Divorced Barbie." It comes with Ken's IRA!)

Mistakes can be easily avoided by regularly updating your IRA beneficiary form. Review each form no less than once a year—even more often if any changes due to life events or new tax laws warrant it. For example, as the estate tax exemption increases over the next few years, you may want to have more of the IRA pass under that exemption, leaving more to your children estate-tax-free.

Most IRA owners today are savvy enough not to name their estate the beneficiary of their IRA, but the estate may have been named years ago when they weren't so savvy. Since they haven't looked at their IRA beneficiary form since, it still is, meaning they will unknowingly lose the stretch by still having their IRA pass through their will. It may turn out that the person they wanted their IRA to go to still gets it, because they're named in the will, but if the recipient is not a designated beneficiary, he or she won't get to stretch. Remember what I keep saying (and repeat it after me): Only a *designated beneficiary* can stretch post-death required distributions over his or her lifetime, and to be a designated beneficiary, that person's name must either be on the IRA beneficiary form or be named through the default provision of the IRA custodial agreement.

Interestingly, many people wouldn't think of losing track of their wills and can locate them right away. They do not realize, however, the importance and long-term significance of the IRA beneficiary designation form, so they can—and often do—lose track of it. The IRA beneficiary form is the key document when it comes to making the most of your IRA and capitalizing on the stretch concept. Even if you have an up-to-date IRA beneficiary form, if no one can find it, it's the same as if you never named a beneficiary for your IRA.

Know Where Forms Are Kept (And Clue in Beneficiaries)

Check to see if a copy of each beneficiary form you've executed is on file with your bank, broker, mutual fund company, or financial advisor, and if so, see that it designates the correct beneficiary—in other words, that it's not blank (you know what that means) or that it names a deceased beneficiary (not uncommon when forms haven't been checked in a while). If they can't be found, don't waste time trying to figure out where they went. You're still breathing, so it's not too late to get new beneficiary forms for each IRA and execute them right away. All prior choices can be changed. The old forms (if ever found) no longer lock in elections as they did under the old rules, and the new forms supercede them.

Keep copies on file in a safe place where you can easily put your hands on them—and leave instructions where they are so your beneficiaries can find them after you're gone.

2. Make Sure Your IRA Custodial Agreement Allows the Stretch

A custodial agreement is a form you sign when you open an IRA with a bank, broker, mutual fund, or financial advisor. This agreement lists all the provisions the bank, broker, or mutual fund that will be holding your IRA assets will allow. It's kind of like their rule book, but many IRA custodians still play by IRA rules more than a decade old, rules predating the creation of the automatic stretch under current tax law.

Let me say it again: *The IRS regulations stipulate that any designated beneficiary can stretch distributions on an inherited IRA over his or her lifetime. Period.*

Nevertheless, having not updated their rule book in ten years, some IRA custodians don't allow the stretch. Is yours one of them? If so, while you still have the leverage, you should move your money *now* to an IRA custodian that does. Your beneficiaries may not be able to after you're gone. How could that be? If your beneficiaries want the money, the IRA custodian has to give it to them, right? True, but if the agreement won't allow the stretch, that money will likely be given to your beneficiaries in a lump sum that gets socked with taxes.

So, the first thing to find out about your existing IRA custodial agreement, or the one you are about to sign, is whether it allows your beneficiaries to stretch the IRA they inherit from you. Most will. But don't take that for granted. *Make sure!*

Here are some other items to check:

- **What is the default option?** I mentioned this earlier. By "default option" I mean the legal provision in the custodial agreement that stipulates what will happen to your IRA at your death if you do not name a beneficiary (which could never happen, of course), or your beneficiary screws up and loses the IRA beneficiary form (which could happen), or the financial institution cannot locate the form (which could also happen, and often does), resulting in an unnamed beneficiary. If the agreement says the IRA goes to the estate, you know that's bad. You want a default option that says if no beneficiary is named then your IRA goes first to your spouse; if no spouse, then to your children; and if no spouse or children, then to your estate. This will help to preserve the stretch option for your heirs if, for whatever reason, no beneficiary is named.

- **Is a per stirpes provision permitted?** For an inherited IRA, the "per stirpes" provision describes how your IRA will pass if your beneficiary dies before you do. This is important to some IRA owners who may leave their IRA equally to three children but want to make sure that if one of the children dies before they do, then that child's share passes to his or her children and not to the remaining siblings. Otherwise, the deceased child's family would be disinherited. Of course, if a beneficiary dies before you, then you can change the beneficiary form and correct the situation yourself. But what if you are incapacitated at that point and unable to make the change yourself or you forget to change your beneficiary form, as too many people do? Then per stirpes is your safety valve. Some agreements will allow you to write it on the form yourself. For example, let's say you are leaving your IRA in equal shares to your three kids, one of whom is Mary Smith. You could simply write: "Mary Smith, per stirpes." This means if Mary Smith (your named beneficiary) dies before you do, then Mary's share of your IRA will pass to her children.

- **Is a customized beneficiary form permitted?** A customized beneficiary form replaces the standard IRA beneficiary form provided by most IRA custodians. You create it with an attorney or financial advisor as a way of ensuring post-death control. It is as close as you can get to naming a trust as your IRA beneficiary without actually doing so. The problem with customized IRA beneficiary forms is that many custodians will not accept them. They often will accept only their own forms. You should find out now, before you go through the trouble and expense of customizing a beneficiary form with your attorney or advisor, whether the custodian will accept it. Even if a custodian does accept it, another problem with a customized beneficiary form is that as events in your life change and you want to go back and recustomize the form to reflect your new wishes, the process can get very expensive, like redoing a trust (or a will). In this case, if you want that much post-death control, you are probably better off naming a trust as your IRA beneficiary in the first place (see Chapter Seven).

- **Is a beneficiary allowed to name a beneficiary?** Why do you care if your beneficiary will be allowed to name a beneficiary? If your beneficiary has, say, a 40-year life expectancy when he or she inherits and then dies prematurely 10 years later, there are still 30 years left on the stretch period, and the IRS will allow a successor beneficiary to stretch withdrawals over that 30 years—unless the custodian says no. In that case, the inherited IRA must go through probate, subjecting it to estate claims and contests, taxes and other costs, likely killing the remaining stretch. The way to avoid all this is to set up your IRA with a custodian that agrees to allow your beneficiary to name a beneficiary. This way, if your beneficiary dies before the IRA is paid out, the named successor beneficiary will receive what's left and be able to continue the stretch based on the original beneficiary's remaining life expectancy at the time of death. If your IRA custodian won't allow this, switch to one that will.

- **Are non-spouse beneficiaries allowed to move investments via a trustee-to-trustee transfer?** You certainly want to give your non-spouse beneficiaries the flexibility to change IRA custodians if they wish. For example, they may want to move the IRA to another bank that might offer different investment choices. They cannot just take the money out and take it to another bank. That's called a "rollover." And tax law prohibits non-spouse beneficiaries (such as your children) from doing a rollover. The only alternative for them—other than accepting a lump sum check and getting hit with taxes—is to move the inherited IRA funds from one custodian to another via what is called a "trustee-to-trustee" (or direct) transfer, meaning the funds are untouched in the transition and are therefore safe from taxes. Make sure your IRA custodian allows this, and if not, pick another that does.

- **Are naming multiple beneficiaries and IRA splitting permitted?** Most institutions will let you open several IRAs and name different beneficiaries on each one, but what I'm talking about here is naming several beneficiaries on one IRA. It is important to know *now* if your custodian will permit you to name multiple beneficiaries (your three children, for example) and allow them to split the IRA into their separate shares after you're gone so that each beneficiary can stretch shares over his or her own life expectancy. If your IRA custodian does not allow splitting, then your beneficiaries must all take distributions over the life expectancy of the oldest one—or to put it another way, they must use the beneficiary with the shortest life expectancy to calculate post-death withdrawals. If you name your three children and they are all around the same age, this won't make much of a difference. But if one beneficiary is 92-year-old Aunt Edna and the other is 2-year-old granddaughter Samantha, the latter will be stuck using Aunt Edna's life expectancy for the stretch period. I don't care how much of a live wire Aunt Edna may still be, according to the IRS Life Expectancy tables she doesn't have that many more years, and the stretch period is based on *her* life expectancy.

- **Will a trust be accepted as beneficiary?** If you want to name a trust as your IRA beneficiary, make sure that your IRA custodian will accept a trust to be utilized and will agree to pay out the inherited IRA according to the terms of the trust. It would be a shame to go through the trouble, time, and expense of naming a trust as your IRA beneficiary, only to have your beneficiaries find out too late (after you are gone) that your custodial agreement does not provide for trusts to be utilized.

- **Is your power of attorney form accepted?** A power of attorney allows the person you designate to act in your place. Bestowing a POA can prove invaluable if for health or other reasons you are unable to act for yourself. Depending upon how much power you give the person you designate, he or she will be able to make investment decisions and execute IRA transactions—including transferring IRA funds, changing IRA beneficiaries on your IRA beneficiary form, making required IRA distributions, and so on. Obviously you would give this broad power only to a spouse, child, or some other trusted family member or friend. It's good to have . . . just in case. Be sure your custodial agreement will accept a POA form allowing you to appoint another person to act on your behalf so as to maintain all stretch options.

- **Is your agreement silent on the issue of divorce?** Here's the situation. You go through a messy divorce (is there any other kind?) and your property and other assets are split up. The divorce papers are signed; you even do up a new will; then you walk away, never to look back because you want to move on with your life. Oops . . . you weren't paying attention when I told you earlier not to forget to revisit your IRA beneficiary form, and so your ex-spouse is still named. While most custodians are silent on the issue, some agreements do contain a provision that says a divorce or legal separation revokes the previous designation of a former spouse as beneficiary, unless the divorce decree stipulates otherwise. I'm not saying your marriage isn't rock solid, but you know the statistics. This provision is a way of making sure your ex-spouse doesn't inherit and get to stretch your IRA instead of your new spouse and children, in case you slip up.

■ **Is there a simultaneous death provision?** How will your IRA custodian handle things should you and your designated beneficiary (your spouse, for example) die at the same time? You'll want to be assured your children (or whoever is next in line) will be named designated beneficiary so they can get the benefit of the stretch. Also, for estate planning purposes, if you and your spouse die together in a car accident or plane crash, it is important to know who is deemed to have predeceased the other. The answer to this determines which estate the IRA goes to and thus who inherits and gets to stretch. For example, if the entire IRA goes to the husband's estate because the wife is deemed to have died first, the husband's beneficiaries will inherit the assets. That's OK if they are the same beneficiary choices as the wife's (your children together, for example). But if you have a blended family or are in a second marriage, the children of one or the other of you could be disinherited entirely, let alone lose the opportunity to stretch. Find out *now* whether your IRA custodian offers a "simultaneous death" provision in your agreement that spells out what happens to your IRA in such a rare case, and tie this into your overall estate plan.

3. Roll Company Plan Funds to an IRA

If you want to guarantee the stretch option for your children, you should roll any funds you may have in a 401(k), 403(b), 457, or other tax-deferred company plan into an IRA as soon as you are permitted, which is usually right after you retire. After you withdraw the funds, you have 60 days to roll them over into an IRA without facing a withdrawal penalty.[7]

---

[7]Beginning in 2002, Congress granted the IRS authority to waive the 60-day rule and give people more time to complete a rollover if you can show your intent to do the rollover on time but were unable due to a clear mistake made by you, your advisor, or financial institution, or if you had health problems that kept you from completing the rollover on time. IRS Revenue Procedure 2003-16 provides guidance in this area. In most cases you'll have to

Better yet, make a trustee-to-trustee transfer (direct transfer—also called a "direct rollover") of the funds so that you do not touch the money. It goes directly from your 401(k) or other company plan into your IRA and you never take possession of the money. This way there is no 60-day rule to worry about, since the 60-day rule only applies when you receive the money. Also, if you do not request a trustee-to-trustee transfer, the company will withhold 20 percent in federal tax, so you will only receive 80 percent of your plan balance to roll over to your IRA. You'll have to make up the rest from other funds if you have them. If you don't, you'll have to pay income tax and a 10 percent penalty (if you are under age 59½ and no exceptions apply) on the 20 percent that was withheld. Yes, you will receive credit for that tax withheld when you file your taxes, but now you have wiped out any stretch possibility on 20 percent of your retirement savings. That will have a devastating impact on the long-term value of the stretch IRA you are setting up now. Rollovers can be done only once every 12 months, but the trustee-to-trustee transfer eliminates that restriction as well. Do the trustee-to-trustee transfer.

If your 401(k) insists on issuing you a check for your account balance (as opposed to doing the direct transfer to your IRA account), the check can still qualify as a trustee-to-trustee transfer if it is made out correctly. Make sure it is *not* made out to you. If your name is Tom Jones, and your IRA is set up with ABC bank—as the place you want to roll your 401(k) funds to—the check should be made out to *"ABC Bank as Trustee of IRA of Tom Jones."* If your 401(k) plan gives you any trouble about this titling on the check, let the plan administrator know that this is *exactly* how the IRS wants the check made out to be considered a trustee-

---

apply to the IRS for a private letter ruling to be granted relief. Then you'll also have to go through the time and expense of the ruling process, which can take anywhere from six to nine months. If the IRS rules favorably, you are able to redeposit the funds—in other words, complete the rollover even though it is well beyond 60 days.

to-trustee transfer (IRS Regulations Section 1.401(a)(31)-1, A-4) so that the 20 percent withholding rule will not apply.

There are several reasons why you should do this rollover. One is that even though the IRS allows the stretch, company plans do not have to offer this option, and typically they do not because they don't want the record-keeping headache of having to keep track of the beneficiaries of deceased ex-employees for payout purposes.

Another reason is that although you may think your company plan will yield a better investment return than an IRA (a debatable point), that short-term higher gain is nowhere near worth the potential millions that may be sacrificed if your beneficiaries are unable to take advantage of the stretch option.

Don't be penny-wise and pound-foolish about fees either. Sure there are fees in an IRA. But do you think there are no fees attached to a company plan such as a 401(k)? You just don't see them. Even if the visible fees in an IRA are slightly higher than the invisible ones in a company plan (another debatable point), not rolling over for that reason is, again, short-term thinking that could cost your family millions in lost tax-deferred compounding.

The bottom line: If you want your family to be able to parlay your retirement wealth into a fortune, roll or transfer your company plan balance to an IRA!

FAQ

Q. Ed, what should I do if I have a Keogh (sole proprietorship) self-employment plan?

A. Same thing. Terminate the Keogh and roll to an IRA and do it *now*. If you wish to keep making contributions, you can set up a SEP-IRA (simplified employee pension). In most cases you can contribute as much to a SEP as you can to a Keogh, and the stretch is guaranteed to nonspouse beneficiaries, such as your children, even if the plan does not outlive you (as is usually the case with sole proprietorships). That's because the SEP not only is your new company plan, but it is already an IRA and can be stretched the same as any inherited IRA. If your spouse is the Keogh beneficiary, there is no problem, because he or she can roll it to an IRA after your death. But if a non-spouse is the Keogh beneficiary, the funds are generally distributed and taxed in full at your death. No stretch.

Slott's Tips

If you cannot do a rollover yet, some smaller company retirement plans—for example, a group of doctors or lawyers who have created a plan for their firm—offer an "in-service distribution" provision allowing you to siphon off some funds and roll them over to an IRA even though you are still working. See if your company allows this. You'll find out in that big book of legalese called the summary plan description every employee receives when joining a company plan. It's in there somewhere. Start with the section on plan distributions. If you don't see it, ask about it. If your plan does not currently offer an in-service distribution, then the plan can be amended to include it.

Supersize Your Stretch with a Roth IRA Conversion

Another reason to roll money from your 401(k) or other company plan over to an IRA is to have that money positioned to be converted to a Roth IRA. You cannot convert to a Roth IRA from a company plan. However, if you die with funds in a company plan such as a 401(k), your spouse beneficiary can roll them to his or her own IRA and then convert them to a Roth.

Between a traditional stretch IRA, which grows tax-deferred, a Roth stretch IRA, which grows tax-free, the Roth stretch IRA is clearly the way to go, especially since you never have to take required distributions (until your Roth is inherited by a non-spouse beneficiary like your child or grandchild). That alone adds years of compounding to the account. But as I've said before, the big benefit of a Roth IRA is that all of this money grows totally income-tax-free for you, and for whomever you leave what's left, to use.

FIVE ■ ■ ■

Who Can—Should—Inherit Your Stretch IRA?

"Inheritance laws regarding IRAs are complex, so it's important to make sure you're not creating a financial headache for your loved ones by not putting enough thought into the designation now."
—Terri Cullen, *The Wall Street Journal*, June 24, 2004

Take Me Out to the Ball Game

It's time for you to decide who will inherit your IRA. You will need to choose both primary beneficiaries and contingent beneficiaries for each IRA or retirement plan you have. The primary beneficiaries will inherit your IRA when you die. The contingent beneficiaries are put in place in case your primary beneficiary dies before you, or if after your death, your primary beneficiary decides to disclaim (refuse) the inheritance for estate planning purposes. Your IRA could then go directly to the contingent beneficiaries you name now.

You wouldn't go a baseball game without getting a scorecard, would you? When it comes to your IRA, you probably already have an idea who your potential beneficiaries are, since most likely they will be close family members. But draw up a scorecard anyway. You'll be surprised who comes to mind—and who may come out of the woodwork after you are gone, especially given today's blended families. Include information on all the players—ages, health, birthdays, residency and future residency, medical or education needs. Residency issues should also be addressed in case you or your beneficiaries have moved to another state or country. You'll want to know if the state protects IRAs from creditors, for example, as well as if there are rules for that state's tax treatment of distributions from retirement accounts (some states have provisions that exempt certain amounts of IRA distributions from state taxation). As of this writing the United States Supreme Court was about to decide whether IRAs will receive federal creditor protection. For the latest on this, go to my website at www.IRAHELP.com.

Start with a simple family tree:

- **Spouse.** Most people name a spouse in order to provide for him or her after his or her death. If you name your spouse, there will be no estate tax on your IRA at death, because property left from one spouse to another is free of estate tax through the use of the marital deduction (if your spouse is a U.S. citizen). Also, naming your spouse as your IRA beneficiary allows the spouse to roll over your IRA and treat it as his or her own. Before you choose this option, though, you should consider the big picture and evaluate all potential beneficiaries and the long-term effects of your choice, including how it fits into your estate plan. The first question you should ask is, "Will my spouse need the money?" If the answer is a definitive yes, then that is the end of the story. Obviously your estate tax concerns should take a backseat to providing financial security for your spouse after your death. However, if your spouse does not need the money, perhaps because he or she has his or her own pension, IRA, or other assets, then that is where real tax planning can parlay your IRA into millions. Even if you name your spouse, the stretch IRA for your children can still be preserved as long as your spouse names them on the IRA beneficiary form as soon as he or she creates his or her own IRA using the IRA inherited from you. Your children can then stretch whatever is left when your spouse dies.

- **Children and/or grandchildren—from current and/or previous marriage(s).** Choosing a younger beneficiary such as a child or grandchild can stretch your tax-deferred IRA another 50 or 60 years, providing them with a powerful financial legacy. Do any of the children or grandchildren have special (education or medical) needs? If so, you may want to leave more of your IRA to that specific person (through a guardian or a trust—see Chapter Seven) to cover these needs.

- **Parents.** If you die and your parents are still living, who will support them? If this is an issue, it would generally be a poor move to name them as your IRA beneficiaries in order to provide support. They are older, will have to withdraw money sooner, and if they are on any government program (Medicaid, for example), the inherited IRA could be lost to nursing home bills. If available, it may be better to use non-IRA money to provide financial support, thereby ensuring the stretch for your spouse or children.

- **Distant relatives.** You want to make sure to have taken into account anyone who may surface after your death to make a claim on your property.

Slott's Tips

Pay attention to family dynamics! This book is about parlaying wealth, but not everything is about money. You may want to leave your IRA equally to your two children, for example, even though one may be a ne'er-do-well and will probably blow it all quickly (just to keep peace in the family). This is just something to keep in mind when planning who gets what. You want to leave your property to the people you feel should receive it, regardless of taxes. But when you do decide, you can also plan how that person can make the most of it and what you may have to do now to make sure this happens.

All the potential beneficiary choices on your scorecard fall into two categories: spouse beneficiaries (wives and husbands) and non-spouse beneficiaries (children, grandchildren, everybody, and every*thing* (estate, charity, or trust) else. Let's consider the ramifications of choosing each one on your IRA's capacity to stretch.

Spouse Beneficiaries

For many people, the first choice is to name their spouse as primary beneficiary and their kids as contingent beneficiaries. Uncle Sam loves spouses. He goes out of his way to please them with tax breaks such as the "spousal rollover." This allows spouse beneficiaries to roll over their deceased spouse's retirement plan into their own IRA, tax-free. Only a spouse beneficiary can do a rollover.

In addition, there are distribution advantages if a spouse is the sole beneficiary. During the IRA owner's lifetime, if the spouse is the sole beneficiary for the entire year and is more than 10 years younger than the IRA owner, the IRA owner can use the Joint Lifetime Expectancy table (see Appendix II) to calculate required withdrawals. This would lower the required minimum distribution amounts and in turn lower the tax and leave more for the IRA owner to use or to pass on to beneficiaries. For the spouse to be able to use these advantages, the spouse must be the sole beneficiary of the IRA. If the spouse is not the sole beneficiary, that spouse is treated for distribution purposes as a non-spouse beneficiary. This is why spouses should never be co-beneficiaries.

A spouse beneficiary of an IRA can also elect to "remain a beneficiary" and not do a spousal rollover or treat the IRA as his or her own. In this case, if the IRA owner dies before his or her required beginning date (RBD) for taking distributions, the inheriting spouse (who remains a beneficiary) can delay required distributions until December 31 of the year the IRA owner would have turned 70½ years old, regardless of the surviving spouse's age. If the IRA owner dies on or after reaching age 70½, then the surviving spouse choosing to remain a beneficiary must begin required withdrawals in the year after the IRA owner's death. But even in that case, spouses who are the sole beneficiary and who elect to remain a beneficiary can take beneficiary payouts based upon their life expectancy, recalculated using the Single Life Expectancy table for inherited IRAs. For example, let's say the IRA owner, whose name is Fred, dies at 68, before his RBD, and names his spouse, Annie, 65, as his sole IRA beneficiary. Annie has two choices. She can elect either to remain a beneficiary or to do a spousal rollover and treat the inherited IRA as her own. If she elects to remain as beneficiary, she does not have to begin taking distributions until December 31 of the year Fred would have reached age 70½. If she chooses a spousal rollover and treats the IRA as her own, she will not have to begin taking distributions until after *she* reaches age 70½. Since she's 65, that gives her five and a half more years to accumulate additional money in the IRA before she has to tap into it.

If Annie were significantly *younger* than Fred, however, it would pay her to elect to remain a beneficiary rather than do a spousal rollover when he dies. For example, if she were *much* younger (say, 40) and wanted to take money out before age 59½, there would be a 10 percent penalty assessed for withdrawing early. But this 10 percent penalty does not apply to retirement account beneficiaries. That's why electing to remain a beneficiary is the better option for her in this instance. After she turns 59½, she still has the option to do the rollover to her own IRA and get all the benefits of that, since the election to remain a beneficiary does not restrict a spouse from doing an IRA rollover later on.

It might also pay Annie to remain a beneficiary if she were older (say, 75) than Fred. In this case, she would not have to draw down from the inherited IRA for another few years (until December 31 of the year Fred would have reached age 70½), thereby accumulating several more years of compounded earnings. And, if Fred was already past his required beginning date when he died, Annie would have the option of using his remaining single life expectancy (if it is longer than hers).

> ## *Slott's Tips*
>
> When spouses are named beneficiary, they should imme-
> diately name beneficiaries of their own as soon as they in-
> herit. The reason for this is that if they should die suddenly
> before having named a beneficiary, the inherited IRA will
> generally pass to their estate, and you should know by now
> what that could mean to the IRA and its stretch capabilities.

Non-Spouse Beneficiaries

As described earlier, a non-spouse beneficiary can be a child, grand-child, brother, sister, parent, friend, trust, estate, or charity. Since only people and not entities[8] can be designated beneficiaries and thus entitled to the stretch IRA, however, I'll focus on them, as this chapter is all about leaving your IRA to whomever will be able to grow it tax-deferred for as long as possible.

Let's look at the following example to see how life expectancy and post-death distributions to individual non-spouse IRA benefi-ciaries are calculated.

Mary names her daughter Jill as designated beneficiary of her IRA. Mary's age doesn't matter because Jill's stretch period (life expectancy) is based on Jill's age in the year after her mother's death. If Mary dies in 2006 when Jill is 50, then Jill would go to the Single Life Expectancy table and look up the life expectancy factor for a 51-year-old (the age Jill will be in 2007, when she must begin taking required minimum distributions). That factor is 33.3 years. This means Jill must withdraw $\frac{1}{33.3}$ (or 3 percent) of her mother's IRA balance as of December 31, 2006. If that balance is, say, $100,000, then Jill must withdraw $3,003 from the inherited IRA by the end of 2007. In 2008 she reduces her life expectancy

---

[8]Trust beneficiaries could be designated beneficiaries if the trust qualifies under certain IRA rules (see Chapter Seven).

factor by one and does the same each subsequent year. So, for 2008, Jill's RMD will be based on the December 31, 2007, IRA balance divided by 32.3 (and so on until the term expires or the entire account balance is withdrawn).

Of course, Jill can always withdraw more, but the way to make the inherited IRA last as long as possible and parlay it to the full extent permitted by law is to withdraw only the minimum amount each year for the rest of her lifetime. That's how the stretch IRA works.

FAQ

Q. Ed, how can I be so sure my designated beneficiary will take advantage of the stretch I've created?

A. I know what you're thinking. The minute you die, maybe your son might take off to Las Vegas with your IRA and bet the whole shebang on red. (Well, he's got almost a 50-50 chance of winning instead of losing!) But hopefully, once you show him the kinds of numbers the stretch can produce, that will be all the incentive he needs. You can lead a horse to water, but you can't make it drink—unless you *force* the issue by naming a trust as your IRA beneficiary (see Chapter Seven) with a provision that requires your wish that the IRA be stretched and only minimum required distributions be taken.

Maximizing the Compounding Power of the Stretch

The best way to take full advantage of the power of the stretch is to leave your IRA to your spouse (assuming he or she needs it to live on) and then have the surviving spouse name your children, grandchildren, or other young family members or loved ones as beneficiary. Once a non-spouse beneficiary inherits, he or she (or they) can stretch distributions based on their own life expectancy factor.

Here are some realistic projections of the power of the stretch depending upon how much is left in your retirement account when it passes to your beneficiaries. To parlay wealth, you must have something remaining in your retirement account, but you don't need to leave much for your family to be able to grow it into a fortune.

These examples are all based on a balance of $100,000 in the IRA when it passes to your beneficiaries. If you already have, or project having, a balance of more or less than that, base the results in each example on whatever multiple, plus or minus, of $100,000 it is. For example, if you do not have $100,000, but have $40,000 that can pass to your family, then your result will be 40 percent of the result in each example. But I have a feeling many of you may have more than $100,000 in IRA funds left for your family to inherit. In that case, your family will end up with much more than I project in these examples. Say you have $300,000 that you can pass on to your beneficiaries; then multiply the results in the examples by 3.

It will be fun to see how much more you can exceed the results these examples show, since in each of them only one spouse has an IRA to pass on, whereas today many married couples each have pensions or IRAs to pass on. In which case you can double the results shown here—assuming again a $100,000 balance for each of you to leave to your family.

Use these examples as an eye-opening guide to the wonders of how much your family can parlay what's left in your IRA into if they seize this golden opportunity you have created for them.

Example 1—Traditional IRA

Steve is 65 years old in 2005 and has an IRA worth $100,000. He names his wife, Debra, who is 62 years old, as his IRA beneficiary. Steve does not have to begin required minimum distributions until he reaches 70½ years of age. Let's assume Steve's IRA grows at an 8 percent rate. After age 70½, Steve begins taking his RMDs on schedule (he wouldn't want to miss an RMD because there's a 50 percent penalty on the amount he should have withdrawn). Now let's further assume that Steve dies in 2025, having lived to the ripe old age of 85. His wife, Debra, inherits, and as soon as she does, she rolls the IRA over, into her own IRA, then immediately names their son Jeffrey as her beneficiary. Debra lives another ten years and dies in 2035 at age 92, when Jeffrey is 57.

Now, look at Table 7 to see what happens to the balance of Steve's original IRA.[9]

	Year	Age	Value of IRA	Life Expectancy Factor (in years)	IRA Required Minimum Distributions (RMDs)	Cumulative IRA Distributions
	2005	65	$100,000	21.0	$0	$0
	2006	66	$108,000	20.2	$0	$0
	2007	67	$116,640	19.4	$0	$0
	2008	68	$125,971	18.6	$0	$0
	2009	69	$136,049	17.8	$0	$0
Steve begins	2010	70	$146,933	27.4	$5,363	$5,363
RMDs	2011	71	$152,896	26.5	$5,770	$11,133
	2012	72	$158,896	25.6	$6,207	$17,340
	2013	73	$164,904	24.7	$6,676	$24,016
	2014	74	$170,886	23.8	$7,180	$31,196
	2015	75	$176,802	22.9	$7,721	$38,917
	2016	76	$182,607	22.0	$8,300	$47,217
	2017	77	$188,252	21.2	$8,880	$56,097

Table 7.

[9]As in all examples shown throughout this book, I am assuming an average 8 percent compounding, which is a quite realistic return over any long-term period.

Table 7. *(continued)*

	Year	Age	Value of IRA	Life Expectancy Factor (in years)	IRA Required Minimum Distributions (RMDs)	Cumulative IRA Distributions
	2018	78	$193,722	20.3	$9,543	$65,640
	2019	79	$198,913	19.5	$10,201	$75,841
	2020	80	$203,809	18.7	$10,899	$86,740
	2021	81	$208,343	17.9	$11,639	$98,379
	2022	82	$212,440	17.1	$12,423	$110,802
	2023	83	$216,018	16.3	$13,253	$124,055
	2024	84	$218,986	15.5	$14,128	$138,183
Steve dies	*2025*	*85*	*$221,247*	*14.8*	*$14,949*	*$153,132*
Debra rolls	2026	83	$222,802	16.3	$13,669	$166,801
over	2027	84	$225,864	15.5	$14,572	$181,373
	2028	85	$228,195	14.8	$15,419	$196,792
	2029	86	$229,798	14.1	$16,298	$213,090
	2030	87	$230,580	13.4	$17,207	$230,297
	2031	88	$230,443	12.7	$18,145	$248,442
	2032	89	$229,282	12.0	$19,107	$267,549
	2033	90	$226,989	11.4	$19,911	$287,460
	2034	91	$223,644	10.8	$20,708	$308,168
Debra dies	*2035*	*92*	*$219,171*	*10.2*	*$21,487*	*$329,655*
Jeffrey begins	2036	58	$213,499	27.0	$7,907	$337,562
RMDs	2037	59	$222,039	26.0	$8,540	$346,102
	2038	60	$230,579	25.0	$9,223	$355,325
	2039	61	$239,064	24.0	$9,961	$365,286
	2040	62	$247,431	23.0	$10,758	$376,044
	2041	63	$255,607	22.0	$11,619	$387,663
	2042	64	$263,507	21.0	$12,548	$400,211
	2043	65	$271,036	20.0	$13,552	$413,763

Table 7. *(continued)*

Year	Age	Value of IRA	Life Expectancy Factor (in years)	IRA Required Minimum Distributions (RMDs)	Cumulative IRA Distributions
2044	66	$278,083	19.0	$14,636	$428,399
2045	67	$284,523	18.0	$15,807	$444,206
2046	68	$290,213	17.0	$17,071	$461,277
2047	69	$294,993	16.0	$18,437	$479,714
2048	70	$298,680	15.0	$19,912	$499,626
2049	71	$301,069	14.0	$21,505	$521,131
2050	72	$301,929	13.0	$23,225	$544,356
2051	73	$301,000	12.0	$25,083	$569,439
2052	74	$297,990	11.0	$27,090	$596,529
2053	75	$292,572	10.0	$29,257	$625,786
2054	76	$284,380	9.0	$31,598	$657,384
2055	77	$273,005	8.0	$34,126	$691,510
2056	78	$257,989	7.0	$36,856	$728,366
2057	79	$238,824	6.0	$39,804	$768,170
2058	80	$214,942	5.0	$42,988	$811,158
2059	81	$185,710	4.0	$46,428	$857,586
2060	82	$150,425	3.0	$50,142	$907,728
2061	83	$108,306	2.0	$54,153	$961,881
2062	84	$58,485	1.0	$58,485	$1,020,366
2063	85	$0		$0	$1,020,366
Totals					**$1,020,366**

Sure, there would be income taxes to pay on each withdrawal, but the withdrawals and the resulting income tax would be low, because Uncle Sam is being made to wait a long time to collect.

And while Uncle Sam is waiting, the IRA is compounding tax-deferred!

Example 2—Roth IRA

Now let's change Steve's IRA to a Roth IRA, which grows income-tax-free forever, and assume that the $100,000 balance he passes on was accumulated either through annual Roth contributions or by converting his traditional IRA to a Roth IRA (see Table 8). Either way, the income tax on that balance will already have been paid. Steve and his wife, Debra, his beneficiary, withdraw nothing from the Roth IRA because no distributions are required during their lives. Otherwise all other details in the example remain the same. Simply by beginning with $100,000 in a Roth IRA instead of a traditional IRA, Steve's family ends up with $2,495,585 more in accumulated growth due to the power of the stretch ($3,515,951 minus $1,020,366 = $2,495,585)—actually more, since the Roth withdrawals are not eroded by income tax. Notice the extra years of compounding due to the fact that Roth IRA distributions are not required until their son Jeffrey inherits.

Table 8.

Year	Roth IRA Beneficiary's Age	Value of Roth IRA	Life Expectancy Factor (in years)	Roth IRA Required Minimum Distributions (RMDs)	Cumulative Roth IRA Distributions
2005	62	$100,000	23.5	$0	$0
2006	63	$108,000	22.7	$0	$0
2007	64	$116,640	21.8	$0	$0
2008	65	$125,971	21.0	$0	$0

Table 8. *(continued)*

	Year	Roth IRA Beneficiary's Age	Value of Roth IRA	Life Expectancy Factor (in years)	Roth IRA Required Minimum Distributions (RMDs)	Cumulative Roth IRA Distributions
	2009	66	$136,049	20.2	$0	$0
	2010	67	$146,933	19.4	$0	$0
	2011	68	$158,688	18.6	$0	$0
	2012	69	$171,383	17.8	$0	$0
	2013	70	$185,094	17.0	$0	$0
	2014	71	$199,902	16.3	$0	$0
	2015	72	$215,894	15.5	$0	$0
	2016	73	$233,166	14.8	$0	$0
	2017	74	$251,819	14.1	$0	$0
	2018	75	$271,965	13.4	$0	$0
	2019	76	$293,722	12.7	$0	$0
	2020	77	$317,220	12.1	$0	$0
	2021	78	$342,598	11.4	$0	$0
	2022	79	$370,006	10.8	$0	$0
	2023	80	$399,606	10.2	$0	$0
	2024	81	$431,574	9.7	$0	$0
Steve dies	*2025*	*82*	*$466,100*	*9.1*	*$0*	*$0*
Debra rolls	2026	48	$503,388	36.0	$0	$0
over	2027	49	$543,659	35.1	$0	$0
	2028	50	$587,152	34.2	$0	$0
	2029	51	$634,124	33.3	$0	$0
	2030	52	$684,854	32.3	$0	$0
	2031	53	$739,642	31.4	$0	$0
	2032	54	$798,813	30.5	$0	$0
	2033	55	$862,718	29.6	$0	$0
	2034	56	$931,735	28.7	$0	$0

Table 8. *(continued)*

	Year	Roth IRA Beneficiary's Age	Value of Roth IRA	Life Expectancy Factor (in years)	Roth IRA Required Minimum Distributions (RMDs)	Cumulative Roth IRA Distributions
Debra dies	2035	57	$1,006,274	27.9	$0	$0
Jeffrey	2036	58	$1,086,776	27.0	$40,251	$40,251
begins	2037	59	$1,130,247	26.0	$43,471	$83,722
RMDs	2038	60	$1,173,718	25.0	$46,949	$130,671
	2039	61	$1,216,911	24.0	$50,705	$181,376
	2040	62	$1,259,502	23.0	$54,761	$236,137
	2041	63	$1,301,120	22.0	$59,142	$295,279
	2042	64	$1,341,336	21.0	$63,873	$359,152
	2043	65	$1,379,660	20.0	$68,983	$428,135
	2044	66	$1,415,531	19.0	$74,502	$502,637
	2045	67	$1,448,311	18.0	$80,462	$583,099
	2046	68	$1,477,277	17.0	$86,899	$669,998
	2047	69	$1,501,608	16.0	$93,851	$763,849
	2048	70	$1,520,378	15.0	$101,359	$865,208
	2049	71	$1,532,541	14.0	$109,467	$974,675
	2050	72	$1,536,920	13.0	$118,225	$1,092,900
	2051	73	$1,532,191	12.0	$127,683	$1,220,583
	2052	74	$1,516,869	11.0	$137,897	$1,358,480
	2053	75	$1,489,290	10.0	$148,929	$1,507,409
	2054	76	$1,447,590	9.0	$160,843	$1,668,252
	2055	77	$1,389,687	8.0	$173,711	$1,841,963
	2056	78	$1,313,254	7.0	$187,608	$2,029,571
	2057	79	$1,215,698	6.0	$202,616	$2,232,187
	2058	80	$1,094,129	5.0	$218,826	$2,451,013
	2059	81	$945,327	4.0	$236,332	$2,687,345
	2060	82	$765,715	3.0	$255,238	$2,942,583

Table 8. *(continued)*

Year	Roth IRA Beneficiary's Age	Value of Roth IRA	Life Expectancy Factor (in years)	Roth IRA Required Minimum Distributions (RMDs)	Cumulative Roth IRA Distributions
2061	83	$551,315	2.0	$275,658	$3,218,241
2062	84	$297,710	1.0	$297,710	$3,515,951
2063	85	$0	0.0	$0	$3,515,951
Totals					**$3,515,951**

The big benefit of the Roth IRA is that while you are the Roth IRA owner, there are no required distributions. Even when a spouse inherits, there are still no RMDs, which do not begin until the Roth is inherited by a non-spouse beneficiary. With a traditional IRA, Steve had to begin RMDs at age 70½, and his wife, Debra, had to continue those distributions after he died. But if Steve begins with a Roth IRA, no distributions are required for the rest of his life or for the rest of Debra's life; they begin in 2036, the year after Jeffrey inherits. Thus, Steve's Roth IRA was able to compound totally income-tax-free for another 25 years before his son Jeffrey ever has to withdraw a dime!

That's why a Roth IRA always builds to so much more than the traditional IRA with the stretch. And that is why you should do everything in your power to contribute to a Roth IRA now and convert your current traditional IRAs to Roth IRAs if you qualify. Yes, you will pay tax now to convert to a Roth IRA, but look at the reward here. The long-term tax-free buildup for you and your family dwarfs any tax you may pay now.

Example 3—Traditional IRA

OK, let's make Steve a bit younger; instead of 65, let's say he's 50 in 2005 and has already accumulated $100,000 in a traditional IRA, and see what happens. His wife, Debra, is 47. As before, Steve still lives to 85 and leaves his IRA to his wife, Debra, who lives until age 92. Jeffrey inherits at age 57. Would just 15 additional years tax-deferred compounding in action, starting with the same $100,000, make that big of a difference? You bet it does! A **$2,216,475** difference, to be exact (see Table 9)!

Table 9.

Year	Age	Value of IRA	Life Expectancy Factor (in years)	IRA Required Minimum Distributions (RMDs)	Cumulative IRA Distributions
2005	50	$100,000	34.2	$0	$0
2006	51	$108,000	33.3	$0	$0
2007	52	$116,640	32.3	$0	$0
2008	53	$125,971	31.4	$0	$0
2009	54	$136,049	30.5	$0	$0
2010	55	$146,933	29.6	$0	$0
2011	56	$158,688	28.7	$0	$0
2012	57	$171,383	27.9	$0	$0
2013	58	$185,094	27.0	$0	$0
2014	59	$199,902	26.1	$0	$0
2015	60	$215,894	25.2	$0	$0
2016	61	$233,166	24.4	$0	$0
2017	62	$251,819	23.5	$0	$0
2018	63	$271,965	22.7	$0	$0

Table 9. *(continued)*

	Year	Age	Value of IRA	Life Expectancy Factor (in years)	IRA Required Minimum Distributions (RMDs)	Cumulative IRA Distributions
	2019	64	$293,722	21.8	$0	$0
	2020	65	$317,220	21.0	$0	$0
	2021	66	$342,598	20.2	$0	$0
	2022	67	$370,006	19.4	$0	$0
	2023	68	$399,606	18.6	$0	$0
	2024	69	$431,574	17.8	$0	$0
Steve begins	2025	70	$466,100	27.4	$17,011	$17,011
RMDs	2026	71	$485,016	26.5	$18,302	$35,313
	2027	72	$504,051	25.6	$19,689	$55,002
	2028	73	$523,111	24.7	$21,179	$76,181
	2029	74	$542,087	23.8	$22,777	$98,958
	2030	75	$560,855	22.9	$24,491	$123,449
	2031	76	$579,273	22.0	$26,331	$149,780
	2032	77	$597,177	21.2	$28,169	$177,949
	2033	78	$614,529	20.3	$30,272	$208,221
	2034	79	$630,998	19.5	$32,359	$240,580
	2035	80	$646,530	18.7	$34,574	$275,154
	2036	81	$660,912	17.9	$36,922	$312,076
	2037	82	$673,909	17.1	$39,410	$351,486
	2038	83	$685,259	16.3	$42,040	$393,526
	2039	84	$694,677	15.5	$44,818	$438,344
Steve dies	***2040***	***85***	***$701,848***	***14.8***	***$47,422***	***$485,766***
Debra rolls	2041	83	$706,780	16.3	$43,361	$529,127
over	2042	84	$716,493	15.5	$46,225	$575,352
	2043	85	$723,889	14.8	$48,911	$624,263
	2044	86	$728,976	14.1	$51,700	$675,963

Table 9. *(continued)*

	Year	Age	Value of IRA	Life Expectancy Factor (in years)	IRA Required Minimum Distributions (RMDs)	Cumulative IRA Distributions
	2045	87	$731,458	13.4	$54,586	$730,549
	2046	88	$731,022	12.7	$57,561	$788,110
	2047	89	$727,338	12.0	$60,612	$848,722
	2048	90	$720,064	11.4	$63,164	$911,886
	2049	91	$709,452	10.8	$65,690	$977,576
Debra dies	*2050*	*92*	*$695,263*	*10.2*	*$68,163*	*$1,045,739*
Jeffrey begins	2051	58	$677,268	27.0	$25,084	$1,070,823
RMDs	2052	59	$704,359	26.0	$27,091	$1,097,914
	2053	60	$731,449	25.0	$29,258	$1,127,172
	2054	61	$758,366	24.0	$31,599	$1,158,771
	2055	62	$784,908	23.0	$34,126	$1,192,897
	2056	63	$810,845	22.0	$36,857	$1,229,754
	2057	64	$835,907	21.0	$39,805	$1,269,559
	2058	65	$859,790	20.0	$42,990	$1,312,549
	2059	66	$882,144	19.0	$46,429	$1,358,978
	2060	67	$902,572	18.0	$50,143	$1,409,121
	2061	68	$920,623	17.0	$54,154	$1,463,275
	2062	69	$935,787	16.0	$58,487	$1,521,762
	2063	70	$947,484	15.0	$63,166	$1,584,928
	2064	71	$955,063	14.0	$68,219	$1,653,147
	2065	72	$957,792	13.0	$73,676	$1,726,823
	2066	73	$954,845	12.0	$79,570	$1,806,393
	2067	74	$945,297	11.0	$85,936	$1,892,329
	2068	75	$928,110	10.0	$92,811	$1,985,140
	2069	76	$902,123	9.0	$100,236	$2,085,376

Table 9. *(continued)*

Year	Age	Value of IRA	Life Expectancy Factor (in years)	IRA Required Minimum Distributions (RMDs)	Cumulative IRA Distributions
2070	77	$866,038	8.0	$108,255	$2,193,631
2071	78	$818,406	7.0	$116,915	$2,310,546
2072	79	$757,610	6.0	$126,268	$2,436,814
2073	80	$681,849	5.0	$136,370	$2,573,184
2074	81	$589,117	4.0	$147,279	$2,720,463
2075	82	$477,185	3.0	$159,062	$2,879,525
2076	83	$343,573	2.0	$171,787	$3,051,312
2077	84	$185,529	1.0	$185,529	$3,236,841
2078	85	$0		$0	$3,236,841
Totals					**$3,236,841**

Example 4—Roth IRA

Now we'll change Steve's traditional stretch IRA to a Roth stretch IRA. Again, we'll base the projected results on his having accumulated $100,000 by age 50 rather than 65. In this case, the Roth will have accumulated an astonishing **$11,153,191** (see Table 10) by the time his 57-year-old son Jeffrey reaches the end of the stretch period.

Table 10.

Year	Roth IRA Beneficiary's Age	Value of Roth IRA	Roth IRA Beneficiary's Life Expectancy Factor (in years)	Roth IRA Required Minimum Distributions (RMDs)	Cumulative Roth IRA Distributions
2005	47	$100,000	37.0	$0	$0
2006	48	$108,000	36.0	$0	$0
2007	49	$116,640	35.1	$0	$0
2008	50	$125,971	34.2	$0	$0
2009	51	$136,049	33.3	$0	$0
2010	52	$146,933	32.3	$0	$0
2011	53	$158,688	31.4	$0	$0
2012	54	$171,383	30.5	$0	$0
2013	55	$185,094	29.6	$0	$0
2014	56	$199,902	28.7	$0	$0
2015	57	$215,894	27.9	$0	$0
2016	58	$233,166	27.0	$0	$0
2017	59	$251,819	26.1	$0	$0
2018	60	$271,965	25.2	$0	$0
2019	61	$293,722	24.4	$0	$0
2020	62	$317,220	23.5	$0	$0
2021	63	$342,598	22.7	$0	$0
2022	64	$370,006	21.8	$0	$0
2023	65	$399,606	21.0	$0	$0
2024	66	$431,574	20.2	$0	$0
2025	67	$466,100	19.4	$0	$0
2026	68	$503,388	18.6	$0	$0
2027	69	$543,659	17.8	$0	$0
2028	70	$587,152	17.0	$0	$0
2029	71	$634,124	16.3	$0	$0
2030	72	$684,854	15.5	$0	$0

Table 10. *(continued)*

	Year	Roth IRA Beneficiary's Age	Value of Roth IRA	Roth IRA Beneficiary's Life Expectancy Factor (in years)	Roth IRA Required Minimum Distributions (RMDs)	Cumulative Roth IRA Distributions
	2031	73	$739,642	14.8	$0	$0
	2032	74	$798,813	14.1	$0	$0
	2033	75	$862,718	13.4	$0	$0
	2034	76	$931,735	12.7	$0	$0
	2035	77	$1,006,274	12.1	$0	$0
	2036	78	$1,086,776	11.4	$0	$0
	2037	79	$1,173,718	10.8	$0	$0
	2038	80	$1,267,615	10.2	$0	$0
	2039	81	$1,369,024	9.7	$0	$0
Steve dies	*2040*	*82*	*$1,478,546*	*9.1*	*$0*	*$0*
Debra rolls	2041	48	$1,596,830	36.0	$0	$0
over	2042	49	$1,724,576	35.1	$0	$0
	2043	50	$1,862,542	34.2	$0	$0
	2044	51	$2,011,545	33.3	$0	$0
	2045	52	$2,172,469	32.3	$0	$0
	2046	53	$2,346,267	31.4	$0	$0
	2047	54	$2,533,968	30.5	$0	$0
	2048	55	$2,736,685	29.6	$0	$0
	2049	56	$2,955,620	28.7	$0	$0
Debra dies	*2050*	*57*	*$3,192,070*	*27.9*	*$0*	*$0*
Jeffrey	2051	58	$3,447,436	27.0	$127,683	$127,683
begins	2052	59	$3,585,333	26.0	$137,897	$265,580
RMDs	2053	60	$3,723,231	25.0	$148,929	$414,509
	2054	61	$3,860,246	24.0	$160,844	$575,353
	2055	62	$3,995,354	23.0	$173,711	$749,064
	2056	63	$4,127,374	22.0	$187,608	$936,672
	2057	64	$4,254,947	21.0	$202,617	$1,139,289

Table 10. *(continued)*

Year	Roth IRA Beneficiary's Age	Value of Roth IRA	Roth IRA Beneficiary's Life Expectancy Factor (in years)	Roth IRA Required Minimum Distributions (RMDs)	Cumulative Roth IRA Distributions
2058	65	$4,376,516	20.0	$218,826	$1,358,115
2059	66	$4,490,305	19.0	$236,332	$1,594,447
2060	67	$4,594,291	18.0	$255,238	$1,849,685
2061	68	$4,686,177	17.0	$275,657	$2,125,342
2062	69	$4,763,362	16.0	$297,710	$2,423,052
2063	70	$4,822,904	15.0	$321,527	$2,744,579
2064	71	$4,861,487	14.0	$347,249	$3,091,828
2065	72	$4,875,377	13.0	$375,029	$3,466,857
2066	73	$4,860,376	12.0	$405,031	$3,871,888
2067	74	$4,811,773	11.0	$437,434	$4,309,322
2068	75	$4,724,286	10.0	$472,429	$4,781,751
2069	76	$4,592,006	9.0	$510,223	$5,291,974
2070	77	$4,408,326	8.0	$551,041	$5,843,015
2071	78	$4,165,868	7.0	$595,124	$6,438,139
2072	79	$3,856,404	6.0	$642,734	$7,080,873
2073	80	$3,470,764	5.0	$694,153	$7,775,026
2074	81	$2,998,740	4.0	$749,685	$8,524,711
2075	82	$2,428,979	3.0	$809,660	$9,334,371
2076	83	$1,748,865	2.0	$874,433	$10,208,804
2077	84	$944,387	1.0	$944,387	$11,153,191
Totals					**$11,153,191**

Steve's Roth IRA will compound for 72 years, until 2077. That's when the last dime will have to be withdrawn by his son Jeffrey.

Could the stretch go on longer? Sure. Let's go to the next example and see what happens if rather than leaving her deceased husband's nest egg to their son Jeffrey, Debra leaves it to someone younger instead. You may have a problem taking in the numbers, since they will resemble a telephone book, including the area codes!

Example 5—Traditional IRA

Let's begin again at the beginning and say that Steve has accumulated $100,000 in his traditional IRA by age 65. His wife, Debra, inherits it when Steve dies at age 85. Debra dies at age 92, but instead of leaving the IRA to Jeffrey, she leaves it to Jeffrey's granddaughter (Debra's great-granddaughter) Victoria, who is born in 2035, the year Debra died. That would make Victoria a 1-year-old in 2036, when she must start taking RMDs on her inherited IRA. What would the compounding schedule look like over Victoria's 81.6-year life expectancy? Like a rocket, that's what (see Table 11).

The IRA will be compounding not only over Victoria's 81.6-year life expectancy, but also over the time it was held by Steve and then by Debra. Thus, the IRA will have a life of 112 years. When the entire account is emptied by the end of that time, **$17,767,255** will have been withdrawn from it!

				IRA	
			Life	Required	
		Value	Expectancy	Minimum	Cumulative
		of	Factor	Distributions	IRA
Year	Age	IRA	(in years)	(RMDs)	Distributions
2005	65	$100,000	21.0	$0	$0
2006	66	$108,000	20.2	$0	$0
2007	67	$116,640	19.4	$0	$0
2008	68	$125,971	18.6	$0	$0

Table 11.

Table 11. *(continued)*

	Year	Age	Value of IRA	Life Expectancy Factor (in years)	IRA Required Minimum Distributions (RMDs)	Cumulative IRA Distributions
	2009	69	$136,049	17.8	$0	$0
Steve begins	2010	70	$146,933	27.4	$5,363	$5,363
RMDS	2011	71	$152,896	26.5	$5,770	$11,133
	2012	72	$158,896	25.6	$6,207	$17,340
	2013	73	$164,904	24.7	$6,676	$24,016
	2014	74	$170,886	23.8	$7,180	$31,196
	2015	75	$176,802	22.9	$7,721	$38,917
	2016	76	$182,607	22.0	$8,300	$47,217
	2017	77	$188,252	21.2	$8,880	$56,097
	2018	78	$193,722	20.3	$9,543	$65,640
	2019	79	$198,913	19.5	$10,201	$75,841
	2020	80	$203,809	18.7	$10,899	$86,740
	2021	81	$208,343	17.9	$11,639	$98,379
	2022	82	$212,440	17.1	$12,423	$110,802
	2023	83	$216,018	16.3	$13,253	$124,055
	2024	84	$218,986	15.5	$14,128	$138,183
Steve dies	***2025***	***85***	***$221,247***	***14.8***	***$14,949***	***$153,132***
Debra rolls	2026	83	$222,802	16.3	$13,669	$166,801
over	2027	84	$225,864	15.5	$14,572	$181,373
	2028	85	$228,195	14.8	$15,419	$196,792
	2029	86	$229,798	14.1	$16,298	$213,090
	2030	87	$230,580	13.4	$17,207	$230,297
	2031	88	$230,443	12.7	$18,145	$248,442
	2032	89	$229,282	12.0	$19,107	$267,549
	2033	90	$226,989	11.4	$19,911	$287,460
	2034	91	$223,644	10.8	$20,708	$308,168

Table 11. *(continued)*

	Year	Age	Value of IRA	Life Expectancy Factor (in years)	IRA Required Minimum Distributions (RMDs)	Cumulative IRA Distributions
Debra dies	*2035*	*92*	*$219,171*	*10.2*	*$21,487*	*$329,655*
1-year-old	2036	1	$213,499	81.6	$2,616	$332,271
Victoria	2037	2	$227,754	80.6	$2,826	$335,097
begins RMDs	2038	3	$242,922	79.6	$3,052	$338,149
	2039	4	$259,060	78.6	$3,296	$341,445
	2040	5	$276,225	77.6	$3,560	$345,005
	2041	6	$294,478	76.6	$3,844	$348,849
	2042	7	$313,885	75.6	$4,152	$353,001
	2043	8	$334,512	74.6	$4,484	$357,485
	2044	9	$356,430	73.6	$4,843	$362,328
	2045	10	$379,714	72.6	$5,230	$367,558
	2046	11	$404,443	71.6	$5,649	$373,207
	2047	12	$430,698	70.6	$6,101	$379,308
	2048	13	$458,565	69.6	$6,589	$385,897
	2049	14	$488,134	68.6	$7,116	$393,013
	2050	15	$519,499	67.6	$7,685	$400,698
	2051	16	$552,759	66.6	$8,300	$408,998
	2052	17	$588,016	65.6	$8,964	$417,962
	2053	18	$625,376	64.6	$9,681	$427,643
	2054	19	$664,951	63.6	$10,455	$438,098
	2055	20	$706,856	62.6	$11,292	$449,390
	2056	21	$751,209	61.6	$12,195	$461,585
	2057	22	$798,135	60.6	$13,171	$474,756
	2058	23	$847,761	59.6	$14,224	$488,980
	2059	24	$900,220	58.6	$15,362	$504,342
	2060	25	$955,647	57.6	$16,591	$520,933

Table 11. *(continued)*

Year	Age	Value of IRA	Life Expectancy Factor (in years)	IRA Required Minimum Distributions (RMDs)	Cumulative IRA Distributions
2061	26	$1,014,180	56.6	$17,918	$538,851
2062	27	$1,075,963	55.6	$19,352	$558,203
2063	28	$1,141,140	54.6	$20,900	$579,103
2064	29	$1,209,859	53.6	$22,572	$601,675
2065	30	$1,282,270	52.6	$24,378	$626,053
2066	31	$1,358,523	51.6	$26,328	$652,381
2067	32	$1,438,771	50.6	$28,434	$680,815
2068	33	$1,523,164	49.6	$30,709	$711,524
2069	34	$1,611,851	48.6	$33,166	$744,690
2070	35	$1,704,980	47.6	$35,819	$780,509
2071	36	$1,802,694	46.6	$38,684	$819,193
2072	37	$1,905,131	45.6	$41,779	$860,972
2073	38	$2,012,420	44.6	$45,122	$906,094
2074	39	$2,124,682	43.6	$48,731	$954,825
2075	40	$2,242,027	42.6	$52,630	$1,007,455
2076	41	$2,364,549	41.6	$56,840	$1,064,295
2077	42	$2,492,326	40.6	$61,387	$1,125,682
2078	43	$2,625,414	39.6	$66,298	$1,191,980
2079	44	$2,763,845	38.6	$71,602	$1,263,582
2080	45	$2,907,622	37.6	$77,330	$1,340,912
2081	46	$3,056,715	36.6	$83,517	$1,424,429
2082	47	$3,211,054	35.6	$90,198	$1,514,627
2083	48	$3,370,524	34.6	$97,414	$1,612,041
2084	49	$3,534,959	33.6	$105,207	$1,717,248
2085	50	$3,704,132	32.6	$113,624	$1,830,872
2086	51	$3,877,749	31.6	$122,714	$1,953,586

Table 11. *(continued)*

Year	Age	Value of IRA	Life Expectancy Factor (in years)	IRA Required Minimum Distributions (RMDs)	Cumulative IRA Distributions
2087	52	$4,055,438	30.6	$132,531	$2,086,117
2088	53	$4,236,740	29.6	$143,133	$2,229,250
2089	54	$4,421,096	28.6	$154,584	$2,383,834
2090	55	$4,607,833	27.6	$166,950	$2,550,784
2091	56	$4,796,154	26.6	$180,307	$2,731,091
2092	57	$4,985,115	25.6	$194,731	$2,925,822
2093	58	$5,173,615	24.6	$210,310	$3,136,132
2094	59	$5,360,369	23.6	$227,134	$3,363,266
2095	60	$5,543,894	22.6	$245,305	$3,608,571
2096	61	$5,722,476	21.6	$264,929	$3,873,500
2097	62	$5,894,151	20.6	$286,124	$4,159,624
2098	63	$6,056,669	19.6	$309,014	$4,468,638
2099	64	$6,207,467	18.6	$333,735	$4,802,373
2100	65	$6,343,631	17.6	$360,434	$5,162,807
2101	66	$6,461,853	16.6	$389,268	$5,552,075
2102	67	$6,558,392	15.6	$420,410	$5,972,485
2103	68	$6,629,021	14.6	$454,043	$6,426,528
2104	69	$6,668,976	13.6	$490,366	$6,916,894
2105	70	$6,672,899	12.6	$529,595	$7,446,489
2106	71	$6,634,768	11.6	$571,963	$8,018,452
2107	72	$6,547,829	10.6	$617,720	$8,636,172
2108	73	$6,404,518	9.6	$667,137	$9,303,309
2109	74	$6,196,371	8.6	$720,508	$10,023,817
2110	75	$5,913,932	7.6	$778,149	$10,801,966
2111	76	$5,546,646	6.6	$840,401	$11,642,367
2112	77	$5,082,745	5.6	$907,633	$12,550,000

Table 11. *(continued)*

Year	Age	Value of IRA	Life Expectancy Factor (in years)	IRA Required Minimum Distributions (RMDs)	Cumulative IRA Distributions
2113	78	$4,509,121	4.6	$980,244	$13,530,244
2114	79	$3,811,187	3.6	$1,058,663	$14,588,907
2115	80	$2,972,726	2.6	$1,143,356	$15,732,263
2116	81	$1,975,720	1.6	$1,234,825	$16,967,088
2117	82	$800,167	0.6	$800,167	$17,767,255
2118	83	$0		$0	$17,767,255
Totals					**$17,767,255**

Example 6—Roth IRA

The compounding ride Steve's traditional IRA took in Example 5 is minor compared to the launch it would receive if it were a Roth IRA instead. It would live on for the same amount of time (112 years), but no distributions would be required until Victoria begins RMDs in 2036. That means 25 more years of additional compounding without having to take any funds from the Roth IRA until she inherits.

At this point Steve's Roth IRA will be worth $1,086,776, and if granddaughter Victoria takes only the Roth RMDs for her full 81.6-year life expectancy, it will grow to **$88,763,001** (see Table 12) by the time she must have withdrawn it all—and every single penny of it will have been income-tax-free!

Table 12.

	Year	Roth IRA Beneficiary's Age	Value of Roth IRA	Life Expectancy Factor (in years)	Roth IRA Required Minimum Distributions (RMDs)	Cumulative Roth IRA Distributions
	2005	62	$100,000	23.5	$0	$0
	2006	63	$108,000	22.7	$0	$0
	2007	64	$116,640	21.8	$0	$0
	2008	65	$125,971	21.0	$0	$0
	2009	66	$136,049	20.2	$0	$0
	2010	67	$146,933	19.4	$0	$0
	2011	68	$158,688	18.6	$0	$0
	2012	69	$171,383	17.8	$0	$0
	2013	70	$185,094	17.0	$0	$0
	2014	71	$199,902	16.3	$0	$0
	2015	72	$215,894	15.5	$0	$0
	2016	73	$233,166	14.8	$0	$0
	2017	74	$251,819	14.1	$0	$0
	2018	75	$271,965	13.4	$0	$0
	2019	76	$293,722	12.7	$0	$0
	2020	77	$317,220	12.1	$0	$0
	2021	78	$342,598	11.4	$0	$0
	2022	79	$370,006	10.8	$0	$0
	2023	80	$399,606	10.2	$0	$0
	2024	81	$431,574	9.7	$0	$0
Steve dies	*2025*	*82*	*$466,100*	*9.1*	*$0*	*$0*
Debra rolls	2026	0	$503,388	82.4	$0	$0
over	2027	0	$543,659	82.4	$0	$0
	2028	0	$587,152	82.4	$0	$0
	2029	0	$634,124	82.4	$0	$0

Table 12. *(continued)*

	Year	Roth IRA Beneficiary's Age	Value of Roth IRA	Life Expectancy Factor (in years)	Roth IRA Required Minimum Distributions (RMDs)	Cumulative Roth IRA Distributions
	2030	0	$684,854	82.4	$0	$0
	2031	0	$739,642	82.4	$0	$0
	2032	0	$798,813	82.4	$0	$0
	2033	0	$862,718	82.4	$0	$0
	2034	0	$931,735	82.4	$0	$0
Debra dies	*2035*	*0*	*$1,006,274*	*82.4*	*$0*	*$0*
1-year-old	2036	1	$1,086,776	81.6	$13,318	$13,318
Victoria	2037	2	$1,159,335	80.6	$14,384	$27,702
begins	2038	3	$1,236,547	79.6	$15,535	$43,237
RMDs	2039	4	$1,318,693	78.6	$16,777	$60,014
	2040	5	$1,406,069	77.6	$18,119	$78,133
	2041	6	$1,498,986	76.6	$19,569	$97,702
	2042	7	$1,597,770	75.6	$21,135	$118,837
	2043	8	$1,702,766	74.6	$22,825	$141,662
	2044	9	$1,814,336	73.6	$24,651	$166,313
	2045	10	$1,932,860	72.6	$26,623	$192,936
	2046	11	$2,058,736	71.6	$28,753	$221,689
	2047	12	$2,192,382	70.6	$31,054	$252,743
	2048	13	$2,334,234	69.6	$33,538	$286,281
	2049	14	$2,484,752	68.6	$36,221	$322,502
	2050	15	$2,644,413	67.6	$39,119	$361,621
	2051	16	$2,813,718	66.6	$42,248	$403,869
	2052	17	$2,993,188	65.6	$45,628	$449,497
	2053	18	$3,183,365	64.6	$49,278	$498,775
	2054	19	$3,384,814	63.6	$53,220	$551,995
	2055	20	$3,598,122	62.6	$57,478	$609,473

Table 12. *(continued)*

Year	Roth IRA Beneficiary's Age	Value of Roth IRA	Life Expectancy Factor (in years)	Roth IRA Required Minimum Distributions (RMDs)	Cumulative Roth IRA Distributions
2056	21	$3,823,896	61.6	$62,076	$671,549
2057	22	$4,062,766	60.6	$67,042	$738,591
2058	23	$4,315,382	59.6	$72,406	$810,997
2059	24	$4,582,414	58.6	$78,198	$889,195
2060	25	$4,864,553	57.6	$84,454	$973,649
2061	26	$5,162,507	56.6	$91,210	$1,064,859
2062	27	$5,477,001	55.6	$98,507	$1,163,366
2063	28	$5,808,774	54.6	$106,388	$1,269,754
2064	29	$6,158,577	53.6	$114,899	$1,384,653
2065	30	$6,527,172	52.6	$124,091	$1,508,744
2066	31	$6,915,327	51.6	$134,018	$1,642,762
2067	32	$7,323,814	50.6	$144,739	$1,787,501
2068	33	$7,753,401	49.6	$156,319	$1,943,820
2069	34	$8,204,849	48.6	$168,824	$2,112,644
2070	35	$8,678,907	47.6	$182,330	$2,294,974
2071	36	$9,176,303	46.6	$196,916	$2,491,890
2072	37	$9,697,738	45.6	$212,670	$2,704,560
2073	38	$10,243,873	44.6	$229,683	$2,934,243
2074	39	$10,815,325	43.6	$248,058	$3,182,301
2075	40	$11,412,648	42.6	$267,903	$3,450,204
2076	41	$12,036,325	41.6	$289,335	$3,739,539
2077	42	$12,686,749	40.6	$312,482	$4,052,021
2078	43	$13,364,208	39.6	$337,480	$4,389,501
2079	44	$14,068,866	38.6	$364,478	$4,753,979
2080	45	$14,800,739	37.6	$393,637	$5,147,616
2081	46	$15,559,670	36.6	$425,128	$5,572,744

Table 12. *(continued)*

Year	Roth IRA Beneficiary's Age	Value of Roth IRA	Life Expectancy Factor (in years)	Roth IRA Required Minimum Distributions (RMDs)	Cumulative Roth IRA Distributions
2082	47	$16,345,305	35.6	$459,138	$6,031,882
2083	48	$17,157,060	34.6	$495,869	$6,527,751
2084	49	$17,994,086	33.6	$535,538	$7,063,289
2085	50	$18,855,232	32.6	$578,381	$7,641,670
2086	51	$19,738,999	31.6	$624,652	$8,266,322
2087	52	$20,643,495	30.6	$674,624	$8,940,946
2088	53	$21,566,381	29.6	$728,594	$9,669,540
2089	54	$22,504,810	28.6	$786,881	$10,456,421
2090	55	$23,455,363	27.6	$849,832	$11,306,253
2091	56	$24,413,973	26.6	$917,819	$12,224,072
2092	57	$25,375,846	25.6	$991,244	$13,215,316
2093	58	$26,335,370	24.6	$1,070,543	$14,285,859
2094	59	$27,286,013	23.6	$1,156,187	$15,442,046
2095	60	$28,220,212	22.6	$1,248,682	$16,690,728
2096	61	$29,129,252	21.6	$1,348,576	$18,039,304
2097	62	$30,003,130	20.6	$1,456,463	$19,495,767
2098	63	$30,830,400	19.6	$1,572,980	$21,068,747
2099	64	$31,598,014	18.6	$1,698,818	$22,767,565
2100	65	$32,291,132	17.6	$1,834,723	$24,602,288
2101	66	$32,892,922	16.6	$1,981,501	$26,583,789
2102	67	$33,384,335	15.6	$2,140,021	$28,723,810
2103	68	$33,743,859	14.6	$2,311,223	$31,035,033
2104	69	$33,947,247	13.6	$2,496,121	$33,531,154
2105	70	$33,967,216	12.6	$2,695,811	$36,226,965
2106	71	$33,773,117	11.6	$2,911,476	$39,138,441
2107	72	$33,330,572	10.6	$3,144,394	$42,282,835

Table 12. *(continued)*

Year	Roth IRA Beneficiary's Age	Value of Roth IRA	Life Expectancy Factor (in years)	Roth IRA Required Minimum Distributions (RMDs)	Cumulative Roth IRA Distributions
2108	73	$32,601,072	9.6	$3,395,945	$45,678,780
2109	74	$31,541,537	8.6	$3,667,621	$49,346,401
2110	75	$30,103,829	7.6	$3,961,030	$53,307,431
2111	76	$28,234,223	6.6	$4,277,913	$57,585,344
2112	77	$25,872,815	5.6	$4,620,146	$62,205,490
2113	78	$22,952,883	4.6	$4,989,757	$67,195,247
2114	79	$19,400,176	3.6	$5,388,938	$72,584,185
2115	80	$15,132,137	2.6	$5,820,053	$78,404,238
2116	81	$10,057,051	1.6	$6,285,657	$84,689,895
2117	82	$4,073,106	0.6	$4,073,106	$88,763,001
2118	83	$0	0.0	$0	$88,763,001
Totals					**$88,763,001**

Example 7—Still a Roth IRA

OK, now let's talk *real money*, as the spendthrifts in Congress might put it, and see what happens if Steve had accumulated a balance of $100,000 in his Roth IRA by age 50 rather than 65. As before, Steve still lives to 85. He dies in 2040 and leaves his Roth IRA to his wife, Debra, who dies in 2050 at age 92. But this time granddaughter Victoria inherits in 2050, the actual year she is born, and she begins taking her RMDs in 2051 when she turns 1 year old. (A guardian would actually take these distributions, or they would be received by a trust set up for her benefit.)

When born, Victoria will have inherited a $3,447,436 Roth IRA; if she takes only the Roth RMDs for her full 81.6-year life expectancy, she will have withdrawn **$281,570,832** (see Table 13) by the end of the stretch period, income-tax-free! She could buy a small country at that point and name it after her great-great-grandpa Steve, who made it all possible!

That extra 15 years of Roth IRA compounding because Steve had accumulated $100,000 by age 50 was worth an additional $192,807,831 to Victoria. Now you know why they say time is money.

			Roth IRA Beneficiary's Life	Roth IRA Required	
Year	Roth IRA Beneficiary's Age	Value of Roth IRA	Expectancy Factor (in years)	Minimum Distributions (RMDs)	Cumulative Roth IRA Distributions
2005	47	$100,000	37.0	$0	$0
2006	48	$108,000	36.0	$0	$0
2007	49	$116,640	35.1	$0	$0
2008	50	$125,971	34.2	$0	$0
2009	51	$136,049	33.3	$0	$0
2010	52	$146,933	32.3	$0	$0
2011	53	$158,688	31.4	$0	$0
2012	54	$171,383	30.5	$0	$0
2013	55	$185,094	29.6	$0	$0
2014	56	$199,902	28.7	$0	$0
2015	57	$215,894	27.9	$0	$0
2016	58	$233,166	27.0	$0	$0
2017	59	$251,819	26.1	$0	$0
2018	60	$271,965	25.2	$0	$0
2019	61	$293,722	24.4	$0	$0
2020	62	$317,220	23.5	$0	$0

Table 13.

Table 13. *(continued)*

	Year	Roth IRA Beneficiary's Age	Value of Roth IRA	Roth IRA Beneficiary's Life Expectancy Factor (in years)	Roth IRA Required Minimum Distributions (RMDs)	Cumulative Roth IRA Distributions
	2021	63	$342,598	22.7	$0	$0
	2022	64	$370,006	21.8	$0	$0
	2023	65	$399,606	21.0	$0	$0
	2024	66	$431,574	20.2	$0	$0
	2025	67	$466,100	19.4	$0	$0
	2026	68	$503,388	18.6	$0	$0
	2027	69	$543,659	17.8	$0	$0
	2028	70	$587,152	17.0	$0	$0
	2029	71	$634,124	16.3	$0	$0
	2030	72	$684,854	15.5	$0	$0
	2031	73	$739,642	14.8	$0	$0
	2032	74	$798,813	14.1	$0	$0
	2033	75	$862,718	13.4	$0	$0
	2034	76	$931,735	12.7	$0	$0
	2035	77	$1,006,274	12.1	$0	$0
	2036	78	$1,086,776	11.4	$0	$0
	2037	79	$1,173,718	10.8	$0	$0
	2038	80	$1,267,615	10.2	$0	$0
	2039	81	$1,369,024	9.7	$0	$0
Steve dies	*2040*	*82*	*$1,478,546*	*9.1*	*$0*	*$0*
Debra rolls	2041	0	$1,596,830	82.4	$0	$0
over	2042	0	$1,724,576	82.4	$0	$0
	2043	0	$1,862,542	82.4	$0	$0
	2044	0	$2,011,545	82.4	$0	$0
	2045	0	$2,172,469	82.4	$0	$0
	2046	0	$2,346,267	82.4	$0	$0

Table 13. *(continued)*

	Year	Roth IRA Beneficiary's Age	Value of Roth IRA	Roth IRA Beneficiary's Life Expectancy Factor (in years)	Roth IRA Required Minimum Distributions (RMDs)	Cumulative Roth IRA Distributions
	2047	0	$2,533,968	82.4	$0	$0
	2048	0	$2,736,685	82.4	$0	$0
	2049	0	$2,955,620	82.4	$0	$0
Debra dies	*2050*	*0*	*$3,192,070*	*82.4*	*$0*	*$0*
1-year-old	2051	1	$3,447,436	81.6	$42,248	$42,248
Victoria	2052	2	$3,677,603	80.6	$45,628	$87,876
begins	2053	3	$3,922,533	79.6	$49,278	$137,154
RMDs	2054	4	$4,183,115	78.6	$53,220	$190,374
	2055	5	$4,460,287	77.6	$57,478	$247,852
	2056	6	$4,755,034	76.6	$62,076	$309,928
	2057	7	$5,068,395	75.6	$67,042	$376,970
	2058	8	$5,401,461	74.6	$72,406	$449,376
	2059	9	$5,755,379	73.6	$78,198	$527,574
	2060	10	$6,131,355	72.6	$84,454	$612,028
	2061	11	$6,530,653	71.6	$91,210	$703,238
	2062	12	$6,954,598	70.6	$98,507	$801,745
	2063	13	$7,404,578	69.6	$106,388	$908,133
	2064	14	$7,882,045	68.6	$114,899	$1,023,032
	2065	15	$8,388,518	67.6	$124,091	$1,147,123
	2066	16	$8,925,581	66.6	$134,018	$1,281,141
	2067	17	$9,494,888	65.6	$144,739	$1,425,880
	2068	18	$10,098,161	64.6	$156,318	$1,582,198
	2069	19	$10,737,190	63.6	$168,824	$1,751,022
	2070	20	$11,413,835	62.6	$182,330	$1,933,352
	2071	21	$12,130,025	61.6	$196,916	$2,130,268
	2072	22	$12,887,758	60.6	$212,669	$2,342,937

Table 13. *(continued)*

Year	Roth IRA Beneficiary's Age	Value of Roth IRA	Roth IRA Beneficiary's Life Expectancy Factor (in years)	Roth IRA Required Minimum Distributions (RMDs)	Cumulative Roth IRA Distributions
2073	23	$13,689,096	59.6	$229,683	$2,572,620
2074	24	$14,536,166	58.6	$248,057	$2,820,677
2075	25	$15,431,158	57.6	$267,902	$3,088,579
2076	26	$16,376,316	56.6	$289,334	$3,377,913
2077	27	$17,373,941	55.6	$312,481	$3,690,394
2078	28	$18,426,377	54.6	$337,479	$4,027,873
2079	29	$19,536,010	53.6	$364,478	$4,392,351
2080	30	$20,705,255	52.6	$393,636	$4,785,987
2081	31	$21,936,549	51.6	$425,127	$5,211,114
2082	32	$23,232,336	50.6	$459,137	$5,670,251
2083	33	$24,595,055	49.6	$495,868	$6,166,119
2084	34	$26,027,122	48.6	$535,537	$6,701,656
2085	35	$27,530,912	47.6	$578,381	$7,280,037
2086	36	$29,108,733	46.6	$624,651	$7,904,688
2087	37	$30,762,809	45.6	$674,623	$8,579,311
2088	38	$32,495,241	44.6	$728,593	$9,307,904
2089	39	$34,307,980	43.6	$786,880	$10,094,784
2090	40	$36,202,788	42.6	$849,831	$10,944,615
2091	41	$38,181,194	41.6	$917,817	$11,862,432
2092	42	$40,244,447	40.6	$991,243	$12,853,675
2093	43	$42,393,460	39.6	$1,070,542	$13,924,217
2094	44	$44,628,751	38.6	$1,156,185	$15,080,402
2095	45	$46,950,371	37.6	$1,248,680	$16,329,082
2096	46	$49,357,826	36.6	$1,348,574	$17,677,656
2097	47	$51,849,992	35.6	$1,456,460	$19,134,116
2098	48	$54,425,015	34.6	$1,572,977	$20,707,093

Table 13. *(continued)*

Year	Roth IRA Beneficiary's Age	Value of Roth IRA	Roth IRA Beneficiary's Life Expectancy Factor (in years)	Roth IRA Required Minimum Distributions (RMDs)	Cumulative Roth IRA Distributions
2099	49	$57,080,201	33.6	$1,698,816	$22,405,909
2100	50	$59,811,896	32.6	$1,834,721	$24,240,630
2101	51	$62,615,349	31.6	$1,981,498	$26,222,128
2102	52	$65,484,559	30.6	$2,140,018	$28,362,146
2103	53	$68,412,104	29.6	$2,311,220	$30,673,366
2104	54	$71,388,955	28.6	$2,496,117	$33,169,483
2105	55	$74,404,265	27.6	$2,695,807	$35,865,290
2106	56	$77,445,135	26.6	$2,911,471	$38,776,761
2107	57	$80,496,357	25.6	$3,144,389	$41,921,150
2108	58	$83,540,125	24.6	$3,395,940	$45,317,090
2109	59	$86,555,720	23.6	$3,667,615	$48,984,705
2110	60	$89,519,153	22.6	$3,961,024	$52,945,729
2111	61	$92,402,779	21.6	$4,277,906	$57,223,635
2112	62	$95,174,863	20.6	$4,620,139	$61,843,774
2113	63	$97,799,102	19.6	$4,989,750	$66,833,524
2114	64	$100,234,100	18.6	$5,388,930	$72,222,454
2115	65	$102,432,784	17.6	$5,820,045	$78,042,499
2116	66	$104,341,758	16.6	$6,285,648	$84,328,147
2117	67	$105,900,599	15.6	$6,788,500	$91,116,647
2118	68	$107,041,067	14.6	$7,331,580	$98,448,227
2119	69	$107,686,246	13.6	$7,918,106	$106,366,333
2120	70	$107,749,591	12.6	$8,551,555	$114,917,888
2121	71	$107,133,879	11.6	$9,235,679	$124,153,567
2122	72	$105,730,056	10.6	$9,974,534	$134,128,101
2123	73	$103,415,964	9.6	$10,772,496	$144,900,597
2124	74	$100,054,945	8.6	$11,634,296	$156,534,893
2125	75	$95,494,301	7.6	$12,565,040	$169,099,933

Table 13. *(continued)*

Year	Roth IRA Beneficiary's Age	Value of Roth IRA	Roth IRA Beneficiary's Life Expectancy Factor (in years)	Roth IRA Required Minimum Distributions (RMDs)	Cumulative Roth IRA Distributions
2126	76	$89,563,602	6.6	$13,570,243	$182,670,176
2127	77	$82,072,828	5.6	$14,655,862	$197,326,038
2128	78	$72,810,323	4.6	$15,828,331	$213,154,369
2129	79	$61,540,551	3.6	$17,094,598	$230,248,967
2130	80	$48,001,629	2.6	$18,462,165	$248,711,132
2131	81	$31,902,621	1.6	$19,939,138	$268,650,270
2132	82	$12,920,562	0.6	$12,920,562	$281,570,832
2133	83	$0	0.0	$0	$281,570,832
Totals					**$281,570,832**

FAQ

Q. Ed, what if my beneficiary dies before the stretch period is complete?

A. The IRS life expectancy tables represent a mean life expectancy. Actuarially, half of the beneficiaries will live out their life expectancies and the other half will not. We just don't know which half is which. So it is likely that at least half the time a beneficiary may not live long enough to collect every year's RMD. If that happens, the stretch does not die with him or her—unless the IRA custodian forces a payout on the death of the beneficiary (the IRS does not require this). As noted in Chapter Four, however, if the custodial agreement allows a beneficiary to name a successor beneficiary, the latter can continue taking RMDs over the deceased's remaining stretch term.

No Spouse Means No Spousal Rollover, But . . .

If you are single or in a domestic partnership with someone, you are probably asking this question: What about me? Can I set up a stretch IRA? The answer is yes. If you are divorced or widowed, have simply remained happily single all your life, or are considered single under the law even though you have a domestic partner, you can name anyone you choose as your designated beneficiary, and he or she will be able to stretch your IRA over his or her life expectancy.

Unfortunately, unmarried people (singles and domestic partners under most state laws) cannot take advantage of the spousal rollover provision, which applies only to legally married people under federal law. Even if you have a domestic partner whom you designate as your IRA beneficiary, your partner will be seen as a non-spouse under federal laws and therefore treated as a non-spouse beneficiary, who cannot roll the IRA over and treat it as his or her own but must remain a beneficiary. Like any other non-spouse beneficiary who lives and breathes, however, once your partner inherits your IRA, he or she can give it a nice stretch. (This is why, if you are single or in an unmarried domestic relationship and have a 401(k) or other company plan, it is just as important—and perhaps even more so—for you to get those funds into an IRA as soon as possible, since most company plans do not allow the stretch.)

Since there is no spousal rollover option available, a domestic partner treated as a non-spouse beneficiary must begin taking required distributions in the year after the IRA owner's death, even if he or she does not need the money to live on, thereby limiting the inherited account's long-term growth potential. Because the potential rewards of the stretch are so much greater, this disadvantage becomes even bigger if the inherited account is a Roth IRA. But at least the distributions will be income-tax-free and the surviving partner will end up keeping more.

OK, now back to some good news. Domestic partners get a benefit with a Roth IRA that is unavailable to legally married couples if they wish to convert from a traditional IRA to a Roth IRA. This benefit may even enable them to build a larger Roth balance than many legally married couples. Here's how:

Married couples cannot convert from a traditional IRA to a Roth IRA if their combined income exceeds $100,000. So, if two married people each have income of $60,000, their joint income is over $100,000 and they cannot convert to a Roth IRA. But if these same two people were unmarried partners (according to the law), the same $100,000 limitation applies separately to each of them. Since they are not legally married, they cannot file a joint return and thus do not have to add their incomes together for Roth conversion or contribution eligibility.

By being able to convert or contribute more, more can be accumulated—and accumulating more means more to leave to a domestic partner (or any other designated non-spouse beneficiary), who can then parlay it to even greater heights, income-tax-free.

SIX

Setting Up a Stretch IRA for Multiple Beneficiaries

Dear Ed,
If I name my two children as beneficiaries of 50 percent of my IRA
and my spouse as the beneficiary of the other half, what will the re-
quired payout be after my death? Is there a way for my children to use
their own lives for calculating required minimum distributions, or does
the IRA have to be split to accomplish that? And if it has to be split,
do I split it into two IRAs—one for my spouse and one for my two
children—or into three IRAs—one for each of my children and one
for my spouse? Please help. My broker is unsure how to answer
these questions.
    —IRA owner

An Iron Rule

Here's an inheritance rule everyone understands: The more money you have, the more beneficiaries there will be. It is sort of like that old adage, "Where there's a will, there's a relative."

If you have more than one beneficiary on your IRA, the stretch period for each will depend on how you set up your IRA now (and on whether each beneficiary knows what to do when he or she inherits, which I'll address in Part Two). Here's why:

The IRS says that when you name multiple beneficiaries on one IRA, the post-death stretch period must be based on the age of the oldest beneficiary (the one with the shortest life expectancy). There is a rule, however, called the "separate account rule," which would allow the inherited IRA to be split into separate inherited IRAs and allow each beneficiary of these separate accounts to use his or her own age to calculate his or her required minimum distributions. Separate inherited IRAs may not be an important issue if your multiple beneficiaries are around the same age. But if one co-beneficiary is 100-year-old Great-Grandma Moses and the other co-beneficiary is 1-year-old Victoria, then little Victoria's stretch period will be dramatically cut short if the IRA is not split.

Even though the life expectancy of a 1-year-old, according to the Single Life Expectancy table, is 81.6 years, if Victoria is a co-beneficiary with her 100-year-old great-grandma, she will be stuck using Great-Grandma's life expectancy stretch period of 2.9 years, according to the Single Life Expectancy table. Therefore, little Victoria's share of the inherited IRA will have to be paid out to her by the time she is 4 years old, resulting in a titanic loss of potential stretch dollars.

We already know from the numbers I showed you in Chapter One that if a 1-year-old child like Victoria inherited a $100,000 IRA by herself and took only the minimum required withdrawals over her 81.6-year stretch term, she would end up with $8,167,629 at an average 8 percent growth rate. But now let's say 1-year-old Victoria inherits the same $100,000, but this time she's co-beneficiary on a $200,000 IRA with 100-year-old Great-Grandma Moses, who gets the other half. Then what? Stuck with a stretch period of 2.9 years rather than 81.6 years, Victoria would end up withdrawing only $107,922 from the inherited IRA (see Table 14), which is a far cry from $8 million!

Table 14. IRA Distributions to Multiple Beneficiaries on the Same IRA

Year	Total IRA Balance	Grandma 50%		Victoria 50%	
		Life Expectancy Factor (in years)	Required Minimum Distributions (RMDs)	Life Expectancy Factor (in years)	Required Minimum Distributions (RMDs)
2005	$200,000	2.9	$34,483	2.9	$34,483
2006	$141,516	1.9	$37,241	1.9	$37,241
2007	$72,396	0.9	$36,198	0.9	$36,198
Totals			**$107,922**		**$107,922**

Of course, the age discrepancy in this example is extreme. Little Victoria and Great-Grandma Moses would be unlikely co-beneficiaries. But it dramatically illustrates my point that sticking a younger co-beneficiary (say, your child) with having to use the life expectancy of an older co-beneficiary (say, your spouse) for the stretch period does considerable damage in dollars to the IRA's stretch potential.

Wow! What a Difference a Split Makes!

If you have one IRA with multiple beneficiaries of different ages, you want to leave it to them in a way that will guarantee each beneficiary the opportunity to use his or her own life expectancy for the stretch rather than be stuck with someone else's. So, rather than naming them as co-beneficiaries, you should create separate accounts (also called "separate shares") for each beneficiary. This is called splitting.

Let's go back to little Victoria and Great-Grandma Moses again and see how things would turn out if the $200,000 IRA were split between them by creating two separate IRAs, with Victoria named sole beneficiary of one $100,000 account and Great-Grandma Moses named sole beneficiary of the other $100,000 account.

There would be no change in Great-Grandma Moses's payout period since her distribution schedule would still be based on her shorter life expectancy. But look at the difference in Victoria's lifetime payout. As she is now the sole beneficiary of her separate $100,000 share, she goes back to receiving an $8 million-plus payout over her own 81.6-year life expectancy (see Table 15). So, whether the IRA is split or not, they each receive $100,000. But if it is split, Victoria can parlay her $100K into an $8 million return!

Table 15. IRA Distributions to Multiple Beneficiaries When the IRA Is Split into Separate Accounts

Year	Total IRA Balance	Grandma 50%		Victoria 50%	
		Life Expectancy Factor (in years)	Required Minimum Distributions (RMDs)	Life Expectancy Factor (in years)	Required Minimum Distributions (RMDs)
2005	$200,000	2.9	$34,483	81.6	$1,225
2006	$177,435	1.9	$37,241	80.6	$1,324
2007	$149,979	0.9	$36,198	79.6	$1,429
2008	$121,340	0.0	$0	78.6	$1,544
2009	$129,380	0.0	$0	77.6	$1,667
2010	$137,930	0.0	$0	76.6	$1,801
2011	$147,019	0.0	$0	75.6	$1,945
2012	$156,680	0.0	$0	74.6	$2,100
2013	$166,946	0.0	$0	73.6	$2,268
2014	$177,852	0.0	$0	72.6	$2,450
2015	$189,434	0.0	$0	71.6	$2,646
2016	$201,731	0.0	$0	70.6	$2,857

Table 15. IRA Distributions to Multiple Beneficiaries
When the IRA Is Split into Separate Accounts *(continued)*

		Grandma 50%		Victoria 50%	
Year	Total IRA Balance	Life Expectancy Factor (in years)	Required Minimum Distributions (RMDs)	Life Expectancy Factor (in years)	Required Minimum Distributions (RMDs)
2017	$214,784	0.0	$0	69.6	$3,086
2018	$228,634	0.0	$0	68.6	$3,333
2019	$243,325	0.0	$0	67.6	$3,599
2020	$258,904	0.0	$0	66.6	$3,887
2021	$275,418	0.0	$0	65.6	$4,198
2022	$292,918	0.0	$0	64.6	$4,534
2023	$311,455	0.0	$0	63.6	$4,897
2024	$331,083	0.0	$0	62.6	$5,289
2025	$351,858	0.0	$0	61.6	$5,712
2026	$373,838	0.0	$0	60.6	$6,169
2027	$397,083	0.0	$0	59.6	$6,662
2028	$421,655	0.0	$0	58.6	$7,195
2029	$447,617	0.0	$0	57.6	$7,771
2030	$475,034	0.0	$0	56.6	$8,393
2031	$503,972	0.0	$0	55.6	$9,064
2032	$534,501	0.0	$0	54.6	$9,789
2033	$566,689	0.0	$0	53.6	$10,573
2034	$600,605	0.0	$0	52.6	$11,418
2035	$636,322	0.0	$0	51.6	$12,332
2036	$673,909	0.0	$0	50.6	$13,318
2037	$713,438	0.0	$0	49.6	$14,384
2038	$754,978	0.0	$0	48.6	$15,535
2039	$798,598	0.0	$0	47.6	$16,777
2040	$844,367	0.0	$0	46.6	$18,119
2041	$892,348	0.0	$0	45.6	$19,569

Table 15. IRA Distributions to Multiple Beneficiaries When the IRA Is Split into Separate Accounts *(continued)*

Year	Total IRA Balance	Grandma 50%		Victoria 50%	
		Life Expectancy Factor (in years)	Required Minimum Distributions (RMDs)	Life Expectancy Factor (in years)	Required Minimum Distributions (RMDs)
2042	$942,601	0.0	$0	44.6	$21,135
2043	$995,183	0.0	$0	43.6	$22,825
2044	$1,050,147	0.0	$0	42.6	$24,651
2045	$1,107,536	0.0	$0	41.6	$26,623
2046	$1,167,386	0.0	$0	40.6	$28,753
2047	$1,229,724	0.0	$0	39.6	$31,054
2048	$1,294,564	0.0	$0	38.6	$33,538
2049	$1,361,908	0.0	$0	37.6	$36,221
2050	$1,431,742	0.0	$0	36.6	$39,119
2051	$1,504,033	0.0	$0	35.6	$42,248
2052	$1,578,728	0.0	$0	34.6	$45,628
2053	$1,655,748	0.0	$0	33.6	$49,278
2054	$1,734,988	0.0	$0	32.6	$53,220
2055	$1,816,309	0.0	$0	31.6	$57,478
2056	$1,899,537	0.0	$0	30.6	$62,076
2057	$1,984,458	0.0	$0	29.6	$67,043
2058	$2,070,808	0.0	$0	28.6	$72,406
2059	$2,158,274	0.0	$0	27.6	$78,198
2060	$2,246,482	0.0	$0	26.6	$84,454
2061	$2,334,990	0.0	$0	25.6	$91,211
2062	$2,423,281	0.0	$0	24.6	$98,507
2063	$2,510,756	0.0	$0	23.6	$106,388
2064	$2,596,717	0.0	$0	22.6	$114,899
2065	$2,680,363	0.0	$0	21.6	$124,091
2066	$2,760,774	0.0	$0	20.6	$134,018

Table 15. IRA Distributions to Multiple Beneficiaries
When the IRA Is Split into Separate Accounts *(continued)*

| | | Grandma 50% | | Victoria 50% | |
| | Total IRA | Life Expectancy Factor | Required Minimum Distributions | Life Expectancy Factor | Required Minimum Distributions |
Year	Balance	(in years)	(RMDs)	(in years)	(RMDs)
2067	$2,836,896	0.0	$0	19.6	$144,740
2068	$2,907,528	0.0	$0	18.6	$156,319
2069	$2,971,306	0.0	$0	17.6	$168,824
2070	$3,026,681	0.0	$0	16.6	$182,330
2071	$3,071,899	0.0	$0	15.6	$196,917
2072	$3,104,981	0.0	$0	14.6	$212,670
2073	$3,123,696	0.0	$0	13.6	$229,684
2074	$3,125,533	0.0	$0	12.6	$248,058
2075	$3,107,673	0.0	$0	11.6	$267,903
2076	$3,066,952	0.0	$0	10.6	$289,335
2077	$2,999,826	0.0	$0	9.6	$312,482
2078	$2,902,332	0.0	$0	8.6	$337,480
2079	$2,770,040	0.0	$0	7.6	$364,479
2080	$2,598,006	0.0	$0	6.6	$393,637
2081	$2,380,719	0.0	$0	5.6	$425,128
2082	$2,112,038	0.0	$0	4.6	$459,139
2083	$1,785,131	0.0	$0	3.6	$495,870
2084	$1,392,402	0.0	$0	2.6	$535,539
2085	$925,412	0.0	$0	1.6	$578,383
2086	$374,791	0.0	$0	0.6	$374,791
Totals			**$107,922**		**$8,167,629**

Slott's Tips

Here's another reason for splitting an IRA to guarantee the stretch. Let's say you've got one IRA and you want to leave it to your two kids and a named charity. At your death, each will collect, but your kids are not guaranteed the stretch option, because one of the named co-beneficiaries is a charity—an entity with no life expectancy—unless they split the IRA themselves in a timely manner (see Chapter Eight). To accomplish your aim of leaving your IRA to different types of beneficiaries without killing the stretch option for those among them who are living and breathing, split your IRA into three separate accounts, naming each child the sole beneficiary of his or her own account and the charity the named beneficiary of the third. This way, each child retains the stretch option and can stretch over his or her individual life expectancy, and the charity can cash out.

Timing Is Everything

The timing of the split is critical to the long-term payout (the stretch) of the IRA for multiple beneficiaries. You as the IRA owner can split your IRA anytime you wish during your lifetime; if you don't, your IRA can still be split into separate IRAs by your beneficiaries when they receive it as their inheritance. However, they must execute the split within a set period that the IRS stipulates as "timely." This means no later than December 31 of the year following your death. If they haven't split the IRA into separate shares by then, they are stuck with a post-death payout based on the age of the oldest beneficiary. If one of those beneficiaries is not a person, then there will be no designated beneficiary and the stretch IRA will be lost. The inherited IRA can still be split later (after December 31 of the year following the year the IRA owner dies), but no separate account treatment will be permitted by the

IRS and the payout will be based on the age of the oldest beneficiary. Separate account treatment means that each beneficiary can use his or her own life expectancy to stretch his or her share of the inherited IRA.

The best way to *guarantee* that each beneficiary will have the opportunity to use his or her own life expectancy is for *you* to do the split. Once done, there will be no question that each beneficiary will be entitled to stretch required distributions over his or her own life expectancy, even if the others decline to stretch at all. This is the cleanest and certainly the most effective way to accomplish separate accounts, and the one I recommend for most IRA owners. It removes any question later on as to whether separate accounts have been created or are created on time. Also, when separate accounts are created by the IRA owner, he or she can allocate specific investments to the IRA for each beneficiary rather than leaving each beneficiary a certain percentage of the entire IRA.

Why do I recommend that "most" IRA owners with multiple beneficiaries do the split themselves, and not "all"? There are practical reasons why some IRA owners leave it up to their beneficiaries to do the split. The most common one is convenience. It's just easier to maintain one IRA with two or more beneficiaries than to maintain, say, five or eight or ten separate IRAs. There is less paperwork, and investments can be managed more easily. For example, if you want to leave your IRA equally to your three children, it's probably easier to have one IRA and name the three children as equal beneficiaries. This way, any appreciation or decline in the account's value is automatically shared equally between your beneficiaries.

Another reason why some IRA owners don't split the account themselves is cost. There may be fees for each account. This is a minor issue, though, compared to the big picture. It may be easier to keep fewer IRAs, but the trade-off is that you will never know if your beneficiaries will split the IRA in time. Don't let fees be the reason you don't do the split. If fees bother you, think of what it would cost if your beneficiaries blew the stretch because for whatever reason the split wasn't done properly or timely after your death. Think long-term. Remember, this is a book about long-term benefits, not saving a few bucks in the short term that will cost your family dearly later on. This is the wrong place to save on fees. If you want to save a few bucks, cut out pizzas instead.

SEVEN

Preserving the Stretch When Naming a Trust as Your IRA Beneficiary

Dear Ed,
My husband and I have a family trust for the purpose of avoiding
probate. Since we have only one child, the trust has one beneficiary.
On our IRAs we designated each other as primary beneficiaries and
the trust as contingent. Would it be better for the contingent beneficiary
on our IRAs to be our child's name instead of the trust? Can you get
the tax benefit of stretching out withdrawals if you name a trust as
your IRA beneficiary?
    —IRA owner

Naming Trusts—When You Should and When You Shouldn't

I'll call her Zelda. I don't know where she got the idea—perhaps from some estate planning seminar on the benefits of trusts, or maybe from her own attorney—but Zelda had her attorney draft a revocable living trust for her. Her attorney correctly pointed out that the trust was no good unless it was funded with assets, and he was right—so far, so good. Zelda placed all of her assets—by which I mean her IRA, worth $850,000—in the trust so it would be properly funded. To do this, she had to take the $850,000 out of her IRA and put it in the trust. Not until Zelda went to have her taxes prepared and her CPA saw the 1099-R form she brought with her showing the $850,000 withdrawal did Zelda realize that even though she was putting the funds in a trust, the withdrawal was a fully taxable distribution. The tax (federal, state, and city, in this case) on that distribution was approximately $380,000! Not only was this a huge bite out of her life savings, it marked the end of any hope she may have had of creating a stretch opportunity for her family.

Luckily there was no 10 percent early withdrawal penalty on top of all that, since Zelda was over age 59½—in fact, she was 82 years and sharp as a tack (too bad her attorney wasn't). She had even said that if she had known this would be taxable, she never would have made the transfer. But she thought by setting up the trust and transferring her IRA to it, she was being prudent in making sure her estate plan would be implemented properly. There was definitely a miscommunication somewhere. If you are doing this type of estate planning (setting up a revocable living trust), that's fine, but you cannot put your IRA into a trust while you are alive, as Zelda did, without opening it up to taxes, thereby killing the stretch. To avoid this, you can *leave* your IRA to a trust by naming the trust as your IRA beneficiary. The question is: Should you?

The benefits of naming a trust to be your IRA beneficiary must outweigh the fact that doing so may cause your family to lose the stretch.

Trusts are not for everyone. Their main purpose is post-death control. For example, you would name a trust as your IRA beneficiary if you wanted to restrict your beneficiary's access to your IRA. If that is your goal, then a trust may be an appropriate tool; still, it must qualify under the various IRS rules in order for your trust's beneficiaries to be able to use their own life expectancy for computing post-death required distributions (the stretch IRA concept). If the trust does not qualify, the stretch IRA option is lost.

There is only one way a trust can help your beneficiaries parlay your IRA into a fortune. That is if you do not trust them to take advantage of the stretch IRA themselves. If you leave your IRA directly to your son, for example, and he is properly named on your IRA beneficiary form, then he has the option to do the stretch and parlay your IRA. But he does not have to, and the IRS will neither encourage nor discourage him. It will just stand on the sidelines, waiting and watching for him to goof up by withdrawing more than the minimum distribution and killing the stretch along the way, or emptying the entire account into his pockets after the funeral. A trust, on the other hand, can *force* your son to do your bidding—even after you die. In effect, it allows you to rule from the grave.

With a trust, you can restrict access to your inherited IRA. You can also include trust provisions that will allow the trustee[10] of your trust to distribute extra funds (in addition to the required minimum distributions) to your son for certain needs—maybe medical or educational, or to buy a home or a business. You can make your trust as rigid or flexible as you wish. The IRS does not care, as long as your IRA pays out at least the required minimum amount each year—an amount that will depend on how the trust is written, specifically in the area of the restricted access provisions.

In addition to easing your mind about the possibility your spendthrift child might blow your entire IRA surfboarding around the world instead of parlaying it like you want him to, here are five other reasons why you might want to name a trust as your IRA beneficiary for post-death control:

- **Your IRA beneficiary is a minor child.** If you have a grandchild or other minor (under 18 or 21, depending on state law) who will be inheriting your IRA, you might want to set up a trust because minors are not able to make tax elections, such as IRA distribution decisions, that will affect the stretch period. If the

---

[10]Whom do you trust? Even if you set up a trust to carry out your instructions after you are gone, you will have to trust somebody to make sure this gets done. That somebody is your trustee, and can be a person or a thing (a financial institution, such as a bank or trust company). Most people who set up a trust to exercise post-death control over their IRA name their spouse as trustee, or perhaps a child (the responsible one), other family member, or friend or professional advisor with whom they feel comfortable to carry out the terms of the trust. Remember, though, if the trustee you name is not a family member, he, she, or it will probably receive a fee to act as your trustee.

minor were named as a direct beneficiary of the IRA, probate court could require a guardian to be appointed. (A custodian could be named as beneficiary on behalf of the minor under the Uniform Gifts to Minors Act or the Uniform Transfers to Minors Act, but the custodian in most states cannot make IRA distribution elections either. The custodian also does not have the same powers that would be granted to the trustee of a trust.) The guardian would make sure that required distributions are taken, but the problem with naming the child directly is that once the child reaches majority (18 or 21 years old), the IRA belongs to the child, with no restrictions. The child might be smart enough to stretch it, but also may not be. Therefore, a trust might be the best way to go in this case.

YOU CAN ALWAYS CHANGE YOUR MIND

Just because any of these situations may exist now does not necessarily mean it will be that way forever. For example, you may want to leave a young child's share in trust, but at some point when the child reaches a certain age (maybe 65!), you might feel he or she can be trusted and you can have it stipulated to remove the trust as IRA beneficiary at that time and to name the child directly. This change can be made at any time and will not increase the beneficiary's required distributions, shrinking the stretch period. The trust does not have to last a lifetime, unless you want it to.

■ **Your IRA beneficiary is disabled or incompetent.** You may need a trust to provide for someone who is not physically or mentally able to care for himself or herself after you are gone. In such a case, you could have an attorney set up a "special needs trust" for this purpose. It's best to use other non-IRA funds to provide for the needs of disabled or other beneficiaries who need care after your death because of required distributions and taxes. But for those of you whose retirement account money may be the only funds available to take care of the special needs of your beneficiaries after your death, a trust may be the way to go.

- **Your beneficiary will need help managing the stretch IRA.** If you feel your IRA beneficiary (even if he or she is an adult) may need help handling your inherited IRA—especially if it is a large one (by which I mean in the multimillions of dollars)—or there are potential divorce issues and you want, say, to protect your adult child's share from his or her ex-spouse, it is generally prudent to leave the IRA to a trust where capable trustees, money managers, and other professional advisors can help your family hold on to this wealth. Even if you are not a zillionaire, naming a trust can still protect a vulnerable or unsophisticated beneficiary from unscrupulous people who might take advantage of him or her, or from creditor problems (though many states already protect IRAs from creditors without need of a trust).

- **You want to make sure that estate taxes are paid.** A trust can be used to hold money for estate taxes if you feel there is a risk that your IRA beneficiary will take the money and run without paying his or her share of the estate tax. When you name an individual as a direct beneficiary of an IRA, the entire IRA goes to that person at your death. There is usually a clause in the will called the "tax apportionment clause" that spells out who is responsible for the estate tax, both on items that pass through the will and on property that passes outside the will (such as an IRA or life insurance). But even if the will's tax clause requires the IRA beneficiary to pay his or her share of the estate tax from the IRA proceeds, it may be too late if the beneficiary has already skipped town with the newly inherited IRA. For example, say there was a guy named Joe who left a large IRA (over $2 million) to several children from his first marriage, and the rest of his property—an equal amount of about $2 million (including a $700,000 house)—to his surviving spouse, Judy. At first blush you might say Judy would inherit her share estate-tax-free because of the unlimited marital deduction (which allows unlimited amounts to pass to a spouse free of estate tax, as long as he or she is a U.S. citizen, which Judy was). That's true. She did receive her $2 million of non-IRA cash and property estate-tax-free. However, there was an estate tax on the amount that passed to the children. (When Joe died, the exemption was only $1 million.) Now, add that the children were named as direct beneficiaries on the IRA and, to put it nicely, were not the stretching kind. They got their money and took off faster than Dick Grasso hightailed it out of the New York Stock Exchange after collecting his almost $200 million paycheck. In such a situation, whom does the IRS say is supposed to pay the estate tax on their share? The children are, if the IRS can find them—but the IRS won't bother looking if it can grab the cash more easily from Judy. You see, the IRS can go after any beneficiary for an estate tax bill, and it will usually go after the easiest target. If, however, there had been a tax apportionment clause in Joe's will that said it was his intent that each beneficiary pay his or her own share of estate tax, then his spouse, Judy, might have been able to get a restraining order from the court stopping payment of any IRA funds to the children until the estate tax bill was covered. But even so, if the children have already skipped town with the money, the IRS is not going to kill itself searching for them when Judy can pay the bill. This type of mess can be avoided by naming a trust as your IRA beneficiary and making sure the trust can escrow money for estate taxes before paying out to your IRA beneficiaries.

THE BIG LIE

Ever hear the one from an estate planner about how a trust will save you on estate taxes? It won't! Trusts don't save on estate taxes; they are used to *control the distribution* of your property after your death. Saving taxes is no reason to name a trust as your IRA beneficiary, because *there is no tax benefit that can be gained with a trust that cannot be gained without one.* Once they've revived from hearing this, some estate tax planners may, of course, say, "But you *must* name a trust, otherwise you will lose the estate exemption." Not true either. You do not have to name a trust to get that exemption. Here's how: Assume you have a $3 million IRA and you want to make sure your family gets the benefit of the first estate exemption of $1.5 million. It's easy. Just split the $3 million IRA into two IRAs. On the first IRA you will name your children. That IRA will pass to them under the estate exemption tax-free. On the other IRA you will name your spouse, who will receive his or her share also estate-tax-free. There. You've received the same estate tax benefit without a trust.

- **Second Marriages.** In a typical second marriage situation (or even with some first marriages), the IRA owner—say, the husband—may want to leave his wife the annual IRA income but, after his wife's death, to make sure the IRA goes to his children and not to, say, her children from a first marriage. A trust can be used to accomplish this. It can also be used to make sure that if your surviving spouse remarries, your IRA goes to your children at your surviving spouse's death and not to his or her new husband or wife. The appropriate trust for these situations is called a QTIP ("qualified terminable interest property") trust. It is used both to qualify for the marital deduction and to give you (the IRA owner and trust creator) control over the trust principal (the IRA) after your death. After your spouse dies, any remaining IRA balance will pass to the beneficiary you named in your trust (most likely your children and not your spouse's). An easier and more effective way to deal with the complications of leaving an IRA in second marriage situations is to use the separate account rule (see Chapter Six) and split the IRA into two or more IRAs with the different beneficiaries on each.

NO SEPARATE ACCOUNTS FOR TRUSTS

Separate accounts for IRA distribution purposes cannot be created when a trust is named as your IRA beneficiary. This means that all trust beneficiaries must use the age of the oldest trust beneficiary, even if the trust terminates after the IRA owner's death and the beneficiaries later transfer (via a trustee-to-trustee transfer) their shares to separate, properly titled inherited IRAs. In contrast, if the beneficiaries were named directly (and not through a trust) and they split their shares by the end of the year after the IRA owner's death, the separate account rule would apply and they could each use their own life expectancy for calculating their required withdrawals. This presents a problem if there is more than one IRA trust beneficiary, which is usually the case (a spouse and several children, for example), as it may negate the stretch for the younger beneficiaries, who will be stuck with using the age of the oldest trust beneficiary to calculate RMDs. For example, if Natalie (the IRA owner) names a trust for her three children as her IRA beneficiary, post-death RMDs would be based on the life expectancy of the oldest of the three children. If you want the whole enchilada, that is, you want each beneficiary to be able to use his or her own age *and* you want to maintain post-death control and protection by naming a trust as your IRA beneficiary—then based on the rigid IRS position in its most recent rulings, you would have to split your IRA into separate shares and set up separate trusts to be the beneficiaries of the separate IRAs—and do it now, during your lifetime. One trust that breaks out into separate sub-trusts won't work. One IRA that names existing separate trusts as beneficiaries (as opposed to one trust that breaks out into separate sub-trusts, as in these rulings) might work, but if you want a sure thing, I would not risk it. I would split the IRAs now and leave them to separate trusts.

When a Trust Can Be a Designated Beneficiary

As I've stressed throughout Part One, only individuals who are named on the IRA beneficiary form (or named through the IRA custodial document if no beneficiary is named on the beneficiary form) can be designated beneficiaries and use their life expectancy to stretch post-death required IRA distributions. Therefore, since a trust is not an individual, it cannot be a designated beneficiary, right? Wrong. If the trust qualifies as a "look-through" (or "see-through") trust, then the individual trust beneficiaries can qualify as designated beneficiaries for IRA distribution purposes. If one of the *trust beneficiaries* is not an individual (a charity, perhaps), however, there will be no designated beneficiary for IRA distribution purposes, even if the trust qualifies as a look-through trust. Clear as mud, huh?

For example, assume the trust qualifies as a look-through. Then you can "look through" the trust and treat the trust beneficiaries as if they were named as direct beneficiaries. But if one of the trust beneficiaries was a charity (and the charity did not cash out its share in a timely fashion), there would still be no designated beneficiary on the IRA, even though the trust qualified as a look-through trust. So, in order for a look-through trust to qualify for the stretch, all of the trust beneficiaries must be individuals; then the life expectancy that will be used to calculate required minimum distributions on the inherited IRA will be based on the age of the oldest of the individual trust beneficiaries.

To qualify as a look-through (or see-through) trust for IRA distribution purposes, the trust must meet the following requirements outlined in Regulations Section 1.401(a)(9)-4, A-5:

1. The trust must be a valid trust under state law.
2. The trust must be irrevocable at death.
3. The beneficiaries of the trust must be identifiable.
4. The required trust documentation has been provided to the plan administrator no later than October 31 of the year after the IRA owner's death.

If these requirements are met, then the trust qualifies as a designated beneficiary and the life expectancy of the oldest trust beneficiary can be used to calculate post-death required minimum distributions. If the trust fails to qualify, then there is no designated beneficiary and trust beneficiaries will not be able to stretch post-death required distributions over the life expectancy of the oldest. In that case, the IRA will be paid out either by the conclusion of the fifth year following the IRA owner's death if he or she died before the required beginning date (RBD) for taking distributions (the so-called "five-year rule") or over the remaining single life expectancy of the deceased IRA owner if death occurred *on or after* his or her RBD.

When an IRA is left to a trust, the trust must abide by the IRA distribution rules just as any other IRA beneficiary. And there can be substantial IRS penalties if the IRA tax rules are not complied with. The fact that the trust may say otherwise will not excuse your beneficiaries from penalties.

For example, if the trust states that only the income is to be paid to the trust beneficiary, but the required distribution is more than the income, a 50 percent excise tax could result on the amount of the required distribution that should have been made but was not. For instance, if the IRA income was $8,000 but the required distribution was $20,000, there would be a $6,000 penalty on the $12,000 that should have been withdrawn from the IRA but was not (50 percent of the $12,000 = $6,000 penalty).

There could also be a tax problem if the correct required distribution of $20,000 (in this example) was made from the IRA to the trust, but still only $8,000 was actually distributed to the trust's beneficiary. In this case, there would not be a 50 percent excise tax, because the correct required distribution was made from the IRA to the trust; however, the trust would be taxed on the taxable IRA distribution (the $12,000) that was not passed through to the trust beneficiary, and at the highest income tax rate.

Slott's Tips

BE CAREFUL, OR THESE TRUST RULES MIGHT COST YOUR FAMILY THE STRETCH

The post-death stretch schedule is based on the life expectancy of your designated beneficiary, but this person—although named by the IRA owner—is not officially crowned designated beneficiary until September 30 of the year following the year of your (the IRA owner's) death—e.g., September 30, 2006, if you died in November 2005. This is to give your beneficiaries a chance to remove an estate or charity (or even themselves, if desired) as a beneficiary. If a non-person (charity or estate, for example) is still a beneficiary on the IRA at that time, however, then your IRA will be deemed to have no designated beneficiary and the stretch for your other beneficiaries will be lost. You can protect your trust from falling into this trap by removing trust language that could lead the IRS to determine that your estate is one of your trust beneficiaries, even though you did not actually name your estate as a trust beneficiary. That can happen, for example, when one of the provisions of the trust is that debts and expenses of the estate can be paid from the IRA and those estate expenses are not paid off by the September 30 beneficiary designation date. (In private letter rulings, the IRS has allowed the estate to be removed as a trust beneficiary where the estate debts and expenses were timely paid.) You should remove that provision so you do not run the risk that IRS might consider your estate as one of the trust beneficiaries. That will mean you have no designated beneficiary and the stretch would be lost for your IRA, even if your IRA trust qualified under the four requirements for a look-through trust. Remove any trust provisions that allow estate debts or expenses to be paid from your IRA trust. That does not mean that they cannot be paid from the IRA funds, but at least you are not forcing them to be paid and risking the loss of the stretch IRA. You are better off having your trust remain silent on the issue. This way the trustee could pay distributions to the trust beneficiary, who can in turn use these distributions to pay estate expenses that may, and probably will, come up.

The Beneficiary Club: Who's In/Who's Out Determines the Stretch Period

A trust generally has both income beneficiaries and remainder (contingent) beneficiaries. For IRA purposes, the lifetime income beneficiary usually receives the required distributions from the trust for life. The remainder beneficiaries receive what's left after the income beneficiary dies. After the income beneficiary dies, either any remaining IRA funds can stay in trust for the remainder beneficiary or the trust can end and pay out the IRA's funds to the remainder beneficiary. So, since the stretch will be based on the age of the oldest trust beneficiary, you need to know who is in the club—the trust beneficiary club that is.

In a typical trust, you might name your spouse as the trust income beneficiary and your children as remainder beneficiaries. That can put a damper on the stretch, though, and that is why many trusts blow the stretch. Most estate planning trusts name the spouse as an income beneficiary to provide security for the spouse, but that backfires if you are looking to use that trust to stretch an IRA. If the spouse is one of several trust beneficiaries, the stretch period will be based on the spouse's life expectancy, and that will most likely be much shorter than the life expectancy of a child beneficiary.

If you are looking to set up your IRA to be stretched over the life of your children or grandchildren, and you are certain you need a trust for them, then you should not use the typical estate planning trusts that name the spouse as income beneficiary. That's fine for other assets. *But for an IRA, you should set up a separate revocable trust to be the IRA beneficiary and name your children (or just the person who needs the trust) as trust beneficiaries of that separate trust.* You'll also name remainder trust beneficiaries, maybe your grandchildren. You want only younger beneficiaries on this trust since the stretch period is based on the age of the oldest trust beneficiary.

Once you get past all of this, you must decide what type of trust you want to qualify as your look-through trust: A "conduit" trust or a "discretionary" trust? Your answer will be based on how much post-death control you want your trustee to have over the IRA distributions paid to the trust and ultimately to your beneficiaries.

Conduit Trusts

This type of trust is merely a "conduit" to pass required minimum distributions (RMDs) from the IRA to the trust beneficiaries. When a conduit trust is the beneficiary of an IRA, the post-death RMDs are first paid from the IRA to the trust and then from the trust to the trust beneficiaries. No IRA distributions remain in the trust. All RMDs that are received by the trust get paid out to the trust beneficiaries as if the trust did not exist. The trust beneficiaries then pay any tax on those distributions at their own personal income tax rates. This type of trust is used as a control mechanism to keep the beneficiaries from invading the IRA beyond the stretch payments.

Trust tax rates for most people are generally much higher than personal tax rates. Conduit IRA trusts eliminate any tax at trust tax rates. If the IRA is a Roth IRA, then trust taxes are not an issue, since all distributions from an inherited Roth IRA will be tax-free (if the account is held for at least five years, including the time the Roth IRA owner held it).

If a conduit IRA trust meets all four of the qualifying trust requirements described earlier, it qualifies as a look-through trust and the trust beneficiaries can be treated as the designated beneficiaries. The distributions will be based on the age of the oldest of those beneficiaries. The life expectancies of contingent or remainder beneficiaries are not considered since they can only receive distributions if the primary beneficiary dies and there is still a balance in the IRA.

Discretionary Trusts

A discretionary trust (sometimes referred to as an "accumulation" trust) does not have to pay out all IRA distributions to the trust beneficiaries. The trustee is given discretion to pay out either some, all, or none of the IRA distributions to the primary trust beneficiaries. Whatever IRA distributions are not paid out, though, are accumulated within the trust and taxed at trust tax rates. IRA owners who want maximum control over the post-death distributions to the trust and to the trust beneficiaries would set up this type of trust. With a discretionary trust, even annual RMDs can be held in trust until certain trust conditions are met—for example, until a child reaches age 30. RMDs must still be paid out from the IRA to the trust, but the trustee does not necessarily have to pay any of these distributions out to the trust beneficiaries. The terms of the trust determine how much or when the trustee will pay out IRA distributions received by the trust to the trust beneficiaries.

A discretionary trust must also meet the four trust requirements to qualify as a look-through trust. You use the age of the oldest trust beneficiary to calculate RMDs on the inherited IRA, but with a discretionary trust you must consider the ages of both the primary and the remainder trust beneficiaries when you look to see who is the oldest beneficiary.

If either the conduit or the discretionary trust does not meet all four requirements to qualify as a look-through trust, the IRA will not have a designated beneficiary and the post-death distributions will be paid out according to the rules that apply when there is no designated beneficiary. In other words, the stretch IRA will be lost.

Impact on the Stretch

If you choose a discretionary trust, you will most likely have to give up on the stretch for each beneficiary (except the oldest of the group), even if you set up separate discretionary trusts and separate IRAs. That may not be enough. Even if you have separate trusts, you still must include contingent beneficiaries in the group of beneficiaries whose lifetimes will be used for RMD purposes. If those beneficiaries are older than your primary beneficiary, then you must use that shorter life expectancy, even though you set up a separate trust and a separate IRA.

With a conduit trust, you can still have it all (the maximum stretch based on each beneficiary's life, and pay only RMDs to the trust beneficiary) by setting up separate conduit trusts and naming them as beneficiaries of separate IRAs you set up during your life. A trust set up under your will qualifies as being established during your life, but I still recommend a separate revocable trust set up to inherit your IRA and only your IRA to avoid any potential problems created with a trust under your will. With a conduit trust, contingent beneficiaries can be disregarded, since all annual RMDs are paid out to the primary trust beneficiaries. That may be reason alone to go with the conduit trust over the discretionary trust, unless you want to restrict your primary beneficiary's access to annual RMDs.

It all comes down to making choices. You should set up your IRA transition plan to accomplish what you feel is most important to you and your family, and then if you are able to also gain the tax and stretch advantages, that would be icing on the cake. If you want or need to control the IRA well past your death ("ruling from beyond the grave"), a trust is the way to accomplish this. Just make sure it's the right move for your family members—because they could be saddled with it for the rest of their lives.

Remove the Trust Tax Problem

For most taxpayers (except the super rich), trust tax rates are substantially higher than individual tax rates. They can quickly wipe out an inherited IRA. The best way to prevent that is by leaving a Roth IRA to your trust. The bottom line is that Roth IRA distributions are not taxable whether they go to a trust or a living beneficiary. So, if you think you will need to name a trust as beneficiary of any part of your IRA for any of the reasons mentioned in this chapter, start planning now to convert as much of it to a Roth IRA and remove the trust tax problem. This will keep more of your IRA growing in the trust for whichever trust beneficiary eventually receives it.

Slott's Tips

IRA TRUSTS MEAN CALLING IN THE EXPERTS, AND EVEN THEN . . .

If you feel you need a trust, you should seek out an attorney who specializes in this highly complex area. It is not enough that the attorney be an estate or trust attorney; he or she must also be familiar with the IRA distribution rules and know how to integrate them within the trust language. It is a relatively new field, and the necessary documents cannot be found in the usual books or attorney software or trust kits. You may want to consult a tax advisor to work with the attorney to get both tax and legal protection for your IRA. A good financial advisor or financial planner will be aware of the IRA trust rules and can also steer you to an attorney who specializes in the IRA trust area, but I must warn you—these types of attorneys are a rare find. For example, I know someone who spent a fortune setting up an IRA trust in his estate plan that included all sorts of instructions, provisions, contingent beneficiaries, you name it. There was one problem. The IRA went to the estate and to beneficiaries other than those meant to receive it in the trust. (I can't wait to see the new TV reality show about this, called *The Battle of the Beneficiaries!*) Also, the stretch was lost because there was no designated beneficiary. Why? Because the attorneys who set up the trust didn't name the trust as the IRA beneficiary on the IRA beneficiary form!

Your Work Is Done! It's Up to Your Beneficiaries Now.

You, the IRA owner, now have everything you need to set up your IRA to be inherited by any type of beneficiary you choose. *Your* work may be done, but the life of your IRA can still be cut short by mistakes made by your beneficiaries. I'll deal with those issues next. You should also read Part Two in order to prepare your beneficiaries for when they will inherit your IRA.

So for now you can take a well deserved break, digest this part—or maybe jump right into Part Two and start a dialogue with your family so that your effort here will not be in vain.

PARLAY IT INTO A FORTUNE

Dear Ed,
Now I know what to do the next time my parents die!
   —An angry beneficiary who lost the opportunity to stretch his
   inherited IRA. (By the time he sought my help, it was too
   late to correct the problem.)

EIGHT

Exercising Your Options—Decisions, Decisions

Dear Ed,
If my father dies and I'm the beneficiary, I know I can do a stretch IRA,
but when do I have to decide to do that? In other words, if I wait
longer than a certain period of time, will I not be able to do a stretch
IRA? I've been looking for that answer for weeks, so any help would be
greatly appreciated. Thank you.
  —IRA beneficiary

Turn, Turn, Turn

If you are an IRA owner, your work planting the seeds of the stretch for your designated beneficiaries is done, but those seeds need care and feeding for the stretch to grow and flourish. Now it's your designated beneficiaries' turn to do the heavy lifting. Here is what *they* must do when they inherit your IRA so that the opportunity you've created for them to parlay your IRA into a fortune will not be lost due to some avoidable technicality or mistake.

FAQ

Q. But, Ed, I don't want to rush things. I'm the named beneficiary (I think), but my parents are still spending their IRAs. After they die and I actually inherit their IRAs is the time to read this section of the book, right?

> **A.** By then it may be too late! Go through it now. Even better, go through it with your parents (or anyone else from whom you may inherit an IRA)—and read Part One, as well—to help guide and reinforce each other as to what you *both* have to do keep the stretch alive.

Inherited IRAs vs. IRAs That Are Inherited

An "inherited IRA" is an IRA inherited by anyone other than a spouse. Does that mean a spouse can never inherit an IRA? Of course a spouse can inherit an IRA—in fact, most IRA owners name their spouse as their IRA beneficiary so the spouse can do a spousal rollover, as recommended in Part One. Only if a spouse beneficiary chooses not to roll over the IRA but elects instead to remain a beneficiary must he or she follow the same yellow brick road as a non-spouse beneficiary (children, grandchildren, family friend, or domestic partner) to ensure the stretch opportunity is not lost.

First Things First

I had a client, a mailman, who was one of several local lottery winners. Although he came to me for advice on how to handle his $1 million payday, he turned a deaf ear to everything I advised and instead fell for every get-rich-quick (or, in his case, get-rich*er*-quick) scam you can name. I apparently was not as convincing as the scam artists who told him what he wanted to hear. Now he's broke and trying to get his job back at the post office.

Many IRA beneficiaries are like him; they wind up broke a short time after hitting the jackpot, wondering what happened to it all because they mishandled it right from the start. The taxman is just waiting for you to make that mistake so he can cash you out, which, of course, will bring an end to the stretch opportunity so skillfully created for you by your benefactor.

So, the stage is set. You've inherited an IRA. What should you do *first* to make sure you don't blow it?

If your spouse, parent, or other benefactor did everything I outlined in Part One to create the stretch opportunity for you, this is easy: Just ask your trusted IRA advisor (see Part Three) to locate the beneficiary form for each inherited IRA to see if indeed your name appears—otherwise you need not read any further, since you should have called or visited the IRA owner more often. Just teasing. Sure, the IRA owner designated you as his or her beneficiary on the form (or forms). If you are not disclaiming[11] the inherited IRA, what's your next move?

Assuming there are estate taxes, they must be settled, of course, but this may have little effect on you because, as a designated beneficiary, you do not have to wait for such formalities. As noted in Part One, the IRA beneficiary form trumps the will and bypasses the probate process. But I will assume that with this, as with everything else I'll be discussing from now on, your benefactor did everything correctly in setting up the stretch for you in Part One, including putting life insurance in place to pay for estate taxes so the IRA itself will not have to be raided. Therefore, the first booby trap you have to avoid so as not to kill the stretch yourself is to make sure you title your inherited IRA properly. Again, you will work closely with your trusted IRA advisor in doing this.

Retitling an Inherited IRA

The minute an IRA you inherit ceases to be an inherited IRA, the account balance becomes taxable and the stretch is lost—because

---

[11]Execute a statement in writing that you do not want all or some part of the inherited IRA (see Chapter Three). The disclaimer treats you as if you had died before the IRA owner and now it passes to the next beneficiary in line—either the contingent beneficiary or another primary beneficiary (if there are multiple primary beneficiaries), who must either take possession or disclaim.

current tax law says the account must be *maintained* as an inherited IRA for the rest of the time that you hold it, as well as the time it is held by a successor beneficiary (the beneficiary's beneficiary), otherwise it is treated as a complete distribution. For the IRA to be retitled properly—and thus maintained as an inherited IRA—the IRS says the name of the person you inherit from (the deceased IRA owner) *must remain* on the account. Even though the deceased IRA owner's name remains on the account, his or her Social Security number should be removed from the account and replaced with yours.

The following are acceptable ways of retitling an inherited IRA under various circumstances according to IRS guidelines. Let's say the IRA owner is Fred Jackson and the beneficiary is his daughter Sandra Jackson. Here is how the inherited IRA account should be titled: **"Fred Jackson, IRA (deceased June 19, 2005) F/B/O**[12] **Sandra Jackson, beneficiary,"** or **"Sandra Jackson, as beneficiary of Fred Jackson, IRA (deceased June 19, 2005)."**

If the beneficiary is Joan Jackson, the surviving spouse of Fred Jackson, and she chooses to remain a beneficiary, she would retitle in the same manner as a non-spouse beneficiary, as follows: **"Fred Jackson, IRA (deceased June 19, 2005) F/B/O Joan Jackson, beneficiary."**

If a trust were named beneficiary (let's call the trustee Adam Hill), the acceptable retitle would go this way: **"Fred Jackson, IRA (deceased June 19, 2005) F/B/O Adam Hill, Trustee of The Jackson Family Trust, beneficiary,"** or **"Adam Hill, Trustee of The Jackson Family Trust, as beneficiary of Fred Jackson, IRA (deceased June 19, 2005)."** Here, though, the Social Security number of the deceased should be replaced by the federal identification number of the trust. If the deceased set up the trust during his or her lifetime, then he or she—or the trustee—may have the number. If not, the trustee must apply to the IRS for a federal identification number on Form SS-4. This can be done online at https://sa1.www4.irs.gov/sa_vign/newformss4.do, or the form can be printed out and mailed or faxed to the IRS.

[12]For the benefit of

FAQ

Q. Ed, what if the estate is the beneficiary?

A. Then obviously the deceased didn't read Part One, and you couldn't steer him or her straight, because you didn't read it either. When an estate is beneficiary, the stretch is lost. But even though there is no stretch, it still pays to keep the account properly titled so that you, as beneficiary of the estate, can withdraw the balance over the time period that applies in this case. If the IRA owner died before his or her required beginning date, then the inherited IRA would have to be withdrawn by the end of the fifth year following the year of the IRA owner's death (the five-year rule). If the IRA owner died on or after his or her RBD, then the inherited IRA can be paid out over the deceased IRA owner's remaining single life expectancy. Under either scenario, there will not be a stretch IRA, but the IRA can at least stay intact for a little while longer. By titling the account properly, as follows, it won't get taxed immediately upon inheritance: "Fred Jackson, IRA (deceased June 19, 2005) F/B/O Estate of Fred Jackson, beneficiary," or "Estate of Fred Jackson, as beneficiary of Fred Jackson, IRA (deceased June 19, 2005)." As with a trust beneficiary, the deceased IRA owner's Social Security number should be replaced by a federal identification number—in this case that of the estate, using the same Form SS-4.

Name Your Successor!

After properly re-titling your inherited IRA, you need to name a beneficiary of your own—a "successor beneficiary," assuming the IRA custodial agreement permits this (which it should if you and the IRA owner read Part One). The reason this is important is that if you die and there are still funds in your inherited IRA, the account will pass to the person you want to have it and not to your estate.

When you name a beneficiary on an inherited IRA, the stretch can be maintained. It cannot be extended beyond the original stretch period, but whoever gets your inherited IRA is permitted to keep the stretch going. He or she can continue the stretch over the remaining number of years that you would have been able to had you lived. This allows the IRA to be parlayed to the max and not be cut down when the beneficiary dies.

For example, Ed dies and leaves his IRA to Natalie. Natalie is 30 years old in the year after Ed's death. She looks up the life expectancy factor for a 30-year-old from the IRS Single Life Expectancy table and sees that her stretch period is 53.3 years. Assume the IRA custodian allows Natalie to name a beneficiary, so Natalie immediately names Seymour as her successor beneficiary (the beneficiary's beneficiary). Natalie then dies after only ten years and there is still a balance in the IRA, plus there were 43.3 years left on her payout term (the 53.3 years less the 10 years she took withdrawals = 43.3 years). Seymour, the successor beneficiary, can still spread his annual required minimum distributions over the remaining 43.3 years. Seymour is now a beneficiary, so he should immediately name a successor beneficiary in case he dies and there are still funds in the IRA. Seymour names Marvin as his successor beneficiary. Seymour dies 20 years later and there are still funds left in the IRA. Since Marvin is the named successor beneficiary, Marvin can take distributions over the remaining 23.3 years (the 43.3 years left when Seymour became beneficiary less the 20 more years Seymour lived = 23.3 years). Marvin should immediately name a successor beneficiary.

FAQ

Q. Ed, I have just inherited an IRA from my aunt, and now I want to name my own beneficiary. Do I have to name my spouse as my beneficiary?

A. Not unless the law of your state requires it.

September 30 Is the Designation Date (DD)

The identity of the designated beneficiary is not determined until September 30 of the year following the year of the IRA owner's death. This is called the "designation date" (DD).

For example, if the IRA owner died in 2005, then the designated beneficiary will be determined on September 30, 2006. The time in between is called the "shake-out" (or "gap") period. It allows for post-death planning by using disclaimers, post-death distributions (cash-outs), and account splitting by beneficiaries. But the beneficiary designation form has to be properly set up to handle this. The beneficiary form must have both primary and contingent beneficiaries and be kept up-to-date; otherwise a disclaimer could backfire and end up negating the stretch IRA. If you disclaimed and there was no contingent beneficiary named or the contingent beneficiary has already died, the IRA could end up going to the estate and having no designated beneficiary.

Removing Beneficiaries

Why would a beneficiary want to be removed? Perhaps so that a better beneficiary (one with a longer life expectancy) can become the designated beneficiary on the designation date, September 30 of the year following the year of the deceased's passing. That would add more long-term value to the stretch IRA. Remember, the longer you can keep the IRA away from IRS, the more your family will accumulate.

A beneficiary can be removed in two ways. He or she can either cash out or disclaim his or her interest in the inherited IRA. A non-designated beneficiary such as an estate, charity, or non-qualifying trust can also be removed. Cashing out means the beneficiary takes his or her share out in a full distribution. A beneficiary cannot do a partial cash-out, because he or she would still be a beneficiary on the part not cashed out. If he or she is one of several beneficiaries, then cashing out can make a difference to the remaining beneficiaries, especially if they are younger (or have longer life expectancies than the beneficiary who cashed out).

Disclaiming is different from cashing out, because it means you refuse your inheritance. With a cash-out, you take your inheritance. That's a big difference. If, after the disclaimer, the IRA passes to a non-designated beneficiary (a charity or estate, for example), then, when the smoke clears on DD, there will be no designated beneficiary on the inherited IRA.

For a 2005 death, you have only until September 30, 2006, to cash out a beneficiary. A disclaimer must generally be made within nine months of the date of death. The September 30, 2006, DD does not extend the nine-month disclaimer period.

Look to see who should be cashed out. If you have several beneficiaries and one of them, for example, is a charity, then make sure the charity cashes out before September 30 of the year following the year of the IRA owner's death. Otherwise, there will be no designated beneficiary on the inherited IRA and the stretch will be lost. If the IRA beneficiaries are a spouse and two children, for example, 50 percent to the spouse and 25 percent to each of the two children, then you may want to have the spouse cash out her share and transfer the funds to her own IRA. The remaining funds would be split into separate inherited IRAs. Then, on DD, each of the children can use his or her own age for the stretch period and not have to be stuck using the mother's shorter life expectancy.

Trust Deadlines

The IRS says that when a trust is named an IRA beneficiary, the trustee must *(by October 31 of the year following the year of the IRA owner's death)* provide the plan administrator with a list of all beneficiaries of the trust and a description of their entitlement. (It's usually easier and more practical just to give the plan administrator a copy of the trust itself, which is what I recommend to clients, since it has all the relevant information.)

Who is this "plan administrator"? (This question reminds me of when kids get their first paycheck and ask, "Who is this guy FICA, and why is he taking my money?") If the deceased's retirement account was in a company plan, it would be the person at the company who has that title and responsibility. It could also be an outside pension administration firm hired by the company to be the plan administrator.

For deceased IRA owners, there really is no plan administrator, so the trustee of the trust would give the documentation to the IRA custodian (the bank, broker, mutual fund company, or insurance company) that is holding the IRA.

A Splitting Headache

If you are one of several beneficiaries on a single inherited IRA and you want to make sure that each of you can stretch over your individual lifetime rather than be stuck with the life expectancy of the oldest in calculating RMDs, you must split the account into separate IRAs (assuming the IRA owner hasn't already done that for you as I advised in Part One). If one of the multiple beneficiaries happens to be a non-person (a charity, estate, or non-qualifying trust) and the inherited IRA is not split, the IRA will not have a designated beneficiary and none of the beneficiaries will be able to stretch their shares.

The mechanics of properly retitling a split IRA is fairly easy. Each IRA will include the name of the deceased IRA owner and the name of the particular beneficiary on that newly split inherited IRA. The IRA will be under the Social Security number of that beneficiary. Then each beneficiary is ready to begin taking required minimum withdrawals over his or her individual stretch period.

> ## CAUTION
>
> An inherited IRA does not actually have to be split into several different IRAs in order to create separate shares. Separate shares will be created if the multiple beneficiaries are willing to have post-death gains and losses on their individual inherited amounts accounted for in a single IRA. However, this will create an ongoing administrative accounting nightmare, and I would not recommend it. If beneficiaries desire separate shares, they should physically split the inherited IRA in a timely fashion.

The regulations state that multiple beneficiaries of an inherited IRA have until December 31 of the year following the year of the IRA owner's death to split the IRA and create separate accounts. That means if the IRA owner has named you and your two siblings as co-beneficiaries on his or her IRA, you can each still be the designated beneficiary on your separate share if the account is split after the September 30 DD (referred to earlier) but before the end of the year. That's plenty of time. Even if the IRA owner died on the last day of the year, you would still have until the end of the following year to split the account.

For example, if the IRA owner dies in 2005, separate shares for RMD purposes can be created, even if the account is split after September 30, 2006, as long as the IRA is split by December 31, 2006. Does this mean that the designated beneficiary can be determined as late as December 31 of the year following the year of death? No. The only explanation then for the two dates is that

September 30 is the date that the designated beneficiary is determined and December 31 is merely an administrative date by which the actual split must be done. To be safe I would split by the September 30 date. That still gives you plenty of time.

It is best to split the IRA by the end of year of death, if that is possible. It is not required, but if you can do this, each of the individual beneficiaries will have a separate account balance in their own inherited IRA as of the end of the year of death. That is the balance you would use to calculate your first required minimum distribution as a beneficiary. If the account was not split until the year after death, it is still okay to create separate shares; you just have to compute your share of total IRA balance for the first year's RMD since it is still all in one account. If the IRA owner died near the end of the year, it would be difficult to split by the end of the year of death. In that case, split as soon as you can in the year after death. But my advice is not to play daredevil and wait until the last possible day.

If a non-designated beneficiary (an estate, charity, or trust) is one of several beneficiaries on a single IRA, I would make sure that either the account is split or the non-designated beneficiary cashes out by September 30 of the year following the year of death. This way there can be no question that the remaining individual beneficiaries can be designated beneficiaries and each use their individual life expectancy for RMDs. Here again, when the rules are not crystal clear, choose the sure thing.

Slott's Tips

The best way of getting rid of a non-designated beneficiary so that it does not taint the inherited IRA gene pool and cause the other individual co-beneficiaries to lose the stretch IRA is to remove it as beneficiary by cashing it out. Let's say it is a charity. You can and should distribute (cash out) the charity's share immediately after the death of the

IRA owner. The cash-out provision works better with a charity (as opposed to an estate) since the charity will want its share immediately and does not have to worry about income tax. If the non-designated beneficiary was the estate, the beneficiaries of the estate might not want to pay tax on the entire amount at once, when they can at least make use of the five-year rule. If the IRA owner died after his or her RBD, the estate beneficiaries could have stretched out even further over the IRA owner's remaining single life expectancy.

Moving Inherited IRA Funds—Proceed with Caution

If you want to move your inherited IRA from its current custodian to some other custodian, before you move one penny, make sure you know *how* to move it. A non-spouse beneficiary (that's you) cannot do a rollover, so the only way you can move an inherited account without opening it up to taxes and killing the stretch is via a trustee-to-trustee transfer.

In Part One, I advised IRA owners to make sure their IRA custodial agreement will let beneficiaries move funds to another IRA custodian in a direct transfer. Hopefully they listened. If not, and the custodian says it must issue you a check to transfer funds to another institution, as long as that check is made out to your inherited IRA at the new bank or broker or fund where you want to move your inherited IRA, and not to you, the move would still qualify as a direct transfer and not be taxable. Even so, my advice is to avoid the check route. Too many things can go wrong; don't take a chance of having the entire inherited IRA become taxable and killing the stretch.

DECISIONS, DECISIONS CHECKLIST

You are an IRA beneficiary (or soon will be). What next? Check each item off as you do it to make sure you don't forget anything.

❐ Get your IRA advisor on board—don't make any unsupervised IRA moves.

❐ If planning to disclaim any of your inherited IRA, do it before any of the IRA funds are touched.

❐ Pay estate taxes (if any) from life insurance or other assets, *not* from the inherited IRA.

❐ Set up your inherited IRA properly—by titling it correctly; putting the inherited IRA in your (the beneficiary's) Social Security number; naming a successor beneficiary; filing for a federal identification number if the beneficiary is an estate or trust.

❐ Know your deadlines for inherited IRAs—the September 30 designation date (DD); the shake-out (or gap) period for removing non-designated beneficiaries; when trust documentation (or a copy of the trust) must be provided to the IRA custodian if a trust is the IRA beneficiary (October 31).

❐ Split the inherited IRA into separate shares if there are multiple beneficiaries of varying ages or different types.

❐ When changing custodians of inherited IRAs, move funds via direct transfer only.

NINE

Taking Inherited IRA Distributions— What to Do When

Dear Ed,

My 79-year-old client died this year before taking her required minimum distribution. The IRA account is going to be split between her two children, and they plan on doing a stretch. Should I do the year of death RMD before the split and divide the proceeds and tax hit between the children, or have them split the IRA then take the RMD from each account?

—Financial advisor

Required Distributions Begin at RBD

Now you are ready to seize the stretch opportunity the IRA owner created for you and that you have properly set up. The only thing that stands in the way of parlaying your inherited IRA into a fortune is *you*. Remember, this is still an inherited IRA and so it can be easily lost. Think of it as an eggshell. Once the eggshell cracks, there's no putting it back together again. The key is to keep it from cracking too much too soon or too late.

FAQ

Q. Ed, I have just inherited an IRA. I am 45 years old. If I withdraw before reaching 59½ years old, won't I be hit with the 10 percent early withdrawal penalty?

A. NO! The 10 percent penalty for taking withdrawals from an IRA or company plan before age 59½ *does not apply to a beneficiary.*

FAQ

Q. Ed, if I withdraw from the inherited IRA, will I be subject to the mandatory 20 percent withholding tax?

A. No. The 20 percent withholding tax rule does *not* apply to IRAs; it only applies to eligible rollover distributions from company plans.

First off, you must know if the person you inherited the IRA from—let's say, your father—was taking required minimum distributions.

The required beginning date (RBD) is when mandatory distributions start for IRA owners. That date is April 1 of the year following the year the IRA owner turns 70½ years old. The IRS rules are clear that if the IRA owner dies before his or her RBD, *no* distributions are required for the year of death, even if the IRA owner died in his or her 70½ year. So, for example, if your father's RBD was April 1, 2006, and he died in March of 2006, he will be treated as having died before his RBD and you (his non-spouse beneficiary) do not have to take a required distribution for 2006 or for his 70½ year (2005).

But if your father lived beyond his RBD and thus already taking required minimum distributions, what happens if he dies before taking his final RMD for the year in which he died? The IRS will know if your father missed an RMD (but is under no obligation to tell you) because the IRA custodian is required under the rules to rat him out to the IRS. And if you fail to take his remaining RMD before you start taking your own, there's a 50 percent penalty on the required amount not withdrawn, and *you* must pay it—because the minute the IRA owner dies, the balance of the IRA belongs to the beneficiary (and not the estate unless, of course, the estate is the beneficiary). It is important not to lose chunks of your newly inherited IRA to 50 percent penalties because a technicality flew by you!

FAQ

Q. Ed, if the IRA owner dies after his RBD and the IRA has no designated beneficiary (the beneficiary is the estate), then how long can the post-death payout go on?

A. Under the new rules, if there is no designated beneficiary and the IRA owner dies after his RBD, distributions can be made using the IRA owner's age in the year of death. The longest possible distribution period for the IRA would be 15.3 years. But 15.3 years would be the factor only if he died in the year he was 71 years old. If he was much older when he died, then the remaining life expectancy would be much shorter. There really is no excuse for not having a designated beneficiary, but things happen. At least the latest round of IRA rules have softened the impact of that somewhat—but 15.3 years is no comparison to being able to use the life expectancy of a designated beneficiary (especially a young one).

If you are one of several beneficiaries and the deceased IRA owner did not take his or her year-of-death RMD, divide the RMD by the number of beneficiaries to determine the share of the RMD you must take. For example, if your father's RMD for the year of his death was $12,000 and there are three beneficiaries (you and your two siblings), each of you will withdraw $4,000 from your separate inherited IRA (assuming the IRA was split) to equal the total of dad's final RMD. This is also why you want to split the IRA and do the split *before* you take that distribution. If you took it from your father's IRA before you split, the IRA would still be under his Social Security number. That would cause problems with the IRS because, as already noted, the beneficiaries are supposed to pay the tax on the IRA owner's year of death RMD.

If the beneficiary is a trust and there are leftover RMDs, they are paid to the trust. The trust terms will then determine if these RMDs will be paid out to the trust beneficiaries. If the trust is a conduit trust, then the RMDs will be paid out from the trust to the trust beneficiaries. If it is a discretionary trust, then it is up to the trustee to decide if the RMD will be paid out to the trust benefici- aries. If the RMD is paid out to the trust beneficiaries, then they must pay the tax on the RMD at their own personal tax rates. If the RMD is not paid out from the trust to the trust beneficiaries and is instead retained in the trust, then the trust pays the tax on the RMD at trust tax rates. These are high tax rates, so a trust that accumulates IRA distributions rather than paying them out to trust beneficiaries will pay a steep tax on those distributions.

Similar to a trust, if the IRA beneficiary is an estate, the estate takes the year-of-death RMD and then pays it out to the benefici- ary(ies) of the estate and that person (persons or entity) pays tax on the distribution.

If the beneficiary is a charity and the RMD remained untaken at the time of the IRA owner's death, the charity takes the remaining distribution (and probably the entire account too), but, being a charity, owes no tax on it.

Now that that's taken care of, let's move on to the distributions you have to take based on your own life expectancy. This begins the stretch IRA, so you might want to stretch first before reading on, just to get in the groove.

Stretch Distributions—Traditional IRAs

As the proud designated beneficiary of your father's IRA, you take *your* first RMD by the end of the year after your dad's death—regardless of whether he passed away before or after his required beginning date. It doesn't matter. If you are a designated beneficiary, it makes no difference when the IRA owner died. And you do not have to clean the inherited IRA out in five years (the five-year rule) no matter what the bank or other financial institution acting as custodian of the account may insist.

To determine the amount of your first year RMD, go to the Single Life Expectancy table (see Chapter One, Table 1) and look up the life expectancy factor for your age in the year *after* the IRA owner's death. (For your second and all future distribution years, you do not have to keep looking up your new life expectancy factor. Just reduce the number by one for each year until the schedule ends or the IRA is completely withdrawn.) Once you have your life expectancy factor, divide the balance of the inherited IRA as of December 31 of the preceding year by that factor to determine the amount of your RMD. You'll owe tax on your withdrawals every year (unless the IRA you inherited is a Roth IRA, which is why I recommended that strategy to IRA owners everywhere in Part One).

For example, John is the IRA owner. He dies in 2005 and his designated beneficiary is his daughter Laurin. Laurin is 50 years old in 2005, when she inherits. The balance in John's IRA at December 31, 2005, is $100,000. Laurin goes to the Single Life Expectancy table. Her age in 2006 (the year after John's death and her first distribution year) is 51. The life expectancy factor for a 51-year-old according to the table is 33.3 *years*. Laurin then looks up the balance in the IRA as of December 31, 2005, which is $100,000. She divides the $100,000 by 33.3 (years) and gets $3,003, the amount of her first year RMD (for 2006).

Assuming an 8 percent growth rate over the year, the new balance as of the end of 2006 is $104,757. How did I get that? The original $100,000 less Laurin's first year RMD of $3,003 = $96,997, plus 8 percent growth brings the new balance at the end of 2006 to $104,757. To calculate her second year RMD (for 2007), Laurin simply reduces her life expectancy factor by one (33.3 years minus 1 = 32.3 years) and divides $104,757 by 32.3, which equals $3,243, her RMD for 2007.

To calculate her 2008 RMD, Laurin starts with the life expectancy factor of 32.3 years and reduces that factor by one to 31.3. Then she looks up the balance in the IRA at the end of the year before the distribution year. In this case that is 2007. On December 31, 2007, the IRA balance, after being reduced by the 2006 and 2007 RMDs and increased with an 8 percent growth rate, is $109,635. Laurin then divides the $109,635 by 31.3 (years) and that equals the RMD for 2008 of $3,503.

Laurin continues this process each year until the end of her life expectancy (according to the table) or until the account is empty. She can always withdraw more than the minimum, but these examples assume she withdraws only the minimum for the full life expectancy schedule. This means that Laurin will eventually withdraw $449,714 from her inherited IRA (see Table 16). Notice how the IRA balance actually increases every year even after taking the RMDs. That's because Laurin only has to withdraw about 3–5 percent for the first 15 years. It goes up a little bit each year as her life expectancy decreases, but during most of the earlier distribution years is when she can really build this account, as long as her return (interest or appreciation) exceeds her RMDs.

Table 16.

Year	IRA Beneficiary's Age	Value of IRA	IRA Beneficiary's Life Expectancy Factor (in years)	IRA Required Minimum Distributions (RMDs)	Cumulative IRA Distributions
2006	51	$100,000	33.3	$3,003	$3,003
2007	52	$104,757	32.3	$3,243	$6,246
2008	53	$109,635	31.3	$3,503	$9,749
2009	54	$114,623	30.3	$3,783	$13,532
2010	55	$119,707	29.3	$4,086	$17,618
2011	56	$124,871	28.3	$4,412	$22,030
2012	57	$130,096	27.3	$4,765	$26,795
2013	58	$135,357	26.3	$5,147	$31,942
2014	59	$140,627	25.3	$5,558	$37,500
2015	60	$145,875	24.3	$6,003	$43,503
2016	61	$151,062	23.3	$6,483	$49,986
2017	62	$156,145	22.3	$7,002	$56,988
2018	63	$161,074	21.3	$7,562	$64,550
2019	64	$165,793	20.3	$8,167	$72,717
2020	65	$170,236	19.3	$8,821	$81,538
2021	66	$174,328	18.3	$9,526	$91,064
2022	67	$177,986	17.3	$10,288	$101,352
2023	68	$181,114	16.3	$11,111	$112,463
2024	69	$183,603	15.3	$12,000	$124,463
2025	70	$185,331	14.3	$12,960	$137,423
2026	71	$186,161	13.3	$13,997	$151,420
2027	72	$185,937	12.3	$15,117	$166,537
2028	73	$184,486	11.3	$16,326	$182,863
2029	74	$181,613	10.3	$17,632	$200,495
2030	75	$177,099	9.3	$19,043	$219,538

Table 16. *(continued)*

Year	IRA Beneficiary's Age	Value of IRA	IRA Beneficiary's Life Expectancy Factor (in years)	IRA Required Minimum Distributions (RMDs)	Cumulative IRA Distributions
2031	76	$170,700	8.3	$20,566	$240,104
2032	77	$162,145	7.3	$22,212	$262,316
2033	78	$151,128	6.3	$23,989	$286,305
2034	79	$137,310	5.3	$25,908	$312,213
2035	80	$120,314	4.3	$27,980	$340,193
2036	81	$99,721	3.3	$30,218	$370,411
2037	82	$75,063	2.3	$32,636	$403,047
2038	83	$45,821	1.3	$35,247	$438,294
2039	84	$11,420	0.3	$11,420	$449,714
Totals					**$449,714**

What would Laurin's stretch IRA look like if she were John's granddaughter rather than his daughter, and if she inherited at, say, age 10 and started taking RMDs at age 11, calculating RMDs in the same manner? Using the same 8 percent average growth rate, she would withdraw a whopping **$4,355,926** over the course of her life expectancy (see Table 17)! That's the power of the stretch IRA, especially with a younger beneficiary.

Table 17.

Year	IRA Beneficiary's Age	Value of IRA	IRA Beneficiary's Life Expectancy Factor (in years)	IRA Required Minimum Distributions (RMDs)	Cumulative IRA Distributions
2006	11	$100,000	71.8	$1,393	$1,393
2007	12	$106,496	70.8	$1,504	$2,897
2008	13	$113,391	69.8	$1,625	$4,522
2009	14	$120,707	68.8	$1,754	$6,276
2010	15	$128,469	67.8	$1,895	$8,171
2011	16	$136,700	66.8	$2,046	$10,217
2012	17	$145,426	65.8	$2,210	$12,427
2013	18	$154,673	64.8	$2,387	$14,814
2014	19	$164,469	63.8	$2,578	$17,392
2015	20	$174,842	62.8	$2,784	$20,176
2016	21	$185,823	61.8	$3,007	$23,183
2017	22	$197,441	60.8	$3,247	$26,430
2018	23	$209,730	59.8	$3,507	$29,937
2019	24	$222,721	58.8	$3,788	$33,725
2020	25	$236,448	57.8	$4,091	$37,816
2021	26	$250,946	56.8	$4,418	$42,234
2022	27	$266,250	55.8	$4,772	$47,006
2023	28	$282,396	54.8	$5,153	$52,159
2024	29	$299,422	53.8	$5,565	$57,724
2025	30	$317,366	52.8	$6,011	$63,735
2026	31	$336,263	51.8	$6,492	$70,227
2027	32	$356,153	50.8	$7,011	$77,238
2028	33	$377,073	49.8	$7,572	$84,810
2029	34	$399,061	48.8	$8,177	$92,987
2030	35	$422,155	47.8	$8,832	$101,819
2031	36	$446,389	46.8	$9,538	$111,357

Table 17. *(continued)*

Year	IRA Beneficiary's Age	Value of IRA	IRA Beneficiary's Life Expectancy Factor (in years)	IRA Required Minimum Distributions (RMDs)	Cumulative IRA Distributions
2032	37	$471,799	45.8	$10,301	$121,658
2033	38	$498,418	44.8	$11,125	$132,783
2034	39	$526,276	43.8	$12,015	$144,798
2035	40	$555,402	42.8	$12,977	$157,775
2036	41	$585,819	41.8	$14,015	$171,790
2037	42	$617,548	40.8	$15,136	$186,926
2038	43	$650,605	39.8	$16,347	$203,273
2039	44	$684,999	38.8	$17,655	$220,928
2040	45	$720,732	37.8	$19,067	$239,995
2041	46	$757,798	36.8	$20,592	$260,587
2042	47	$796,182	35.8	$22,240	$282,827
2043	48	$835,857	34.8	$24,019	$306,846
2044	49	$876,785	33.8	$25,940	$332,786
2045	50	$918,913	32.8	$28,016	$360,802
2046	51	$962,169	31.8	$30,257	$391,059
2047	52	$1,006,465	30.8	$32,677	$423,736
2048	53	$1,051,691	29.8	$35,292	$459,028
2049	54	$1,097,711	28.8	$38,115	$497,143
2050	55	$1,144,364	27.8	$41,164	$538,307
2051	56	$1,191,456	26.8	$44,457	$582,764
2052	57	$1,238,759	25.8	$48,014	$630,778
2053	58	$1,286,005	24.8	$51,855	$682,633
2054	59	$1,332,882	23.8	$56,003	$738,636
2055	60	$1,379,029	22.8	$60,484	$799,120
2056	61	$1,424,029	21.8	$65,322	$864,442
2057	62	$1,467,404	20.8	$70,548	$934,990

Table 17. *(continued)*

Year	IRA Beneficiary's Age	Value of IRA	IRA Beneficiary's Life Expectancy Factor (in years)	IRA Required Minimum Distributions (RMDs)	Cumulative IRA Distributions
2058	63	$1,508,604	19.8	$76,192	$1,011,182
2059	64	$1,547,005	18.8	$82,288	$1,093,470
2060	65	$1,581,894	17.8	$88,870	$1,182,340
2061	66	$1,612,466	16.8	$95,980	$1,278,320
2062	67	$1,637,805	15.8	$103,659	$1,381,979
2063	68	$1,656,878	14.8	$111,951	$1,493,930
2064	69	$1,668,521	13.8	$120,907	$1,614,837
2065	70	$1,671,423	12.8	$130,580	$1,745,417
2066	71	$1,664,110	11.8	$141,026	$1,886,443
2067	72	$1,644,931	10.8	$152,308	$2,038,751
2068	73	$1,612,033	9.8	$164,493	$2,203,244
2069	74	$1,563,343	8.8	$177,653	$2,380,897
2070	75	$1,496,545	7.8	$191,865	$2,572,762
2071	76	$1,409,054	6.8	$207,214	$2,779,976
2072	77	$1,297,987	5.8	$223,791	$3,003,767
2073	78	$1,160,132	4.8	$241,694	$3,245,461
2074	79	$991,913	3.8	$261,030	$3,506,491
2075	80	$789,354	2.8	$281,912	$3,788,403
2076	81	$548,037	1.8	$304,465	$4,092,868
2077	82	$263,058	0.8	$263,058	$4,355,926
2078	83	$0		$0	$4,355,926
Totals					**$4,355,926**

If Laurin (now age 50 again) inherits two or more IRAs from her father, John, then her RMDs are based on the total of all of these inherited IRAs. She can withdraw the RMD from any one or a combination of the IRAs, but would be better off consolidating the inherited IRAs into one. If a beneficiary like Laurin inherits IRAs from several different people—which is not as uncommon a situation as one might think (she could inherit an IRA from her dad and then another IRA from her mom), these inherited IRAs must stay separate. They cannot be combined, because they were inherited from different IRA owners. Laurin must take RMDs for each inherited IRA separately and keep separate distribution schedules and calculations. She cannot combine the balances in IRAs inherited from different people.

Now let's say Laurin dies before the September 30 DD. Although she is not officially crowned designated beneficiary until then, if she is the named beneficiary on the IRA beneficiary form when the IRA owner dies, and then she dies before DD, she automatically becomes the designated beneficiary and the post-death stretch IRA schedule will still be based on the age she would have reached in the year after the IRA owner's death. That's the power of being a designated beneficiary. *Your life expectancy schedule can outlive you!*

Laurin's beneficiary then takes the RMDs Laurin would have taken had she lived. That is why it is so important for a beneficiary to immediately name a beneficiary. If upon inheriting, Laurin immediately names, say, Jeffrey as her beneficiary, then Jeffrey will take the RMDs based on the same stretch IRA term that Laurin would have had. Jeffrey's age does not matter, because distributions on the inherited IRA are not based on his age. Jeffrey should now immediately name a beneficiary in case he dies before the payment schedule ends and there is still a balance in the IRA. Lets say that his beneficiary is Gregory. Gregory would continue Laurin's original remaining stretch period. Gregory's age also does not matter, since RMDs are still based on Laurin's age and not Gregory's. A beneficiary's beneficiary cannot extend the post-death distribution schedule based on his or her life expectancy. If, in this example, Jeffrey was only 22 when he inherited, he still must take distributions over Laurin's remaining life expectancy from her original schedule. According to the Single Life Expectancy table, the life expectancy of a 22-year-old is 61.1 years, but Jeffrey cannot tack that on when he inherits and start taking distributions based on a 61.1-year term. If he does that, he will be taking out too little and will be subject to the 50 percent penalty that applies to any RMD not taken. This is true even if the beneficiary's beneficiary is older. If Laurin's beneficiary was, say, her grandmother Flo, who was 100 years old when she inherited Laurin's IRA, Grandma Flo could still continue on whatever is remaining of Laurin's 33.3-year stretch schedule, even though it is not likely Grandma Flo would live that long.

If Laurin neglects to name a beneficiary before she dies, the payment schedule would not change, because her life expectancy is locked in. But the IRA would most likely pass to her estate, and the financial institution might just pay it all out to her estate and end the stretch. Also, if the IRA is paid to the estate, it becomes a probate asset and must go through that process. It can also be subject to will contests and may not even go to Jeffrey or Gregory if they are not specifically named in the will or someone has a better claim. I know I sound like a broken record here, but this, again, is why it is so important for you, once you become a beneficiary, to make sure that you name a beneficiary (a successor beneficiary) to inherit your share of the inherited IRA—in case you die prematurely and there is still a balance remaining in the inherited IRA.

FAQ

Q. Ed, can an IRA beneficiary's RMD be taken in stock? In other words, if most of the inherited IRA is invested in stocks, do you have to sell those stocks to take your RMD, or can you just withdraw the RMD in stock?

A. An IRA beneficiary (and any IRA owner) can take distributions "in kind," meaning in stock or other property. For example, if all you had was real estate in your IRA, you could take your RMD by withdrawing a piece of the property—even though that may be tedious since you would have to deed a part of the property out each year, it can be done. You don't have to sell the property to take a distribution from your IRA or your inherited IRA. If you do decide to withdraw stock from your inherited IRA (or any IRA), you will pay income tax on the value of the stock or other property that you withdrew. Once you withdraw the stock from your IRA, the amount that you paid tax on becomes your new *basis* (your cost) for figuring gain or loss when you eventually sell that stock (see Chapter Ten). If you withdraw stock from your IRA, you are not selling it. You are merely transferring the stock to a taxable brokerage account. When you do this, make sure you update the basis of the stock in your taxable brokerage account to the value that you already paid tax on. It's the value of the IRA distribution. If you do not update this value, you can end up paying tax twice on the same increase in stock value.

Stretch Rules for Look-Through (See-Through) Trusts as Beneficiaries

If you are the beneficiary of a look-through trust that has been named as a beneficiary of the inherited IRA, then the post-death rules may be different, depending on whether the trust is a conduit or a discretionary trust (see Chapter Seven). A conduit trust says that all RMDs are paid from the IRA to the trust and then from the trust to the primary (income) trust beneficiaries. If that is the case, then the post-death distribution (stretch IRA) schedule is based on the age of the oldest primary trust beneficiary in the year after the year of the IRA owner's death. If the trust is a discretionary trust, then it is a bit more involved. In this case, as you may recall from Chapter Seven, the IRS opens up the beneficiary club to include all potential trust beneficiaries, not just the primary income beneficiaries. This club would now include remainder beneficiaries. The rule is the same, though. You still use the age of the oldest trust beneficiary. It's just that with a discretionary trust the number of beneficiaries you have to include (to find the oldest one) will be greater, because it must also include remainder beneficiaries. If one of those remainder beneficiaries is not a person, your trust fails and has no designated beneficiary. The stretch is lost. If all of the members of the newly expanded trust beneficiary club are people, then you use the age of the oldest of that group to determine RMDs. The stretch period thereafter is the same as if the trust beneficiary were named directly and not through the trust. But there is a key difference: Only the RMD is paid from the IRA to the trust and not the entire IRA balance. Here is an actual (and not uncommon) horror story about how a defective IRA trust plan and an incompetent advisor destroyed an inherited IRA due to ignorance of that key difference:

This story came to me from an accountant, Jill, who called me after attending one of my IRA seminars for advisors. It was tax season, and she was preparing the taxes for a widow. The widow's husband died the year before. He left an IRA of just over $600,000. Jill called because she feared the worst. While going through the widow's tax information, Jill came across a 1099-R form for the exact balance that was in the deceased husband's IRA. Jill's first thought was, "How could this be? This should be a $600,000 tax-free rollover!" Her gut reaction was that something had gone terribly wrong and the entire $600,000 balance might be taxable. She asked me if this was possible. My answer was, "Not only is it possible, the situation is much worse. The $600,000 is taxable at the highest tax rates that can be assessed—trust tax rates!" This is what happened.

The IRA owner was terminally ill. Since his wife knew he did not have long to live, she thought she would review his estate plan to make sure that everything was in order when the time came. That sounds prudent, for sure. He had this $600,000 IRA. The wife was the beneficiary on a properly completed IRA beneficiary form. Since the named beneficiary was a spouse, after her husband's death she could roll the $600,000 IRA over to her own

IRA, tax-free, and then name their children as her IRA beneficiaries. After her death the children would be able to stretch required IRA distributions over their lives. During her remaining life, the inherited IRA would be treated as her IRA in all respects. She would have to take required distributions after she turned age 70½ and pay tax only on those distributions each year at her own personal tax rates. After her death, the children would set up inherited IRAs and stretch out required distributions based on their own lives. That was a fine plan for her terminally ill husband's IRA. Everything was set up properly.

But then she went to see her attorney. The problem was that even though the attorney called himself an estate planning specialist, he did not really understand the tax nuances of IRA transition planning. But he thought he did because he had just come from a seminar for lawyers on naming trusts. So he advised her to change the beneficiary of her terminally ill husband's $600,000 IRA from her to a trust. Soon after, her husband died. She went back to the attorney to see how to deal with the $600,000 IRA, which was left to the trust. The attorney advised her to pay the IRA to the trust since the trust was the beneficiary. It turns out that the trust did not include provisions for inheriting an IRA, because the estate planning specialist/attorney who'd drawn it up for her had simply downloaded a template (boilerplate trust) from his computer (again, not uncommon). When she asked him what happens to the IRA, the attorney figured since the beneficiary was this new trust he created, he advised her to pay the IRA to the trust. She did that. She distributed the entire $600,000 into the trust. Then because the trust did not allow required distributions to be paid to her, the $600,000 remained in the trust. This dealt a fatal blow to her stretch IRA dreams when tax time came around. Since the IRA money remained in the trust, the $600,000 IRA distribution was taxable at trust tax rates (the highest tax rates you can pay). Combined with state trust tax rates (also high), the poor woman had to pay more than $240,000 in taxes, all in one year!

The big mistake here was not establishing the trust, but paying the entire $600,000 from the IRA to the trust. That is never supposed to happen, but it often does. The average attorney thinks, "Well, the trust is the beneficiary, so I'll just take the IRA and pay it to the trust." That's fine for other assets, like a house, for example, or other non-IRA bank accounts or stocks. But once you remove the funds from an IRA, you pay tax on the amount withdrawn, even if the funds go directly to a trust. The only time an IRA withdrawal is tax-free is when the funds are rolled over to another IRA, which could have been the case here, but the beneficiary was changed from the spouse to the trust. An expert IRA advisor would have made a big difference here, which is why Part Three of this book is such a key step in being able to parlay your IRA into a fortune.

Stretch Rules for Spouses Who Remain a Beneficiary

If you are a spouse who is the sole beneficiary of an inherited IRA and you choose not to roll the IRA over and make it your own but instead elect to remain (be treated as) a beneficiary, you do not always have to take required distributions beginning in the year after the IRA owner's death as other non-spouse beneficiaries must. Your RMDs do not have to begin until the later of (1) December 31 of the year the IRA owner would have turned 70½ years old, or (2) December 31 of the year following the year of the IRA owner's death.

For example, Larry is the IRA owner and is 55 years old in 2006. His wife and sole IRA beneficiary is Annie who is 50 years old in 2006. Larry dies in 2008 and Annie chooses not to do the spousal rollover but instead remain a beneficiary. She does not have to take any distributions until 2021—the year that Larry would have been 70½ years old had he lived. Any distributions she takes before then are purely voluntary. She'll pay tax but no penalty on those distributions. If Larry was over age 70½ when he died (after his required beginning date), then Annie would have to begin RMDs in the year after Larry's death, the same as any other non-spouse beneficiary.

Here's another benefit for a spouse who chooses to remain a beneficiary: To calculate her first-year RMD, Annie looks up her age in that year for her life expectancy factor, just as any other non-spouse beneficiary would. But for her second-year RMD, she does not reduce that factor by one (as a non-spouse beneficiary must do); she can "recalculate," which means that she can go back to the single life table and look up her new life expectancy factor each year. That will reduce her RMDs and will make sure that she never runs out money (assuming her IRA investments don't tank). When a non-spouse reduces his or her life expectancy factor by one each year, eventually that term will end, in theory at the same time the beneficiary takes a last breath. But if a non-spouse beneficiary outlives his or her stretch term, all IRA funds must be withdrawn. That cannot happen with a spouse beneficiary, because no matter how long he or she lives, the table will still have a remaining life expectancy. That's the benefit of recalculating. Even a 110-year-old spouse beneficiary has a life expectancy of 1.1 years.

Stretch Distributions—Roth IRAs

Contrary to popular misconception, non-spouse beneficiaries of Roth IRAs *are* subject to required minimum distributions. Only, spouse beneficiaries of Roth IRAs do not have to take RMDs, provided they roll the account over or treat it as their own.

When the designated beneficiary of a Roth IRA is a non-spouse (a child, for example), the RMD rules are the same as those for a traditional IRA. The only difference with a Roth IRA is that post-death distributions are generally tax-free. If Roth IRA owners die without a designated beneficiary, RMDs are the same as those for traditional IRA owners who die before their required beginning date (RBD), regardless of how old they were in the year of death. The reason for this is that since there are no required lifetime distributions for Roth IRA owners, there is no RBD.

To better understand the distribution possibilities—and thus the stretch opportunities—for Roth IRA beneficiaries, you need to know the basic tax and penalty provisions that apply to Roth IRA distributions. Here's a quick review:

In order for Roth IRA distributions to be income-tax-free they must be what the tax law calls "qualified distributions." A qualified distribution is a withdrawal from a Roth IRA made after the Roth has been held for five years[13] (beginning on the first day of the first year in which a contribution was made) *and* that meets any *one* of the following criteria:

- The distribution is made on or after the original Roth IRA owner reaches age 59½.
- The distribution is made due to a severe long-term physical or mental disability, likely to end in death or leaving the person unable to work. In other words, you'd better have at least one foot in the grave to qualify here (and be able to prove it), and if that is the case, taxes are the least of your concerns.
- The distribution is used to buy, build, or rebuild a first home. For this provision, a first-time home buyer is someone who has not owned a home for two years prior to acquiring the new home. This provision is limited to a $10,000 lifetime maximum, almost enough to pay some of the closing costs on today's homes. If you are married, your spouse must also have not owned a home for the past two years.
- The distribution is made to a beneficiary after the death of the Roth IRA owner.

Spouse as Beneficiary

For example, Mr. Bond . . . James Bond (aka 007) converts $100,000 of his traditional IRA to a Roth IRA in November 2005 when he is 40 years old. However, unlike in the movies, in 2006 he gets too cocky and is killed on a mission, at age 41. He has named his wife, Tracy, as his Roth IRA beneficiary (that's right, in this

---

[13] A Roth IRA beneficiary tacks on the time the deceased Roth IRA owner held the account. The five years do not restart with the beneficiary. For example, if the Roth IRA owner dies after holding the account for three years, the beneficiary needs to hold the account for only an additional two years to meet the five-year holding provision.

story Tracy doesn't get killed by Bond's archenemy Blofeld on their wedding day). Tracy is 30 years old when she inherits 007's Roth, which carries a value of $110,000 ($100,000 in contributions plus $10,000 in earnings). For this to be a qualified distribution, the five-year holding period begins on January 1, 2005, even though the conversion of funds was not done until November of that year. This means that Tracy must hold the Roth IRA until January 1, 2010, to satisfy the five-year provision for tax-free distributions— or she must marry another secret agent with a better pension plan so she won't have to withdraw from this one before being able to get her distributions tax-free.

So, if Tracy rolls 007's Roth IRA over into her own Roth IRA and withdraws the entire $110,000 account balance in 2006, the distribution will not be a qualified distribution, because the Roth was not held the required five years. The $10,000 of earnings will be subject to income tax. Furthermore, she will incur a 10 percent early withdrawal penalty of $11,000 (10 percent of the entire value of the account). This is because, by rolling it over and treating it as her own account, she does not remain a beneficiary; therefore, as with a traditional IRA, she leaves herself open to the early withdrawal penalty that only *beneficiaries* can escape. Even if Tracy rolls over and waits until 2016 when she is 40 years old to withdraw the entire account balance—which has now grown to $250,000—the $150,000 of earnings on the account would be taxable, and, in addition, she would again be subject to a 10 percent early withdrawal penalty of $15,000 on the $150,000 of earnings because she is under 59½. But there is no 10 percent penalty on the original $100,000 in the inherited account, because the converted funds have been held for more than five years. However, if Tracy rolls it over and waits until 2036, when she is 60 years old, to withdraw the entire account balance (which has grown to $700,000), the distribution will be tax-free because it has long met the five-year holding requirement *and* penalty-free because she has met the age requirement as well.

Penalties and taxes can eat up the stretch on a Roth IRA pretty quickly. So, let's see what happens if Tracy Bond doesn't roll over the original $110,000 Roth IRA she inherited from 007 but chooses instead to remain a beneficiary. If she takes a full distribution of the $110,000 account balance in 2006, she faces no early withdrawal penalty (she's still a beneficiary), but she will still pay income tax on the $10,000 of earnings *because the account was not held the required five years.* If she elects to remain a beneficiary and waits until 2016, when she is 40 years old, to take a full distribution of the entire account balance (which is now $250,000), the entire distribution will be both penalty-free because she's a beneficiary and tax-free because the five-year holding period has (long) been met.

Non-Spouse (Child) as Beneficiary

Distributions are required for non-spouse Roth IRA beneficiaries. Failure to take RMDs will result in a 50 percent penalty on the required amount that was not withdrawn, even if the Roth IRA distribution would have been tax-free to the beneficiary. As with traditional IRAs, RMDs for Roth IRAs are based on the non-spouse beneficiary's age in the year after the year of the Roth IRA owner's death, which is the first required distribution year. Let's look at some numbers.

For this example, our hero Mr. Bond . . . James Bond and his beloved wife, Tracy, have produced a child, Jimmy, whom 007 has named beneficiary of the same $110,000 Roth IRA. Jimmy is 10 years old in 2007, the first required distribution year. This is the same as with a traditional IRA, where RMDs also begin the year after the owner's death. As with a traditional IRA, the first-year RMD will be based on the Roth IRA account balance as of—in this case—December 31, 2006, the year of 007's unexpected demise. (Or is 007 just fooling us again and off somewhere looking for Blofeld?) The required distribution for year 2007 is $1,511 ($110,000 divided by 72.8 years). The next year, 2008, the life expectancy factor drops by one year to 71.8 years; the third year, 2009, it's 70.8 years, and so on until the 72.8-year term is completed. If Jimmy Jr. happens to die before the term ends, then his successor beneficiary can continue the remaining term.

Jimmy Jr. can always take more than the required amount (unless otherwise restricted—with a trust, for example). But if he acts like his old man and says, "Damn the torpedoes, full speed ahead," and just withdraws the entire $110,000 account balance in 2006, while he faces no 10 percent penalty (because he's a beneficiary), tax will be owed on the $10,000 of earnings on the account because the Roth IRA was not held for five years. Again, no tax is due on the original $100,000, because that tax would have been paid in full by dear dead dad.

But if Jimmy Jr. takes only the minimum required distributions for the entire 72.8-year term, at an estimated 8 percent return within the inherited Roth IRA, 82-year-old Jimmy Jr. will have withdrawn $5,105,240 . . . all tax-free! Not too shabby.

FAQ

Q. Ed, what's the stretch look like if an estate is Roth IRA beneficiary?

A. What stretch? You should know by now that naming an estate as beneficiary—or rather, by not naming anyone and the estate's becoming beneficiary by default—is the worst of all possible scenarios for either a traditional IRA or a Roth IRA. The estate must withdraw the entire balance in the Roth IRA within five years—in the case of the estate of the late Mr. Bond . . . James Bond (who died in 2006), that would be by December 31, 2011, the fifth year after the year of 007's death.

Now that you, the beneficiary, have done everything right to take full advantage of the stretch opportunity that your traditional IRA or Roth IRA benefactor created for you, turn the page and I'll show you how you can take even fuller advantage of that opportunity—by keeping Uncle Sam at bay!

TEN

Tax-Cutting Strategies for IRA Beneficiaries

"The Internal Revenue Code is a Kafkaesque maze of complexity that confounds millions of Americans every single year."
—Representative Steny Hoyer

"It's good that our tax laws are so complicated. Deep within that convoluted maze is a virtual treasure chest of tax-saving opportunities for everybody, including IRA beneficiaries, which most people (including those in Congress who make our tax laws) don't know exist. (Let sleeping dogs lie!)"
—Ed Slott

Uncle Sam Is Counting on You

If I were to ask you to make a big fat voluntary contribution to the IRS, what would you say? I'm not talking about crumbs here. I mean writing out a check for a few thousand dollars. Would you say, "Sure, how much does Uncle Sam need?" I'm guessing that would not be your answer—I couldn't print what you would probably say. Yet IRA beneficiaries like you are constantly contributing part of an IRA inheritance to Uncle Sam in the form of missed tax-saving opportunities.

Uncle Sam is not really your relative, so you do not have to provide any more support than you are legally required to. If you do not take advantage of these tax breaks, it's the same as making a voluntary contribution to the IRS. So, stop giving when you don't have to and help your stretch IRA to keep growing. Remember, the key to parlaying your IRA into a family fortune is keeping Uncle Sam's paws off it not only for as long as possible but also for as much as possible.

Slott's Tips

If you have inherited an IRA, be sure to look for state tax provisions that can reduce the tax on your distributions also. Most of these tax cutting opportunities will not say "for inherited IRAs or plans," since they are for plan owners. But in most cases, these tax breaks carry over to beneficiaries also. For example, in my state of New York, if you inherit an IRA from someone who was over 59½ years old, the first $20,000 of distributions are tax-free to you. So, in New York, if your RMDs as a beneficiary are less than that amount, which many are, then you pay no state income tax on those distributions. Some states, in fact, exclude *all* retirement distributions. Check your state, and you may find opportunities to trim your taxes when you withdraw from an inherited IRA so it stays more intact and you can keep it growing.

Inherited IRA Basis—It's Tax-Free!

You only have to pay income tax once with an IRA. That's true for traditional IRAs as well as Roth IRAs. The difference is that with a Roth IRA, the money that is contributed has already been taxed and will not be taxed again when withdrawn.

Traditional IRA contributions can be either deductible or non-deductible, depending on whether the IRA owner is active in a company plan and how much income he or she reports. If the money in the IRA is deductible, then it has not yet been taxed. If it is a non-deductible IRA contribution, then the money contributed has already been taxed. To put it another way, if the IRA owner has already paid the tax, as is the case for contributions made to a Roth IRA and non-deductible traditional IRA contributions, then that money is called "after-tax" money because it has already been taxed and is not to be taxed again. If the IRA owner has not already paid the income tax, as is the case for deductible contributions to a traditional IRA, then that money is called "pre-tax" money.

Money that has already been taxed (after-tax funds) is basis—i.e., the amount used for figuring any gain or loss when property is sold. If you are inheriting an IRA or other retirement account with basis, that basis is tax-free when it is withdrawn. Beneficiaries who do not know to ask if the IRA or plan they inherited contains basis could be overpaying their taxes on the distributions from those inherited accounts. Money that has not already been taxed (pre-tax funds) is *not* basis. It's important to know whether the retirement funds you inherit have already been taxed or not. It makes a big difference when you take withdrawals.

Slott's Tips

If you are the beneficiary of a company plan as opposed to an IRA, the IRA distribution rules still apply. But the problem is that most companies do not have to abide by them, and they generally do not. They do not have to allow the stretch IRA. That is why in Part One I made an emphatic plea to all IRA owners to roll their company plan balances to an IRA as soon as they can. If you did not and you are inheriting the company plan, you are stuck with that plan's options, which at best may be a five-year payout and, at worst, a forced lump sum distribution, meaning you will you have to pay all the tax at once if you are a non-spouse beneficiary. So, if you are inheriting from someone who is still alive, urge that person to roll over that company plan into an IRA *now*! If the person is still working, urge him or her to ask about the plan's in-service distribution rules and to not just to assume that an IRA rollover is not yet permitted. Some company plans do allow withdrawals for a rollover to an IRA while the plan participant is still working. In fact, this practice is becoming more and more popular.

To figure out if there is basis in the distributions you are receiving from an inherited IRA, you will have to find out if the person you inherited from ever made any non-deductible IRA contributions. You can discover that by looking for Form 8606 (Non-deductible IRAs) attached to any of his or her income tax returns. Form 8606 shows the basis (the amount of non-deductible IRA contributions made).

If there is basis, then as you withdraw from the inherited IRA, the portion of the withdrawal that is a return of the basis is tax-free, the same as it would have been for the person you inherited from. It is rare that even a professional tax preparer thinks to ask if there was any non-deductible IRA contributions made by the person you inherited from. That's why you'll have to find out for yourself.

If no Form 8606 is found, it does not automatically mean that no non-deductible IRA contributions were made. It may mean that the form was never filed. You can still find any non-deductible contributions by checking IRA statements to see if prior-year contributions were made. You may also be able to track down Form 5498 (IRA contribution information) for prior years, which would also show if IRA contributions were made. Then you look at the tax return for the year of the contribution to see if a deduction was claimed for that IRA contribution.[14] If not, then you can assume that a non-deductible contribution was made. Keep any documentation at least three years

[14]Non-deductible IRA contributions began in 1987, so do not bother checking returns for prior years. It was not until 2002 that after-tax money in a company plan could be rolled over to an IRA, so you don't have to look too far back in the deceased IRA owner's returns to find that information either.

after you file your own return, in case the IRS asks you to show how you came up with the amount of non-deductible contributions. To claim the tax-free portion of distributions from your inherited IRA, you will also have to file Form 8606, just as the IRA owner did, or should have.

For example, Louis dies and leaves his traditional IRA to his friend Ilana. Louis made only non-deductible IRA contributions. At Louis's death his IRA had a balance of $20,000, of which $16,000 came from non-deductible IRA contributions and $4,000 was interest earned. If Ilana withdraws the entire $20,000, she should pay tax on only the $4,000, not the full $20,000, because $16,000 is basis and can now be withdrawn tax-free by Ilana. If Ilana withdraws the $20,000, she will receive a 1099-R form reporting the $20,000 as a gross distribution. When she has her taxes prepared, it is very likely that she will pay tax on the full $20,000 since she probably did not know to point this out to her accountant and there is a good chance that her accountant (or whoever prepares her taxes) would not even think to ask whether Louis ever made non-deductible IRA contributions. In fact, unless the accountant looked very carefully at this 1099-R form, he would not even know that this was an inherited IRA.

If Ilana reports the full $20,000 as income, she will have over-reported her income by $16,000 and thus significantly overpaid her taxes. Assuming a combined federal and state tax rate of 30 percent, Ilana will have overpaid her taxes by $4,800 ($16,000 of overreported income times the 30 percent tax on that extra income). No one would find this error, since Ilana is reporting the exact amount of income reported on the 1099-R. That is why this is so often missed—because the tax return looks correct as is. It is up to Ilana to file Form 8606 and show that $16,000 was from non-deductible contributions so that she will pay tax on only the $4,000.

This example assumes Ilana withdraws the entire balance at once. If Ilana does the stretch IRA over her lifetime, then each withdrawal contains a portion of the tax-free basis, based on the percentage of non-deductible contributions made to the entire IRA balance. Ilana cannot just withdraw the $16,000 of basis and pay no tax. That is the case only if she withdraws the entire $20,000. If she withdraws only $16,000, then $12,800 will be tax-free and $3,200 will be taxable. IRS rules require that every withdrawal from an IRA that contains basis must include a percentage of that basis. In this example, that percentage is 80 percent based on $16,000 of basis divided by the total IRA balance of $20,000 ($16,000 divided by $20,000 = 80 percent),[15] so 80 percent of every dollar withdrawn will be tax-free (a return of basis) and 20 percent of every dollar withdrawn will be taxable. If Ilana withdraws the entire $20,000, then she shows 80 percent of that, or the entire $16,000 basis, as tax-free and pays tax on the 20 percent, or $4,000 of earnings. If she only withdraws $16,000, then she shows 80 percent of the $16,000, or $12,800 as tax-free and 20 percent of the $16,000, or $3,200, as taxable. Every dollar Ilana withdraws from this IRA will be 80 cents tax-free and 20 cents taxable. Form 8606, which Ilana will need to attach to her tax return to claim the tax-free basis, will take her through this calculation. But the form won't help if she does not know if any of her inherited IRA contains basis.

All Roth IRA contributions are nondeductible, so if you have inherited a Roth IRA, all of the contributions are basis and can be withdrawn tax-free. The earnings can also be withdrawn tax-free, as long as the account was held for more than five years (including the time the person you inherited from held the Roth IRA).

For example, you inherit a Roth IRA in 2005 from your aunt Gertrude. She first contributed to her Roth IRA in 2002 and died in 2005. All distributions of contributions are tax-free whenever they are withdrawn, but the income is not tax-free until 2007, when the Roth IRA will have been held for more than five years.

---

[15]If you inherit a company plan that has after-tax money, you do not have to go through this percentage calculation. You can withdraw the after-tax plan money directly from the plan tax-free, but it is likely that the plan will force a lump sum distribution anyway, so you still won't be able to withdraw only the after-tax funds first and pay no tax. You'll have to withdraw the entire plan balance, but you'll only pay tax on the pre-tax funds.

Assume Aunt Gertrude contributed $10,000 to the Roth, and the Roth is now worth $12,000. If you withdraw the entire balance of $12,000 in 2006, then $10,000 will be tax-free and the $2,000 of income earned will be taxable. If you withdraw only $10,000 in 2006, it is all tax-free, since IRS rules say that the contributions are the first dollars withdrawn. If you withdraw all $12,000 in 2007, then it is entirely tax-free, because the Roth IRA has been held more than five years. Even though you, the beneficiary, have not held the Roth for more than five years, you add the time it was held by your aunt.

The bottom line: If you are an IRA or plan beneficiary, make sure to find out if the person you inherited from had any basis in that retirement account. If yes, then you want to get this information to your financial advisor and tax preparer to make sure that you do not overpay your tax here. Most beneficiaries do.

CAUTION!

Your basis for the federal return may be different from the basis you can claim on the state tax return. The person you inherited from may have received a federal tax deduction for his or her IRA contribution but may have filed state taxes in a state that does not allow a deduction for IRA contributions. If that is the case, then for state tax purposes the IRA distribution may be partially tax-free, even though it may have been fully taxable on the federal tax return. So, if you are an IRA beneficiary, see if the IRA contributions made by the person you inherited from were deductible on his or her *state* tax returns. If not, you have state basis, and part of your inherited IRA distributions may be tax-free on your state tax return.

The IRD Deduction—It's Not to Be Missed!

The biggest tax break available to an IRA beneficiary is the "income in respect of a decedent" (IRD) deduction, referred to by the IRS on the tax forms as the "estate tax deduction." But guess what? It's almost always missed because many advisors do not know enough to ask about it, and most beneficiaries do not bring it up because they are unaware this deduction exists.

IRAs are subject to both income tax and estate tax. That's outright double taxation, and the federal tax code is aware of this. That is why there is a tax deduction in the code that is specifically intended to partially offset the double taxation. IRAs, annuities, 401(k)s, and other retirement plans are among a special group of items the tax code calls "income in respect of a decedent" (IRD). When these items are inherited, the beneficiary who withdraws from the account must pay income tax the same as if the deceased IRA owner would have had to had he lived. The deceased IRA owner, however would not have also paid the estate tax, since he was still alive. But the IRA beneficiary does get hit with both taxes. For that reason, the tax code provides an income tax deduction for beneficiaries of IRD items (like IRAs and pensions) for any *federal* estate tax paid on the IRA. Note that the IRD deduction is only available for federal estate tax paid on an IRA, not state estate tax. So there is still double tax on a state level. But the federal tax is generally the big tax and generates the big IRD tax deduction.

The IRA beneficiary takes the deduction whenever he or she withdraws from the IRA. This is something to have an expert IRA advisor (see Part Three) help you with. This advisor can either make the calculation for you or work with your accountant to make sure you receive this tax deduction. The deduction is generally either the largest or one of the largest deductions on an IRA beneficiary's tax return, depending on the size of the inherited IRA and how much of that IRA is withdrawn each year. Not to be missed, as witnessed in the following almost-a-horror story:

Linda inherited a $1,866,968 IRA from her father. The total estate including the IRA was $2,747,334. The father's estate paid a federal estate tax of $863,654, and it was all due to the IRA. If there had been no IRA in the estate, there would have been no estate tax, so all of the $863,654 in federal estate tax was because of the IRA. That means that the entire $863,654 federal estate tax is the IRD deduction. Linda had just filed her tax return and was clearly upset that the combined estate and income tax on her inherited IRA could be so high (just over 80 percent). The IRS was receiving four times more of her father's IRA than she was. Linda felt something must be wrong. She was correct. The IRD deduction was missed.

When I mentioned that to Linda, she said she had done some research on her own and came across the IRD deduction and told the accountant who had prepared her tax return. She told me he was not familiar with this and said it "probably wouldn't make a difference." He obviously had no clue or might have felt that it was some esoteric part of the tax code that would not apply anyway. I asked Linda to send me a copy of the income tax return she just filed, as well as a copy of her late father's estate tax return, which was also recently filed. It arrived in the mail a few days later. It took me three seconds to see that an $863,654 tax deduction was missed. If Linda had not been so diligent and persistent, no one would have ever known. She would have licked her wounds, paid the tax thinking that must be the way it works out—just as the accountant who prepared her taxes must have thought—and walked away leaving IRS with a huge voluntary contribution.

The IRD deduction is usually around 45 percent of the amount withdrawn. In Linda's case, the deduction came out to 46.26 percent ($863,654 of estate tax on the inherited IRA divided by the total value of the IRA, $1,866,968 = 46.26 percent). That meant 46.26 percent of every dollar withdrawn from the inherited IRA can be taken as a tax deduction on Linda's tax return each year as she withdraws from the IRA until she eventually deducts the full $863,654. If she decided to withdraw the entire $1,866,968 IRA she inherited, she would claim the entire $863,654 as a legitimate tax deduction on her tax return. That might set off a few bells and whistles at the IRS, but no problem. This is a perfectly legitimate deduction. IRS might even be impressed that you know about it!

Linda was sharp enough to know to stretch her inherited IRA for all it was worth, however, and she took only the required minimum distribution based on her age, withdrawing $92,256 from the inherited IRA. Although she was entitled to an IRD deduction of $42,678, as I said, she had not taken that deduction on the return she filed because her accountant had missed it. We prepared an amended income tax return for Linda to claim the missed deduction. She will take this deduction on her income tax return every year as she takes her required minimum distributions until the entire $863,654 IRD deduction is used up. Can you imagine missing an $863,654 tax deduction? That's what could have happened here.

If you die before the entire inherited IRA is withdrawn, the IRD deduction carries to your successor beneficiary. If your estate is large enough to trigger an estate tax, your successor beneficiary could double the IRD deduction by claiming the remaining IRD deductions you were claiming plus the IRD deduction from your estate.

If you are one of several IRA beneficiaries, and the IRD deduction applies, then each of you can claim your share of the tax deduction when you withdraw from your inherited IRA. If you withdraw, say, 6 percent of your inherited IRA, then you claim 6 percent of the IRD deduction. Then you keep track of the deduction as you claim a portion of it each year until the entire IRD deduction is used up. This can take years, especially if you stretch your IRA out. The IRD deduction can really take a meat cleaver to your tax bill every year. What's better than having a built-in tax deduction every year?

There is no tax form to use to compute the deduction. Uncle Sam would never give you that kind of clue to a deduction this large, no sir. The IRS expects you to find this for yourself. In fact, it is rarely mentioned in IRS tax information, forms, or publications. The only IRS publication that refers to the IRD deduction and goes through the calculation is Publication 559 "Survivors, Executors, and Administrators" (available at www.irs.gov), but who would ever think to look there?

Not every IRA beneficiary can claim the IRD deduction. For example, if there is no federal estate tax, then there is no IRD deduction. But every IRA beneficiary should check to make sure. You can receive the IRD deduction—even if someone else paid the federal estate tax—as long as you inherited the IRA. You can also receive it if the federal estate tax has not yet been paid—in which case just submit your best estimate. What a deal!

The IRD deduction is claimed as a "miscellaneous itemized deduction" on your taxes, but it is so much more valuable than other deductions in that category because it is not subject to the 2 percent "adjusted gross income" (AGI) limit and is exempt from the dreaded "alternative minimum tax" (AMT) as well. This may be part of the problem. The IRD deduction often looks so large that many beneficiaries and their tax preparers (assuming they are aware of it in the first place) believe it is too good to be true and must be a mistake. But the only mistake is not to take it—because if you don't claim it, you lose it!

FAQ

Q. Ed, do Roth IRA beneficiaries qualify for the IRD deduction too?

A. Generally no—because there must be a double tax to get the deduction. The Roth is subject to estate tax, but the inherited Roth IRA distributions are generally not subject to income tax. If there is no income tax on the Roth IRA distributions, there can be no IRD deduction.

The Annuity Solution

In most qualified plans, if the beneficiary is a non-spouse, the plan must end and the plan funds must be completely distributed and taxed. This problem is especially acute for single-owner Keogh plans, which are sponsored by many doctors, professionals, and other sole proprietorship businesses. There are many of these types of entities, and when the beneficiaries are non-spouses, they are at risk of having their qualified plan money taxed soon after the business owner dies. In some cases, the business owner or professional practitioner will die while he or she is still working and the funds are still in the plan.

For example, a retired doctor dies at the age of 66. He was sole practitioner with a Keogh plan but had not yet rolled over the plan assets to an IRA. He wanted to leave the money in the plan to his wife. However, his wife had suffered an injury that cast doubts on her ability to handle large sums of money (the Keogh plan held over $2 million). Therefore, the doctor had named a trust as his Keogh plan beneficiary, preferring to have a trustee be responsible for such a substantial amount. The surviving spouse was named as the beneficiary of this trust. After her death, any assets were to be held in trust for the benefit of the physician's son from a previous marriage and for the son's children (the late physician's grandchildren). As it turns out, the surviving spouse dies just two months after the doctor, at age 55. Thus, the trust for the benefit of the doctor's son (in his late 30s) and the grandchildren inherited the account balance . . . and a tax headache. Because the doctor was a sole practitioner, his Keogh plan had no continuing sponsor, so the plan died with him. According to the IRS, the trust has to withdraw all the money from the plan and pay tax on the full amount right away—unless there is an alternative solution.

As it happens, there is. And it is to be found in an obscure corner of the tax code regarding nontransferable annuities.

According to the tax code a retirement plan can buy and distribute a non-transferable annuity[16] without triggering a tax bill. A non-transferable annuity is one that can't be sold, given away, assigned, or pledged as collateral for a loan or other obligation once the beneficiary holds it. It must pay out at least the required minimum distribution the beneficiary would have to take each year under RMD rules and get IRS approval for the extended tax deferral. The bottom line is that it re-creates a stretch IRA that was not available from the Keogh plan (and also makes it possible for the beneficiary to take out even more money if that should be desirable).

In our example, the plan trustee (the late doctor's executor) will use the trust's money to buy the non-transferable annuity; then transfer the annuity to the trust that has been named as the Keogh plan's beneficiary. This transfer of the annuity from the plan to the plan beneficiary will be tax-free. Then the Keogh can terminate.

The trust for the benefit of the doctor's son and the grandchildren will receive annuity payments that conform to the IRS Single Life Expectancy table guidelines for RMDs. Because the doctor's wife is the oldest trust beneficiary, the distributions will be made over a life expectancy of 28.7 years (based on her age—age 56—in the year after her death).

The son and grandchildren will pay income tax on the full amount of each distribution received from the trust. The trustee may permit larger amounts to be withdrawn from the trust, if desired.

The annuity will actually be a deferred variable annuity so the payment amounts will vary from year to year, based on investment performance within the contract, as well as on the minimum distribution life expectancy table. In this case, the trustee has the responsibility for making investment decisions within the variable annuity.

If you are a non-spouse beneficiary and have inherited a company plan, such as a Keogh, that must be terminated because of the sponsor's death, forcing a large lump sum distribution, this strategy may help you avoid the immediate tax on that lump sum and instead let you pay taxes over your lifetime similar to a stretch

---

[16]A yearly payment of money

IRA. How large must an inheritance be to warrant such an effort? That's hard to know, but the amount should be substantial enough that the additional tax deferral is worth the money spent on professional advice and the application to the IRS for a "private letter ruling" in your favor (which is likely). My feeling is that the company plan should be well into six figures before such an effort would be justified.

Slott's Tips

If you trade in your old Keoghs for a SEP-IRA (simplified employee pension) or a SIMPLE-IRA (savings incentive match plan for employees), you can preserve the stretch for your named beneficiaries—because SEP and SIMPLE plans are IRAs, and a designated beneficiary on an IRA (but not a Keogh plan) gets the stretch. Mention this to any Keogh plan owners you know so they make the change and not stick their beneficiaries (like you) with a lump sum payout that will kill the stretch.

Turning an Inherited Roth IRA Loss to Your Advantage

Once you inherit a Roth IRA, you are in the best possible position for the tax-free stretch, so I would generally never advise you to give that up. But if the market value of the Roth IRA you inherited declines substantially and you see no end in sight, let alone an opportunity for future growth, there are two ways to recoup some of that loss. Both ways require you to end your inherited Roth IRA— and if you decide to do this, you cannot get that inherited Roth IRA back again.

The two ways of taking a tax loss on an inherited Roth IRA gone south are to "cash out" or to "recharacterize" (undo the original Roth conversion as if it never took place). In both cases you'll receive tax benefits.

Cash Out

This requires emptying your entire inherited Roth IRA balance to be able to claim a loss. For example, Jeb converts $75,000 of his traditional IRA to a Roth IRA and later dies with the $75,000 in the Roth IRA. His son George inherits the $75,000 Roth IRA and decides to get in on the hottest tech stocks. His timing is poor and the Roth he inherited is now worth just a measly $1,000—a $74,000 drop in value! George can claim the loss if he withdraws the remaining $1,000, thus emptying the inherited IRA. In this case, it would really pay to do that because the Roth is already just about worthless anyway, with no sign of return. Once he withdraws the $1,000, he is able to claim a loss of $74,000 on his personal tax return.

Not everyone can claim this loss, though, even if they agree to empty their Roth IRA. *First you must have a loss.* That means the value of the Roth IRA you inherit must be less than its original basis—i.e., the contributions made to the Roth IRA by the person you inherited from. If so, this means only that you are a *candidate* for the loss deduction. Once you have emptied the inherited Roth IRA and established a loss, you must determine if you can actually claim the deduction. You see, the loss can only be deducted on Schedule A of your 1040 form as a miscellaneous itemized deduction subject to the 2 percent adjusted gross income limit and subject to alternative minimum tax. You must itemize to be able to claim the deduction. If you do not have enough deductions to itemize, you cannot claim the tax loss for your Roth. A large enough loss—like the $74,000 in this example—would enable you to itemize, in which case that loss would be worth over $20,000 in both federal and state tax savings. The deduction, though, could be reduced by the 2 percent AGI limitation, or completely eliminated if you are subject to AMT.

FAQ

Q. Ed, where does it say that you can deduct a Roth IRA loss? I thought you cannot deduct a loss *within* your IRA.

A. That's right, which is why the IRS requires you to empty your Roth IRA before any loss can be taken. The authority for the tax deduction is in IRS Publication 590 under the heading "Recognizing Losses on Investments." (For the authority on deducting traditional IRA losses, see the heading "Recognizing Losses on Traditional IRA Investments" in the same IRS publication.)

Recharacterize

The second way to seize a tax opportunity from a decline in the value of the Roth IRA you inherit is to undo the original Roth conversion as if it never happened. You will receive a refund of any tax paid on the conversion (by the original owner). Even though the Roth IRA balance may have declined, at least you can get the tax back that was paid on value that no longer exists.

The post-death recharacterization can only be done (1) if the IRA owner dies in the year of the conversion, or (2) in the following year, but before October 15 of that year. If the inherited Roth IRA had been converted from a traditional IRA in 2005, for example, the last day to recharacterize would be October 15, 2006. If the Roth IRA owner died after October 15, 2006, the beneficiary could not recharacterize.

For example, assume your dad converted $300,000 to a Roth IRA in 2006 and died later that year. When you inherit, the value of the Roth falls to $100,000. Your dad already paid tax on the $300,000, and now it's worth only $100,000. You can leave it alone, hoping it will go back up, or you can recharacterize it as a traditional IRA and get back all the tax you paid on the conversion. You have until October 15, 2007, to recharacterize and re-move the tax as if the conversion never happened—even if your dad's 2006 tax return has already been filed. Once you do this, the Roth IRA you inherited will now be a traditional IRA and you cannot convert it to a Roth IRA again.

Slott's Tips

If you inherit a Roth IRA—or any investment—from some-one and its value drops six months later, you may be able to use the lower value to lower the estate tax bill. This tax election is called "alternate valuation." If you elect to take it, you must use it on all estate assets, not just your IRA. You cannot elect it on only a part of the property. Anytime the market takes a dive, keep this post-death tax tactic in mind, especially if you will be inheriting an IRA (or are a professional advisor or estate planner). It's a way to get Un-cle Sam to really feel your pain—and share it.

In addition to a situation where you may *want* to recharacterize in order to recoup a loss, there is another situation where you may *have* to recharacterize, regardless of whether the inherited Roth IRA is losing or gaining in market value, or face some stiff tax penalties.

This situation occurs when those from whom a Roth IRA is in-herited were not eligible to convert their retirement funds to a Roth IRA in the first place. How could this be? Perhaps, they might not have known they weren't eligible when they converted, and the il-legal Roth conversion wasn't discovered until after their death.

For example, Ida converts her IRA to a Roth IRA in June 2006 and then dies in August 2006. Ida named her son Harvey as the beneficiary of her Roth IRA. When Ida's year of death (2006) tax return is prepared in 2007, the accountant realizes that Ida's in-come exceeded $100,000, so she was not permitted to convert. At the time she converted, she did not realize her income would exceed $100,000 or did not know about the limitation. The conversion now must be undone. Since Ida would have had up to October 15, 2007, to undo this conversion (had she lived long enough), the tax law[17] allows the executor of her estate—who in this example, as well, I'll say is Harvey—to recharacterize on her behalf by that date. Otherwise there will be tax consequences, and not good ones. If not undone, Ida's ineligible conversion will be treated as a taxable distribution (from the traditional IRA she converted); furthermore, there will be a 6 percent penalty applied to the excess amount (the entire Roth IRA balance, since the Roth should not have existed in the first place) for each year the Roth remains. So, Harvey the executor better get moving and recharacterize the illegal Roth IRA in a timely fashion so it will be treated as a traditional IRA and Harvey the beneficiary can keep stretching to his heart's content.

Slott's Tips

If you are a Roth IRA beneficiary and want to or must recharacterize, but the October 15 deadline has passed, your expert IRA advisor can help you apply to the IRS for a private letter ruling. The IRS will most likely rule on your behalf and allow you more time to recharacterize, especially in a situation where there was a death and/or you were not aware of the problem until it was too late.

At this stage, if you are an IRA owner, you have all the information you need to be able to create a stretch IRA opportunity for your beneficiaries, and if you are the beneficiary of an inherited IRA, you have all the information you need to parlay your inheritance into a fortune (as well as seize every tax break possible to increase the size of the pie by trimming Uncle Sam's share). Now it's time to make it all happen—by working closely with your expert IRA advisor to clear the way to IRA wealth.

[17]Roth IRA Regulations Section 1.408 A-5, A-6 (c)

CHOOSE THE RIGHT IRA ADVISOR

Dear Ed,

My brother died, and I inherited an IRA from him. The bank's IRA de-partment advised me to withdraw the IRA. They told me that the only one who could inherit an IRA and avoid a tax on the total amount re-ceived would be a spouse. Thus, I was assessed close to $18,000 on the full amount of $52,378 received on the IRA from my brother. It turns out later—too late—that the bank advice was wrong. I could have taken the IRA out over the rest of my life because my brother named me as his IRA beneficiary. I am nearly 70 years old and could use the nearly $18,000 that the bank's wrong IRA advice cost me!

—IRA beneficiary

ELEVEN

Why You Need an IRA Advisor

"Dear Reader,
I know what you're thinking: 'Ed, you have given me everything I
need to know about growing my IRA for generations. So why do I
need to find an expert IRA advisor?' The answer is simple: Even a top-
flight surgeon wouldn't operate on himself (or herself). And as Honest
Abe Lincoln once put it about his own profession: 'The lawyer who
hires himself has a fool for a client.'"
   —Ed Slott

The Last Vital Link

Any serious IRA owner needs the expert assistance of a professional financial advisor to help make sure the estate plan for
his or her IRA is set up correctly so that assets pass intact without
a hitch—then, after you've gone to that big retirement party in the
sky, to work with your family members in making sure they inherit
properly and can build your legacy into a fortune. The fact that
you are now well educated in this area just means you are better
equipped to *choose* an advisor and won't fall for the promise of
the sizzle instead of the steak.

Purchasing estate planning services is very different from buying
most anything else, *because when the plan goes into effect, you
won't be around to know if you've gotten your money's worth.*
With most other goods or services, you get to see if you've bought
a pig in a poke—sometimes right away or sometimes later, but you

find out. If you buy a TV and it blows a gasket when you turn it on, you find out PDQ whether the warranty is worth the paper it is printed on. And if you dine out at a restaurant and have a bad meal, you'll know it faster that you would have wished.

With estate and IRA planning, however, only your beneficiaries know if the advice you got pans out. By then it is often too late to correct things, as is usually the case with the IRA tax rules. An experienced and knowledgeable *IRA advisor* is your best—indeed your *only*—defense against putting your retirement assets at risk in this transitional no-man's-land between death and taxes. That's why choosing the right advisor is so important: it is the last vital link in our three-link chain.

How to Find an IRA Advisor

Rule #1 in finding a right advisor is this: Steer clear of any financial advisor without a professional designation!

A professional designation shows that advisors are subject to certain professional standards and must maintain a level of general education in the field in order to meet those standards. Typically, they are accountable for meeting state and local regulations as well, or risk losing their professional license.

While a membership designation in a professional organization such as the College of Financial Planning may be a valuable indicator that certain standards of professional excellence have been achieved, it is no guarantee of competence in IRA planning and inheritance.

Strangely enough, there is no requirement for any professional financial advisor (including CFPs, CPAs, insurance professionals, and attorneys) to possess even a minimum knowledge of the complex IRA tax rules—even though most working people today have most of their savings in some type of retirement account. I can see you shaking your head in disbelief and asking, "But *why* don't these organizations make it a point for their members to know these IRA rules?" Good question. I ask the same thing.

Part of the problem is that since not all of their members deal with IRAs, the boards of these organizations do not want to impose strict standards of IRA knowledge and experience upon them. That certainly makes sense—to them. But it doesn't help you to discern which members are indeed IRA experts.

Two Methods

The financial advisor industry is no different from most other industries. You will always have your top people, the top 1 percent, who have a passion for their business and seize the day to become the best in all areas of that business, including—indeed especially, given the stakes for their clients—IRA distribution and inheritance planning. You can discern these folks in two ways:

- **Method One** involves testing and evaluating your current or prospective IRA advisor with a set of questions and giving them a pass/fail grade.

- **Method Two** enables you to locate an IRA advisor in your region or state whose expertise I can vouch for, because the advisor has been personally trained in all things IRA *by me* (of course, the lawyers want me to make sure to tell you to first read the disclaimer in Chapter 13, before you select one of these advisors). You may even use a combination of the two methods. For example, you can select an expert IRA advisor from among those on my list, then submit that person to an evaluation when you contact them. Don't feel at all reluctant to put them to the test. Asking to do so will not offend them or put them off. On the contrary, they will *love* that you want to test them, because they can't wait to tell you how much they know about IRAs!

Given the vicissitudes of life, one can never be guaranteed of anything, of course—including competence—but at least these two methods will show you how to identify the incompetents and separate the wheat from the chaff. Either of these methods will help you choose an IRA advisor more efficiently—and more wisely— than relying on someone's professional designation alone.

Now you are ready to proceed to choose the right IRA advisor. I won't wish you luck because you won't need it. With either of these two methods you will at last no longer be dependent on luck!

TWELVE

Is Your Advisor an IRA Expert? Let's Find Out!

"All expert IRA advisors are professional financial advisors, but not all professional financial advisors are IRA experts. It's sort of like that old saying: All cats are animals, but not all animals are cats."
—Ed Slott

Professional Financial Advisors vs. Expert IRA Advisors

To use an old-fashioned term, this chapter will help you "separate the men from the boys"—i.e., the expert IRA advisors from among all those who call themselves professional financial advisors.

It is the job of the advisor representing the financial institution where your IRA assets are held to smoothly transition these assets from one generation to the next, enabling beneficiaries to grow them into a fortune through future compounding. So much rides on the knowledge and experience of the advisor that if the ball gets dropped at this stage, tremendous tax breaks and opportunities for income and growth may be lost to your heirs and beneficiaries forever. There is usually only one opportunity to get it right.

Here is a true story from a woman who found this out the hard way. One day I got the following letter from her (I've changed the names and some of the details to protect the innocent, as well as the guilty, but the truth remains):

Dear Mr. Slott,

I have read about you several times recently. I wish I knew about you in 2001, when my father passed away. I received so much contradictory advice and still am confused about certain things. I am appealing to you as an expert to confirm that I am handling things properly. Here are the facts.

My father was born 1/19/1930 and died 2/23/2001. He had started taking withdrawals from his IRA, even though he died before 4/15/2001, which I understand was the required beginning date. On the Tuesday after his death, my two brothers and I visited the office of Dad's attorney to review the will and discuss the procedures of probate. There we discovered that when setting up the IRA, Dad's broker had filled out the paperwork leaving the IRA to Dad's estate rather than directly to us—his three children and the beneficiaries of his estate. During that same week, I asked Dad's broker why she had made the estate the beneficiary of the IRA instead of us. She told me it was best to do it this way in "complicated situations" where there could be confusion over the secondary beneficiary. As I may want to change beneficiaries over the years, it is easier to revise the will than remember to contact each IRA holder, she said, adding that it really made no difference anyway in terms of distributions.

After extensive attempts at research and the opinions of at least five professionals, including attorneys, CPAs, and financial advisors, it appeared that my brothers and I were limited to the five-year rule in distributions. On advice, I split the account into three equal accounts. One brother took his entire distribution in 2002. I have taken small distributions in 2002 and 2003. The other brother has taken nothing to date. Distributions have required liquidation of the funds in the account so that a check can come to the estate. I deposit the check in the estate checking account and write a check in the same amount to the specific beneficiary.

My question is: Am I correct in abiding by the five-year rule? Am I correct in selling the shares in the accounts as needed for cash and depositing the funds in the checking account and making a similar check to the beneficiary? Thank you for any help you can provide.

Sincerely, Sherry Trout

After taking this real live (and unfortunately all too common) IRA horror story in, I wrote back to Sherry to give her the bad news. She was stuck with the five-year rule, I told her, because—advisor mistake number one—the estate was named beneficiary and her father had died just short of his required beginning date.

As you will recall from my discussion of the five-year rule earlier in this book, the entire inherited IRA must be completely withdrawn by the end of the fifth year following the year of death, which in Sherry's case (her father having died in 2001) would be by the end of 2006. So she and her brothers really didn't have to withdraw anything until the end of 2006 if they hadn't wished to, but they did so—advisor mistake number two.

Unfortunately, her family received bad advice all the way around. As a result, not only was the chance to parlay Dad's IRA into a fortune lost, the inheritance was decimated by estate taxes, probate costs, broker and other fees, plus taxes on withdrawals. I explained that it was too late to go back and undo all the mistakes that had been made. All I could offer were the details of what *should* have been advised but wasn't. Regrettably, Sherry and her brothers were out of luck.

Sherry whipped off a letter to the advisor at the brokerage firm who steered things so wrong. She copied me on it. And get things off her chest she did, venting as follows:

Dear Judy [name changed],
Just a reminder that it has been two years to the day since my father passed away. Two years for us to mourn him and two years for us to deal with the mess you created through your ignorance and incompetence. Two years of paying extra attorney fees, brokerage fees, and accounting fees. You made a good deal of money from our family. In return, you cost us thousands of dollars since you were not informed enough to know not to leave an IRA to an estate. Every professional that has heard what you did to us has been amazed at your incompetence. I would think, being the good Christian that you claim you are, you would have made some attempt at apology and restitution. Instead you remind us that there are hypocrites in all walks of life. Since we are

going to be reminded of your negligence for years to come, I think it is only fair that you remember too. I will remind you each year of my father, when we have to file another estate tax return and pay more taxes and fees. Before you advise any client regarding estate planning, remember the horror that you caused our family. I hope you learned something from it. I hope you took some extensive courses and educated yourself in order to spare others the terrible grief and additional expense you caused us. Better yet, I hope you found another line of work. Maybe selling used cars or snake oil would be more appropriate.
Until next year . . .

    Sherry Trout

As it turns out, not long after, the advisor did go into another line of work—probably to escape Sherry's letters!

As Sherry's story demonstrates, it is not enough for a financial advisor to simply know how to invest retirement money wisely, important though that is. As you've learned from reading Parts One and Two of this book, the endgame is keeping that money intact so beneficiaries can grow it for generations into a windfall rather than lose it early on to avoidable taxes and other costly mistakes—which is where the importance of having an *expert IRA advisor* comes in.

In spite of what it may seem, this step in my three-step system for parlaying your IRA into a fortune is actually advisor-friendly— but only to those advisors who deserve to be managing people's IRA money by having fully developed their IRA education and taking IRA distribution planning seriously.

Most advisors (more than 95 percent) who accept IRA money from clients to manage do not have the IRA expertise to retain those IRAs and will most likely make costly, irreparable blunders when the IRA funds move into transition at rollover time and, especially, at the IRA owner's death when the IRA is inherited. Often, these mistakes will kill any chance the beneficiaries may have of capitalizing on the IRA tax rules to parlay their inheritance. So, the point of this step in the book is to guide you, the consumer, to the best and most prepared IRA advisors (or to make sure your advisor measures up).

Types of Professional Financial Advisors

I use the umbrella term "professional financial advisors" to refer to the following specialized groups of people and what they do:

- *Financial Planners*

    The term "financial planner" is a broad-brush term for a true melting pot that includes numerous types of advisors. It is likely (but not a given) that your expert IRA advisor will come from this group whose members may carry designations from diverse professional groups such as: FPA (Financial Planning Association), NAIFA (National Association of Insurance and Financial Advisors), CFP (Certified Financial Planner from the College of Financial Planning), NAPFA (National Association of Personal Financial Advisors), SFSP (Society of Financial Service Professionals), and Estate Planning Councils (made up of members from the banking, legal, accounting, and insurance professions). Beware of anyone who calls himself or herself a financial planner but has no professional designation. A professional designation of some kind is the minimum acceptable standard of certification. Without it, the advisor has literally nothing to lose (like a license) if he or she messes up. But you have plenty to lose.

- *Insurance Professionals*

    I am a big believer in the concept of using life insurance to cost effectively protect an IRA, especially a large IRA that may be subject to both estate and income taxes, and parlay it into a fortune, because the leverage life insurance provides is unbeatable. Insurance professionals today do more than just sell insurance. They are among the most motivated and professional financial advisors you can find. Are they all IRA experts? No, but insurance companies are moving to become leaders in the IRA marketplace and, in turn, are educating their representatives to become versed in the IRA rules. They see the strong connection between IRAs and life insurance, and so many insurance professionals are quickly taking the lead among advisors to become IRA experts. The savviest insurance professionals in the world belong to the MDRT (Million Dollar Round Table), one of the most respected professional groups in the financial services industry. Then there is the elite of MDRT called TOT (Top of the Table). The aforementioned NAIFA is an insurance-related industry group whose members are not required to be insurance professionals. For example, I am a member of this group, but I do not sell insurance.

- *Certified Public Accountants (CPAs)*

  Many CPAs have gone into the financial services market so they can provide advice and services to their tax and accounting clients. For example, members of AICPA (the American Institute of Certified Public Accountants) who take additional training in financial planning can earn a designation as a PFS (Personal Financial Specialist).

- *Attorneys*

  You need an attorney specializing in estate and trust work to develop your overall estate plan, to prepare the required legal documents (wills, trusts, and so on), and to work with your executor in distributing your estate assets. Not all estate planning attorneys are expert IRA advisors, though, nor do they wish to be; some prefer to work as a team with your financial advisors and leave the IRA expertise up to them. On the other hand, many estate attorneys see this as a natural extension of their field and are becoming IRA experts as well.

- *Brokers*

  Today, many brokers call themselves an FA, short for "financial advisor." This again is a broad term that really does not give you a clue as to whether they specialize in anything, including IRAs. But many of the large brokerage firms do have IRA specialists within the firm that can serve as a resource to your individual broker. Brokers are still making the transition from being transaction-oriented sales people to professional financial advisors who can handle IRA planning issues.

- *Trust Companies*

    Trust companies cater to wealthier clients. All financial advisors want wealthy clients, but private bank and trust companies seem to attract more of them, because these firms have many professional resources and employ highly trained professional advisors. Chances are, if you are working with one of these companies, they will have expert IRA advisors in-house or will be able to refer you to several.

- *Bank Advisors*

    Many banks have key people who are excellent IRA advisors, but you may have to ask around the bank to find out who they are. I am not referring to the nice folks who are tellers, loan specialists, or those who sell you mutual funds and other investments. I am talking about seasoned advisors who know their stuff. These advisors may not be present at each branch of a big bank, but you still may gain access to them if you ask. Having a ton of cash at the bank also helps ferret out their best people.

- *Pension Actuaries*

    These are often backroom geniuses that know a ton about the retirement account tax rules, but it is unlikely they will be available directly to consumers without going through the financial services company that employs them.

If you wind up involving a team of advisors from these various groups to develop your overall estate plan—i.e., to assist in building, investing, retaining, and passing on your IRA or other retirement accounts to your family, that's fine—*as long as at least one of them is an expert IRA advisor as well!*

What Should Your IRA Advisor Know
to Be an Expert?

He or she should be *fluent* in the IRA distribution rules, which is a challenge by itself. But also, he or she needs to know how to integrate your IRA with your overall estate plan and how to deal with IRAs in transition—i.e., any period when funds are removed from their IRA tax shelter and become vulnerable to Uncle Sam.

As noted elsewhere in this book, IRAs fall into transition during three major events in your life: (1) when you retire (or change jobs) and move retirement money from a company plan to an IRA; (2) when you reach the age (generally after age 70½) at which you must begin taking your required minimum distributions (RMDs); and (3) when your beneficiaries inherit your IRA after you pass on. These three key transitional periods must be dealt with very carefully, or the roof will come off the tax shelter and the opportunity to parlay your IRA into a family fortune will be lost. Our tax code shows no mercy when it comes to adhering to the rules about exactly how and how much of your IRA must be withdrawn, and when.

An expert IRA advisor is aware of all the IRA tax traps in your path and how to avoid them, which means that it is not enough for him or her to just be up on the *current* rules. Regular income tax rules change maybe once a year, but the IRA rules are an evolving species. Congress and the IRS change or redefine their positions on these rules on a regular—sometimes *weekly*—basis. This is why I write a monthly newsletter dedicated to the changing IRA tax rules.

Good Signs or Bad Vibes?

Before asking your existing professional financial advisor—or hiring one—to set up your IRA for inheritance or to negotiate the transfer of retirement account assets you will be inheriting, make sure the person will be able to measure up to the task by putting him or her to my Official Expert IRA Advisor Detector Test. The answers you get back to the questions on this test will help you gauge the person's knowledge, experience, comprehension of the IRA distribution rules (and how to apply them to your benefit and goals), and ability to translate these rules for you in a language you can understand.

B***S*** DETECTOR!

Being able to explain complicated concepts in terms anyone can comprehend is a skill that can be acquired; it simply demands that whoever is doing the explaining understands the concepts himself or herself. Advisors who say, "It's too technical to explain" or "You won't understand it because it's so complicated," are really saying *they* don't understand. Don't fall for it.

Ed Slott's Official Expert IRA Advisor Detector Test

Question 1: What resources or publications does the advisor use to keep up-to-date with changing IRA distribution rules?

These resources should include IRA reference books, newsletters, tax service advisories, IRS Publication 590 (the IRA bible every advisor should have handy), and so on. See how long it takes the advisor to find them. If they are not within arm's reach, or even closer, and not well thumbed—the pages covered with highlights, Post-it notes and handwritten notes—it's a bad sign. If a reference book makes a cracking sound when the advisor opens it, this is a very bad sign; it means the book has likely never been opened before. At least some of these materials should be well worn; having them but not using them helps neither the advisor nor you.

B***S*** DETECTOR!

Beware the full-color company brochure on inherited IRAs shown to back up claims of knowledge and expertise. Typically this is just evidence of sizzle rather than steak. (If the company produces its own newsletter on inherited IRAs, however, that is impressive, and a good sign.) Likewise, if the advisor pulls out a full-color brochure on inherited IRAs from another company to show you, it may indicate that he or she knows of no other resource.

Question 2: When was the last time the advisor attended a seminar or training session on IRAs?

Any good advisor should be attending IRA seminars or IRA training programs on a regular basis. If the advisor does not like going to seminars because he or she wants to spend more time with clients like you, that's fine, but there are still ways to keep one's IRA education current without leaving the office or home—for example, continuing education classes in IRAs conducted online or by mail. The best part about attending live seminars and workshops, though, is that the advisor gets to meet and network with other advisors who have IRA clients. This interaction almost always spurs new ideas and an awareness of the most recent changes in the IRA rules. I cannot emphasize enough that to be an IRA expert, the advisor MUST ALWAYS be up to date on the latest changes in the IRA rules. It could spell disaster for you if a key new ruling or change is missed.

B***S*** DETECTOR!

It's not enough to just *ask* the advisor about recent IRA seminars or training he or she attended; *request proof.* Following Question 2, ask the advisor to show you the course manuals. If the advisor can't show you a recent one (or any), then you know how fresh his or her knowledge and training are.

Question 3: What is the last new IRA ruling or tax law change the advisor is aware of?

If, say, it's April 2005 and the advisor shows you the new IRA rules from April 2002, it's good that he or she has the rules on hand but not so good that they're old and bewhiskered. New rulings and changes in the tax laws come out on the average of once a week. In fact, as I am writing this, a major new IRS private letter ruling was released that could have a dramatic impact on almost every trust named as an IRA beneficiary. Does the advisor know about this? He or she certainly should, especially if you have named a trust as your IRA beneficiary.

Question 4: What factors does the advisor recommend his IRA clients consider in deciding what to do with their lump sum distribution from their company retirement plan?

The typical (and often the best) move is a direct IRA rollover, but a good advisor won't just assume this is the best move. He or she will ask questions of you first, the answers to which will determine whether the best move *for you* is an IRA rollover, a direct trustee-to-trustee transfer to an IRA (he or she should know the difference between the two), to leave the lump sum in your current plan, to roll it to a new plan, or to take the money and pay the tax. There are sound reasons for choosing any of these options. A good advisor should be able—and willing—to lay them all out for you in layman's terms so that you understand the advantages and disadvantages of each and can make a fully informed decision. For example, one of the options I mentioned was to take the lump sum and pay the tax. When would it ever be a wise decision to do this? Answer: When you qualify for ten-year averaging tax rates and when the tax break for "net unrealized appreciation" (NUA) on employer securities can be used. These special tax breaks may or may not apply to your situation, but the advisor won't know whether they do or don't if he or she isn't even aware they exist!

Question 5: Whom does the advisor recommend you should name as your IRA beneficiary? And what factors does the advisor suggest you consider in making that decision?

An expert IRA advisor's immediate response should be: "To whom do you *want* to leave your IRA?" Not everything is about taxes. Once the advisor knows what *you* want, he or she will more effectively be able to explain the advantages and disadvantages of each beneficiary choice, as follows in Question 6. Naming an IRA beneficiary is a simple function, and yet I have seen it messed up countless times with disastrous results because the advisor just says, "Sign here, here, and here," without taking the time to discuss the tax ramifications of each beneficiary choice.

A good advisor *advises* on this all-important matter by laying out the pros and cons and all the options available to each type of beneficiary for keeping the account growing. This means the advisor must know how to do a post-death rollover when a spouse is the beneficiary, as well as understand what the effect of naming one type of beneficiary for your IRA will have on the distribution of other types of assets in your estate to other beneficiaries—in other words, how to integrate your decision with your overall estate plan.

It would be a mistake if the advisor just says, "Name your spouse," as many advisors do without asking for more information about your personal and financial situation. Naming your spouse as your IRA beneficiary may or may not be the best choice for you and your family, but a good advisor will want to know more about you before rattling off the usual advice. A good advisor also will make sure you name a contingent beneficiary so that additional options are available after your death.

Question 6: How does the advisor keep track of clients' IRA beneficiary forms?

In other words, *where* does the advisor keep them, *who* also has a copy, and *when* should they be updated—will the advisor know, or is that left up to the client to remember?

The IRA beneficiary form is the key to the concept of parlaying the account into a fortune tax-deferred (or tax-free with a Roth IRA) for decades. It therefore must be available, filled out correctly, and up-to-date. An expert IRA advisor will ask to be kept informed of any major changes in your life—a birth, a death, a marriage, or a divorce—that may affect your IRA bequest so that he or she will be able to revise your IRA beneficiary forms accordingly and keep that information current *at all times*. The advisor should also be proactive and call you when, for example, there are changes in the tax laws or new IRA rules that might warrant a change to your IRA beneficiary form.

At a *minimum*, the advisor should keep a copy of your IRA beneficiary form in his or her files and know that it agrees with the copy that should be on hand at the financial institution where the account is held. Most IRA problems, come inheritance and distribution time, stem from a beneficiary form's not having been filled out properly, not having been updated (especially when a previous beneficiary has died), or having gone just plain missing. In such cases, the problem is often insurmountable and permanent!

Question 7: Can the advisor show you the IRS life expectancy tables used to calculate required IRA distributions for both IRA owners and beneficiaries?

Similar to the response to Question 1, a good advisor should have this material close at hand. If he or she does not, this means the advisor probably doesn't do much work in the IRA distribution area and just dabbles in it. That's a danger sign. After all, you wouldn't entrust a critical operation on your body to a doctor who just dabbles in surgery, would you?

Also, the advisor should know which distribution table applies to lifetime distributions and which table applies to post-death distributions from an inherited IRA. Many errors arise from using the wrong table or an outdated one. As you know from this book, the table most IRA owners will use to compute their lifetime required distributions is the Uniform Lifetime table (see Appendix II). The Single Life Expectancy table (see Chapter One) is for inherited IRAs. (There is also the Joint Life Expectancy table, which is used for lifetime distributions where a younger spouse is sole beneficiary—see Appendix II for details.)

Question 8: Does the advisor know what will happen to your IRA after your death?

Much of the litigation that ensues today over inherited IRAs stems from the mishandling of them by advisors who simply don't know enough. Do not work with an advisor who is unfamiliar with the material covered in this book, among the most important of which are: (1) how to properly title an inherited IRA; (2) what the required minimum distributions are that the beneficiary will be subject to (and how these distributions are computed); and (3) that the beneficiary may be entitled to a valuable income tax deduction (income in respect of a decedent).

The last thing you want for your family is a post-death surprise. A good advisor will be able to make sure that does not happen by explaining to you now how your IRA will be paid out after death. If the advisor cannot explain these options, find one who can.

For example, remember the story in Chapter One that involved a huge financial institution and a particular broker in the firm who were unable to stretch an inherited IRA for one of their clients *because they did not know the option existed!* Instead, the broker delivered checks for $90,000 to each beneficiary with the result that the beneficiaries had to pay all the income tax on the IRA in one year rather than have the option of spreading the taxes out and growing the account while doing so. This triggered a huge lawsuit against the broker and the firm by the beneficiaries, as well it should have. How can anyone who holds himself or herself out to be a financial *advisor* not know about this option, which is basically a part of setting up a plain vanilla inherited IRA? I was shocked, but not as shocked as the beneficiaries when they found out what their share could have been worth over the next 40 years if they had not lost so much of their inherited IRA to taxes.

Question 9: Does the advisor have an estate planning process for your IRA?

If the advisor is not an expert in estate planning as well as IRA planning, this can be OK, provided he or she is willing to work for your benefit with other professionals who have this expertise. This is where networking with other professionals becomes a real asset to an advisor and, in turn, to you.

The big picture for your IRA is how it will be inherited along with your other estate assets. This is the estate plan for what may be your largest single asset—your retirement account. This cannot be done in a vacuum without considering your other assets and beneficiaries. Does the advisor have at least a general knowledge of estate planning (including when to name an IRA trust as your IRA beneficiary) and how to integrate an IRA into an overall estate plan?

Ask the advisor when he or she would recommend naming a trust as IRA beneficiary. If you recall from our detailed discussion on this topic in Part One of this book, the answer to this question generally relates to the degree of control you want to have over how your IRA is distributed to your beneficiary(ies) after your death. The advisor should have at least a basic understanding of when a trust should or should not be named as IRA beneficiary and, if so, of what happens—for example, that the stretch option may be lost. I find that lots of advisors have their clients' name trusts as their IRA beneficiary (often unnecessarily) and then, after death, the advisors do not know how to distribute the IRA or the required distributions to the trust.

You also want to know how the advisor intends to make the most efficient use of the federal estate tax exemption. Also, as we have seen, life insurance can play a huge role in an IRA estate plan. Is the advisor versed in setting up life insurance or willing to work with an insurance professional on this?

Question 10: Whom does the advisor call or turn to for help when he or she has questions about inherited IRA distributions?

As I've tried to emphasize, many decisions in the unforgiving world of inherited IRAs are irreversible. The damage cannot be undone. Good advisors need not only print and online resources, but also outside experts they can turn to for added help on perplexing questions. Good advisors let their clients know that they have ready access to authorities in this area on a regular basis for questions that arise. At the seminars in which I participate, advisors are always coming up to me and seeking answers to complex questions about their clients' situations. Many times when I give them the answer, they will say, "That's what I thought, but I just wanted to make sure before I advise my client." That is the kind of advisor you want!

B***S*** DETECTOR!

An answer from the advisor such as, "I know this stuff cold; I don't have to call anyone," is a sure indicator that he or she is blowing smoke. I study IRA distribution planning full-time and I still have questions that I discuss with other IRA experts, who will be the first to say the same thing about themselves. It's a complex field—the IRS likes it that way! If your advisor can't name at least a few experts such as an outside attorney or accountant that he or she draws upon as an additional resource, then you have the wrong advisor. A good advisor will have these contacts.

Bonus Question: Is the advisor familiar with the name Ed Slott?

The answer to this bonus question is arguably the most critical of all in determining whether the advisor is truly in the know! (Just kidding. Well, mostly.)

These are the questions today's smart consumers are asking their financial advisors. Any financial advisor worth his or her salt will welcome this test from you and be able to pass it with flying colors.

B***S*** DETECTOR!

You may be wondering why I don't include the question, "How long has the advisor been in business?" It's because the answer is irrelevant *if the advisor knows his or her IRA stuff.* Some firms have wisely just begun to specialize in this area, and although they may not have been in business long, they are right up-to-the-minute as IRA experts. So, beware advisors who tout how long they have been in operation. Business longevity is not necessarily an indicator of IRA expertise and should not be a factor in considering the advisor's competence as an IRA expert.

Rate the Advisor

To get a fix on the advisor's IRA savvy, rate him or her on each pair of phrases, based on the answers you receive on the test, by deciding how you feel the advisor rates on each of the ten questions using a rating scale of 1 (stinks) to 10 (great). Then add up the totals from each column, and refer to the scoring key that follows.

	1	2	3	4	5	6	7	8	9	10	
My advisor does NOT maintain adequate IRA resources											My advisor does maintain adequate IRA resources
My advisor does NOT regularly attend IRA training seminars											My advisor does regularly attend IRA training seminars
My advisor does NOT keep current with the changing IRA tax rules											My advisor does keep current with the changing IRA tax rules

	1	2	3	4	5	6	7	8	9	10	
My advisor is NOT well versed in IRA and plan rollover options											My advisor is well versed in IRA and plan rollover options
My advisor does NOT have a system for helping me determine who to name as my IRA beneficiary(ies)											My advisor does have a system for helping me determine who to name as my IRA beneficiary(ies)
My advisor does NOT have a system to keep track of my IRA beneficiary forms											My advisor does have a system to keep track of my IRA beneficiary forms
My advisor does NOT have the current IRA life expectancy tables immediately available and is NOT sure which tables apply											My advisor does have the current IRA life expectancy tables immediately available and is sure which tables apply
My advisor is NOT very knowledgeable about the IRA distribution rules and tax options for inherited IRAs											My advisor is very knowledgeable about the IRA distribution rules and tax options for inherited IRAs
My advisor does NOT have an estate planning process for my IRA											My advisor does have an estate planning process for my IRA
My advisor does NOT consult with other IRA advisors											My advisor does consult with other IRA advisors
ADD COLUMN TOTALS											TOTAL SCORE _____

B***S*** DETECTOR PENALTY!

If you catch the advisor on your B***S*** Detector, deduct 30 points right away! No amount of B***S*** will help you or your family clean up this advisor's mess.

What the Score Means

Assume you had to have surgery. What score would you hope your doctor got on his medical exam? Because it indicates you will have a better than 50-50 chance of coming off the operating table alive, would you think any score over 70 is probably sufficient? Is that good enough for you? It's the same with your IRA. How accurate would you want your advisor to be in setting up your account so it can be parlayed into a fortune? Wouldn't you hope that he or she knew every possible IRA move and tax strategy down to the last detail?

No doctor or financial advisor is perfect, of course, but you can and should demand the expertise necessary to ensure you'll not only survive the operation, but emerge from it in good health, and that your hard-earned nest egg won't crack.

It's your money. You are the judge and jury here; it's your standards that matter most.

SCORING KEY

0–70 points: You've got a dentist when you really need a cardiologist—i.e., your IRA is doomed.

71–80 points: You'll survive the operation, but it won't be pretty. There'll be some bumps and bruises along the way. In other words, unless the advisor is your brother-in-law and you have no other choice without causing a family feud, you and your IRA can still do better.

81–90 points: You are well on the way to recovery—i.e., this is an impressive score but still shows that there is room for improvement, depending upon how high your standards are.

91–100 points: You're not only the picture of health, you're better than new—and 30 years younger, to boot! In other words, the advisor is truly among the best in the business, a genuine IRA expert worth every cent. Be sure your beneficiaries stay connected to this advisor after you're gone.

THIRTEEN

The Green Berets of IRAs

Choose an Advisor I've Already Screened

My second method for choosing an expert IRA advisor is to select one I have already screened for you from among an elite list I call the "Green Berets of IRAs."

These people are financial advisors from all across the country practicing diverse disciplines with a variety of professional designations. I have personally instructed this elite team in my workshops and seminars to become Ed Slott–trained expert IRA advisors. I've already given them the test in Chapter 12, which they have all passed with flying colors. I can call them an elite team because I have no board or bureaucracy hovering over my shoulder to account to in affixing such a title—just you, my readers—to whom I am providing this exclusive list, the only one of its kind in existence since I created it, because it is sorely needed.

It is not easy for advisors to get on this list. They cannot pay their way on. Many financial advisors e-mail me with their credentials, begging to be included on this list. But they do not get listed without attending one of my seminars or workshops to enhance their IRA education and be personally trained by me. Furthermore, they must sign an affidavit to the effect that they attended my training—and I personally check their attendance record! In other words, they cannot just pay for the training, then not show up for it, call themselves an IRA expert, and get listed.

FAQ

Q. Ed, are these the only financial advisors out there who really know their IRAs?

A. I would not be so presumptuous as to state that if a financial advisor has not been trained by me, then he or she cannot be considered an IRA expert. I am sure that there are other financial advisors around who have gained IRA expertise on their own or through other types of continuing education, but are not on my list. Finding them is the difficulty, which is where the test in the previous chapter comes in.

A Word About Financial Advisor Fees

No, I am not going to give you the usual nonsense you see everywhere about how to pay less for expert professional advice. Cheap expert professional advice does not exist! I know that every magazine and Internet site says it does—even professional IRA advice—but it doesn't. You get what you pay for in this life—and that's especially true when it comes to specific, high-level IRA expertise that can dramatically impact your life savings.

The advisors on this list are not inexpensive; that's because they are *experts*. Whether you choose your advisor from this list or elsewhere, remember this: You cannot afford to hire an advisor who is *not* an expert. If you shop fees, you're being penny-wise and pound-foolish. You are missing the big picture—where saving a tenth of a percent in advisor fees may turn out to be a drop in the bucket if the advisor you hire makes a mistake that costs your family your retirement savings. As I've stressed so often in these pages, the IRA battlefield area is loaded with land mines, and if an advisor makes a mistake, it can be costly as well as irreversible.

FAQ

Q. Ed, do you get a cut of their income by putting them on your list?

A. That certainly is a fair question. The answer is **absolutely not**. In fact, I make each person on the list sign an affidavit that says that I am not a partner in any way in any income or fees they receive as a result of being listed as an Ed Slott–trained expert IRA advisor. My mission is to motivate more financial advisors to become IRA experts by taking my training (which is how I make my living) and thus become qualified for this list.

FAQ

Q. Ed, how can you be sure these folks won't ever make mistakes too?

A. I can't be sure. All I can do is offer you guidance. What I have done here is to narrow the field to a list of advisors I believe are the best trained in IRAs based on my professional opinion and expertise in the IRA area. Choosing an advisor is still *your* responsibility, and you do so at your own risk—just as with selecting any kind of consultant or advisor. The key is to choose wisely. (Please see the disclaimer that follows here.)

ED SLOTT–TRAINED EXPERT IRA ADVISORS

To make it easier for you to locate the expert IRA advisor, trained by me, nearest you and not a zillion miles away, the following list is presented alphabetically—first by state, then by the name of the individual advisor. Who knows—there might even be one in your neighborhood!

This is a fast-paced world. People move—especially good IRA advisors whose businesses are always expanding. They move, change phone numbers, fax numbers, e-mails, and Web sites. Sometimes they add an office in another location. Also, I am constantly adding more expert IRA advisors to my list as more of them take my intensive IRA training courses. So while this list is as accurate in all details as possible at the time we went to press, for any corrections as well as additions to the list in the future, please refer to the "Advisors" page of my Web site, **www.irahelp.com,** for updates.

LEGAL DISCLAIMER

For your general information, Ed Slott, CPA, www.irahelp.com, Ed Slott's IRA Advisor, and E. Slott and Company maintain a list of financial advisors who have attended an intensive full-day training seminar with Ed Slott, CPA, on IRA distribution planning, including the latest IRA distribution rules, court cases, IRS rulings, planning strategies, retirement account rollovers, inherited IRAs, estate planning for retirement accounts, and related tax provisions. These financial advisors are not affiliated with Ed Slott, CPA, www.irahelp.com, Ed Slott's IRA Advisor, and E. Slott and Company. These financial advisors conduct their own practices, which are independent of Ed Slott, CPA, www.irahelp.com, Ed Slott's IRA Advisor, and E. Slott and Company, and they are not representatives, agents, partners, employees, or contractors of, and are not otherwise associated with, Ed Slott, CPA, www. irahelp.com, Ed Slott's IRA Advisor, and E. Slott and Company. Any representation made to the contrary by any of the financial advisors named in this list or in this Web site is false.

Ed Slott, CPA, www.irahelp.com, Ed Slott's IRA Advisor, and E. Slott and Company are not responsible for any financial advice or any other services provided by any of the financial advisors named in this list or in this Web site. You are responsible for your choice of a financial advisor. You should carefully interview one or more potential financial advisors, ask for and check references, and otherwise carefully assess your choice of a financial advisor.

The financial advisors you may access through this list or this Web site have attended a training seminar presented by Ed Slott, CPA. This "training" is not conferred or certified by any government agency or any professional group (such as, for example, groups that confer the title "certified financial planner"). Any representation made to the contrary by any of the financial advisors named in this list or in this Web site is false. Ed Slott, CPA, www.irahelp.com, Ed Slott's IRA Advisor, and E. Slott and Company grant training to financial advisors who attend an approximately seven-hour training seminar regarding IRA distribution planning and the IRA distribution tax rules. Financial advisors pay a fee to Ed Slott, CPA, for attending this seminar. At the seminar they receive certain instructions, IRA information, and various written materials that may help them apply the principles of planning IRA distributions to the affairs of a particular client. Ed Slott, CPA, www.irahelp.com, Ed Slott's IRA Advisor, and E. Slott and Company have not conducted any background checks and have not in any way qualified any of the financial advisors who attend its seminars and who are named in this list or in this Web site. Ed Slott, CPA, www.irahelp.com, Ed Slott's IRA Advisor, and E. Slott and Company make no representations regarding the financial advisors named in this list or in this Web site or the quality of the service they provide. In other words, the term "Ed Slott–Trained IRA Expert Advisor" as used in this book, in this list, or in this Web site means solely that the financial advisor has attended the above-described seminar.

Ed Slott, CPA, www.irahelp.com, Ed Slott's IRA Advisor, and E. Slott and Company do not consult with, advise, or help financial advisors as they work with their clients. In other words, any advice or services you may receive from a financial advisor, whether listed here or on this Web site or not, is not the advice of or services by Ed Slott, CPA, www.irahelp.com, Ed Slott's IRA Advisor, and E. Slott and Company. Ed Slott, CPA, www.irahelp.com, Ed Slott's IRA Advisor, and E. Slott and Company do not control or review, and are not responsible for, the advice you may receive from a financial advisor you learn of through this list or Web site. Ed Slott, CPA, www.irahelp.com, Ed Slott's IRA Advisor, and E. Slott and Company are not responsible for such a financial advisor's action or failure to act on your behalf. Ed Slott, CPA, www.irahelp.com, Ed Slott's IRA Advisor, and E. Slott and Company do not guarantee and are not responsible for the results of any investments you may make with the advice of or through any such financial advisor.

Your use of a financial advisor named in this list or in this Web site is strictly at your own risk. By accessing or using the list of financial advisors in this list or in this Web site you agree that neither Ed Slott, CPA, E. Slott and Company, nor Ed Slott's IRA Advisor is responsible or liable for any advice given by, actions taken by, failures to act by, negligence of, or other misconduct of any type of any of the financial advisors named in this list or in this Web site. If you accept these terms and conditions, you waive and release, and you agree to indemnify and hold Ed Slott, CPA, E. Slott and Company, and Ed Slott's IRA Advisor harmless from any and all claims, liabilities, and losses arising from or related to your use of any financial advisor named in this list or in this Web site.

ALABAMA

Cox Associates, Inc.
Anne C. Jewell
115 Manning Drive, Suite 202B
Huntsville, AL 35801
256-533-0001
http://www.coxassociatesinc.com
ajewell@hiwaay.net

SeniorsLTC, LLC
Brad Williams, CSA
115 Manning Drive,
    Suite 202B
Huntsville, AL 35801
256-536-3075
http://www.askbradwilliams.com
brad@seniorsltc.com

ALASKA

Shilanski & Associates, Inc.
John C. Coffman, Ph.D., JD
431 W. 7th Avenue, Suite 100
Anchorage, AK 99501
907-278-1351
http://www.shilanski.com
john@shilanski.com

Shilanski & Associates, Inc.
Floyd Shilanski, RFC, CSA
431 W. 7th Avenue, Suite 100
Anchorage, AK 99501
907-278-1351
http://www.shilanski.com
floyd@shilanski.com

Shilanski & Associates, Inc.
Micah Shilanski, CSA

431 W. 7th Avenue, Suite 100
Anchorage, AK 99501
907-278-1351
http://www.shilanski.com
micah@shilanski.com

ARIZONA

Heritage Financial Place, Inc.
Darel T. Crosby, CSA
3131 E. Camelback Road,
    Suite 200
Phoenix, AZ 85016
800-867-2838
http://www.heritagefinancial
    place.com

Harris Capital Planning
A. Wayne Harris
417 E. LeMarche Avenue
Phoenix, AZ 85022
602-863-0472
wharris@fwg.com

Hoopes Capital Network
Rick Hoopes, CEPS, CSA
5215 N. Sabino Canyon Road
Tucson, AZ 85750
520-577-5117
hoopesgrp@aol.com

American Express Financial
    Advisors
Kirk G. Kaprelian, CFP®
14300 N. Northsight Boulevard,
    Suite 114
Scottsdale, AZ 85260
480-473-0376, ext. 210
karekin.g.kaprelian@aexp.com

Kramer & Kramer, LLC
Robert Kramer, CEP
12211 W. Bell Road, Suite 100
Surprise, AZ 85374
623-974-1966

McDowell Estate Planning
Michael McDowell
PO Box 6115
Sun City West, AZ 85376
623-388-2097
runningfox@earthlink.net

Southwest Capital Advisors, LLC
Theodore (Ted) Mietzner, CEP,
  CSA
3130 N. Arizona Avenue,
  Suite 105
Chandler, AZ 85225
480-503-0999
southwestcapital@msn.com

Lincoln Financial Advisors
Anthony R. Pennacchio, MBA,
  CHBC, CSA
5343 N. 16th Street, Suite 400
Phoenix, AZ 85016
602-744-5879
tpennacchio@lnc.com

Kramer & Kramer, LLC
Jay K. Perry, CEP
12211 W. Bell Road, Suite 100
Surprise, AZ 85374
623-974-1966
jayperry@qwest.net

Mark D. Rosenfeld, CPA, PC
Mark D. Rosenfeld, CPA
3200 N. Hayden Road, Suite 230
Scottsdale, AZ 85251
480-947-4443
http://www.markrosenfeld.com
mark@markrosenfeld.com

Heritage Financial Place, Inc.
J. Blake Taylor, CFP®, ChFC,
  RFC, CSA, LUTCF
3131 E. Camelback Road, Suite
  200
Phoenix, AZ 85016
800-867-2838
http://www.heritage
  financialplace.com

W. H. Wilkinson & Co., Inc.
William H. Wilkinson, III, CFP®,
  ChFC, CLU
15849 N. 71st Street,
  Suite 100
Scottsdale, AZ 85254
480-281-3870

ARKANSAS

Jordan Woosley Crone & Keaton
Leslie Ballentine, CPA
144 Sunshine Valley Place
Pearcy, AR 71964
501-624-5788
ballentine@hotsprings.net

Jones & Associates
Mary L. Jones, CPA
4501 N. Highway 7, Suite E
Hot Springs Village, AR 71909
501-984-5301
maryj@arkansas.net

Community First Trust Company
William L. Kerst, Jr., CPA
135 Section Line Road,
  Third Floor, C-1
Hot Springs, AR 71913
501-520-3660
http://www.communityfirsttrust.
  com
bill@communityfirsttrust.com

CALIFORNIA

Baiz-Adams Retirement Planning
Tracie L. Baiz-Adams, CRPC
10152 Carmel Valley Way
Elk Grove, CA 95624
916-714-0073
http://www.baiz-adams.com
Tracie@baiz-adams.com

Kit Batina
1200 Sixth Avenue, Suite 103
Belmont, CA 94002
650-622-9144
http://batinafinancial.com
kitbatina@juno.com

Guardian Advisory Services, LLC
LeRoy E. Blanchard
24544 Avenida Arcante
Murrietta, CA 92562
909-696-0536
royblan@dslextreme.com

The Annuity Store
Lowell D. Bundy, CSA
1337 Howe Avenue, Suite 250
Sacramento, CA 95825
916-924-9601
lowell@theannuitystore.com

Ronald B. Caballero &
    Associates
Ronald B. Caballero, CLU
11141 Briarcliff Drive
San Diego, CA 92131
888-775-3425
http://www.advtaxstrategies.com
rcaballero@advtaxstrategies.com

Commonwealth Financial
    Network
Marjorie Determan, Investment
    Advisor Representative
14651 Greenwood Circle

Nevada City, CA 95959
530-265-9272
http://www.fsnca.com
mfd@fsnca.com

Stan DiLiberto, CPA, CFP®, Inc.
Stan DiLiberto, CPA, CFP®
12535 Seal Beach Boulevard,
    Suite 220
Seal Beach, CA 90740
714-969-1040
stan@cpaadvisor.com

Jerry Galloway, CSA
3125 Kaywood Drive
Escondido, CA 92026
760-741-3035
http://asset-advisors.com
didocrew11@cox.net

Hartwell Financial Services
Philip Hartwell, CFP®
2790 Skypark Drive, Suite 200
Torrance, CA 90505
310-257-0744
phil@wealthmgmt4u.com

Jim Hilbe
PO Box 3659
Rancho Cucamonga,
    CA 91729-3659
909-238-8400
jim.hilbe@verizon.net

Michael Hsu, JD
1855 O'Toole Avenue,
    Suite D-202
San Jose, CA 95131
800-800-0280
http://www.888ira.com
atisf@aol.com

Kennedy Financial & Insurance
    Services
Mark S. Kennedy, CSA

21550 Oxnard Street,
  Third Floor
Woodland Hills, CA 91367
888-805-1541
http://www.markkennedyonline.
  com
ira@markkennedyonline.com

Lau Financial Services
John Lau
181 Second Avenue, Suite 600
San Mateo, CA 94401
888-957-1100
http://www.laufinancial.com
jlau@laufinancial.com

W & H and Associates, LLC
Marol Liguori
3280 E. Foothill Boulevard,
  Suite 130
Pasadena, CA 91107
626-304-2888
http://www.lpl.com/kelly.bob
marol@sbcglobal.net

Leisure Werden & Terry Agency
Peter Lopez, RFC
200 S. Los Robles Avenue,
  Suite 200
Pasadena, CA 91101
626-304-1300, ext. 231
peterlopez@lwtagency.com

Veritas Advisory
George E. Mahoney
5075 S. Bradley Road, Suite 235
Santa Maria, CA 93455
805-934-7117
http://www.veritasadvisory.com
george@veritasadvisory.com

QRS & Associates
Dennis N. Mainard, CFP®
11770 Bernardo Plaza Court,
  Suite 205

San Diego, CA 92128
858-546-9991
http://www.discerninginvestor.
  com
dennis@discerninginvestor.com

Jefferson Pilot Financial
Glenn A. McKinney
1 World Trade Center, Suite 800
Long Beach, CA 90831-0800
562-983-8164
http://www.glennmckinney.com
glennmckinney@msn.com

John Padilla, CSA
5420 Chester Street
Los Angeles, CA 90032
213-364-3449
ten31@msn.com

Merrill Lynch
Gary J. Sampson, CFP®
5080 California Avenue,
  Suite 102
Bakersfield, CA 93309
800-937-0722, ext. 756
gary_sampson@ml.com

Cliff Slaten, EA, CSA, CAA
501 N. Brookhurst Street,
  Suite 318
Anaheim, CA 92801
800-698-2560

Taylor Wealth Management
Douglas E. Taylor, CFP®, CPA
600 Avenue D
Redondo Beach, CA 90277
310-995-8803
http://taylorwealthmanagement.
  com
doug@taylorwm.com

W & H and Associates, LLC
Kelly Waring, CFP®

3280 E. Foothill Boulevard,
Suite 130
Pasadena, CA 91107
626-304-2888
http://www.lpl.com/kelly.bob
kwaring@sbcglobal.net

Terrie Will, EA, CSA, CAA
501 N. Brookhurst Street,
Suite 318
Anaheim, CA 92801
800-698-2560

COLORADO

Fred A. Barbeito, CLU, ChFC
1775 Sherman Street, Suite 2700
Denver, CO 80203
303-860-7519
fbarbeito@rmininc.com

C. Chance Carson & Associates
C. Chance Carson
5373 N. Union Boulevard,
Suite 101
Colorado Springs, CO 80918
719-268-0800
chance.carson@intervestintl.com

Chambers & Associates
John M. Chambers
225 N. 5th Street, Suite 520
Grand Junction, CO 81501
888-540-8655
http://www.chambersand
associates.com
john@chambersandassociates.
com

Dasgupta & Perron
Sanjoy Dasgupta
5445 DTC Parkway, Penthouse 4
Greenwood Village, CO 80111
303-486-6984

http://www.dasgupta-perron.com
sanjoy@dasgupta-perron.com

Hallmark Consulting Group, Inc.
Don Hartmann
2121 South Oneida Street,
Suite 248
Denver, CO 80224
303-756-8900
http://www.hallmarkconsulting.
com
dhartmann@hallmarkconsulting.
com

Dasgupta & Perron
Susan Perron
5445 DTC Parkway, Penthouse 4
Greenwood Village, CO 80111
303-486-6984
http://www.dasgupta-perron.com
sue@dasgupta-perron.com

Safe Money Solutions, Inc.
Les Simpson
6900 W. Grant Ranch Boulevard,
#61
Littleton, CO 80123
303-579-6881
les520@earthlink.net

CONNECTICUT

John E. Ackerman, CPA
John E. Ackerman, CPA, CFP®,
CLU, ChFC, CSA
1204 Durham Road
Guilford, CT 06437
203-453-8825
jeabilly@comcast.net

David Gagnon, CPA, CFS,
RFC, CSA
17 Wall Street
PO Box 1070

Madison, CT 06443
877-245-0017
http://www.davidgagnonplanning.
   com
davegagnoncpa@netscape.net

Warner Financial Group
James W. Warner
2 Trap Falls Road, Suite 105
Shelton, CT 06484
203-929-5999
james.warner@lpl.com

Warner Financial Group, Inc.
William F. Warner, CFP®, ChFC,
   RFC, CSA, LUTCF
2 Trap Falls Road, Suite 105
Shelton, CT 06484
203-464-4966
william.warner@lpl.com

FLORIDA

Wealth Preservation Group
Susan L. Ames, CLU, ChFC
800 Fairway Drive, Suite 370
Deerfield Beach, FL 33441
954-354-1183
slames@inc.com

Eugene D. Ashman, CPA/PFS,
   ChFC
Eugene D. Ashman
1366 Pinehurst Drive, Suite 1366
Spring Hill, FL 34606
352-666-5557
edacpa@yahoo.com

Baron Silver Stevens, Financial
   Advisors, LLC
Howard Baron
5555 Anglers Avenue, Suite 1B
Ft. Lauderdale, FL 33312
954-962-3332

http://www.bssfa.com
hsbaron@bssfa.com

Classic Tax and Financial
   Services, LLC
Paul P. Belshaw, CSA
2107 W. Cass Street, Suite B
Tampa, FL 33606-1233
813-258-6446
http://www.classictaxes.com
pbelshaw@classictaxes.com

Certified Financial Group, Inc.
Joseph F. Bert, CFP®
1111 Douglas Avenue
Altamonte Springs, FL 32714
407-869-9800
http://www.financialgroup.com
joe@financialgroup.com

Alan H. Blecker, CLU, ChFC,
   CFP®, CPA/PFS
3111 University Drive, Suite 901
Coral Springs, FL 33065
954-796-3833
bleckera@bellsouth.net

Dennis Martino & Associates/
   Raymond James Financial
   Services, Inc.
John A. Bozza, CPA
362 Scotland Street
Dunedin, FL 34698
727-738-6101
john.bozza@raymondjames.com

Douglas A. Brown
2020 NW 150th Avenue
Pembroke Pines, FL 33028
954-538-4424
dbrown@p1cu.org

Bill Burns
151 Mary Esther Boulevard,
   Suite 407

Mary Esther, FL 32569
850-244-8933
burnsb@insuranceconsultants.net

Julia Burns
151 Mary Esther Boulevard,
  Suite 407
Mary Esther, FL 32569
850-244-8933
burnsj@insuranceconsultants.net

Stuart Financial Group
James P. Chiras, CFP®, CSA
7000 SE Federal Highway,
  Suite 303
Stuart, FL 34997
772-221-7933
http://www.stuartfinancialgroup.
  com
jchiras@stuartfinancialgroup.com

Earl & Associates/NFP Securities
Paul E. Cloutier
1120 Belcher Road South
Largo, FL 33771
727-532-9995
pcloutier@earlandassociates.com

Financial Planning for Life's
  Transitions
Luana Mobley Corral, CFP®,
  CFS, CLTC
2699 Stirling Road, Suite A200
Ft. Lauderdale, FL 33312
954-983-5600, ext. 19
http://www.lmcorral.com
luana@lmcorral.com

IMS Partners, Inc.
Julie M. Decker
5240 Babcock Street NE,
  Suite 218
Palm Bay, FL 32905
321-837-0741

http://www.imsagency.com
julie@imsagency.com

Raymond James Financial
  Services, Inc.
David Fontaine, Financial
  Advisor, CSA
9010 SW 137th Avenue,
  Suite 231
Miami, FL 33186
305-386-7667
http://www.dfontaine.com
david.fontaine@raymondjames.
  com

JB Hanauer & Co.
Richard A. Freiman, CFP®,
  CPA, EVP
704 E. Hallandale Beach
  Boulevard
Hallendale Beach, FL 33009
954-458-4900
http://www.jbh.com
rfreiman@jbh.com

Senior Benefit Group of FL, Inc.
Bill Heiman
240 N. Washington Boulevard,
  Suite 400
Sarasota, FL 34236
941-952-0030
vettedad1@aol.com

David Hixson
16100 NE 16th Avenue, Suite B
North Miami Beach, FL 33162
305-944-7001, ext. 207
davidh@hmdcpa.com

Sycamore Group, Inc.
Wally Mackey, RFC, CSA,
  President
10419 Croy Lake Drive
Tampa, FL 33647

813-986-6500
http://www.sycamoregroupinc.
  com
sycamoregr@aol.com

SenioResources Group, Inc.
Mark E. Nichols, CSA
4700 Tamiami Trail North, Suite 6
Naples, FL 34103
239-263-7333
messagedepot@ureach.com

Advanced Estate Services
Michael M. Niedbala, CES,
  CEP, MBA
3982 Wellington Parkway
Palm Harbor, FL 34685
727-773-9688
http://www.advanced
  estateservices.com
mniedbala@verizon.net

Retirement Services
Harold J. Rogers, CFP®, CSA
8596 Arlington Expressway
Jacksonville, FL 32211
904-725-0556
hal@retserv.net

Baron Silver Stevens, Financial
  Advisors, LLC
Michael J. Silver, CFP®, CLU
5555 Anglers Avenue, Suite 1B
Ft. Lauderdale, FL 33312
954-962-3332
http://www.bssfa.com
msilver@bssfa.com

Smithsonian Group
Larrye A. Smith
160 NW 176th Street, Suite 205
Miami, FL 33169
305-790-3200
larryeasmith@aol.com

GEORGIA

Merrill Lynch Retirement
  Group
Michael Breyel, CRPC
333 North Point Center East
Alpharetta, GA 30022
770-360-6067
michael_breyel@ml.com

Capital Planning
R. Leslie Hammock, RFC, CSA
PO Box 8108
Warner Robins, GA 31095
478-329-0339
http://www.retirebydesign.com
leslie@cpwealth.com

Planning Concepts of Ga., Inc.
Frank M. Miller, CLU
6467 Wright Circle NE
Atlanta, GA 30328
404-851-1810
shakeloose@aol.com

Morgan Stanley
Steven J. Moore, CIMA
950 E. Paces Ferry Road,
  Suite 2700
Atlanta, GA 30326
404-365-3650
steven.moore@morganstanley.
  com

BPC Financial Advisors
Ray P. O'Connell, CSA
300 Park Brooke Place,
  Suite 320
Woodstock, GA 30189
770-592-4800
http://www.bpcfa.com
ray@bpcfa.com

IDAHO

The H Group, Inc.
Chyrle Pinkerton, CFP®
5995 W. State Street, Suite B
Boise, ID 83703
208-853-7770
http://www.thehgroup.com
cpink@spro.net

ILLINOIS

Richard Barr & Associates
Richard G. Barr
318 W. Half Day Road,
    Suite 333
Buffalo Grove, IL 60089
847-634-0072
http://www.barr-gneuhs.com
dick@barrfinancial.com

Nardulli Tax Advisory Group
Jim Blanchard, CSA
33 Higgins Road, Suite 510
South Barrington, IL 60010
847-519-7925
jim@ntag-tax.com

Rey Cruz, Inc.
Rey Cruz, CFP®
151 S. Lincoln Avenue
Aurora, IL 60505
630-897-0333
http://www.reycruz.com
money_mgr@msn.com

Frank Advisory Services
Michael Frank, CPA, CFP®
501 W. Main Street
St. Charles, IL 60174
630-513-1337
http://www.lpl.com/michael.frank
michael.frank@lpl.com

Lighthouse Financial Group, Inc.
John S. Groleau
2 Hankes Road, Suite A
Aurora, IL 60506
630-859-2633
jgroleau@summitbrokerage.com

Guthoff, Mehall, Allen & Co.,
    PC
Ronald R. Guthoff, President
2710 E. Lincoln Street
Bloomington, IL 61702
309-662-4356
http://www.guthoff.com
rguthoff@guthoff.com

Byron Bank Financial Services
Gene Hartzell, CFP®
200 N. Walnut Street
Byron, IL 61010
815-234-4075
eugene.hartzell@uvestmail.com

AMIC
John Herzog, CSA, CEPC
21104 Washington Parkway
Frankfort, IL 60423
815-464-1730
john_herzog@hotmail.com

Kovacic Financial Assoc., Inc.
William F. Kovacic, CFP®
7480 W. College Drive,
    Suite 102
Palos Heights, IL 60463
708-923-1290
wfkcfp@aol.com

Lubkeman Investment Group
Marc R. Lubkeman, CFP®
505 Orchard Street, Suite 100
Antioch, IL 60002
847-838-3167
marc.lubkeman@wachoviasec.com

C & M Financial Group, Inc.
Curtis D. Mase, CEPP, CEP, CSA
176 Rosin Street
Glen Carbon, IL 62034
618-288-2392
mrfixit62034@yahoo.com

McNeily & Associates
Thomas E. McNeily
15 Salt Creek Lane, Suite 122
Hinsdale, IL 60521
800-592-2064
tommcneily@msn.com

Maureen O'Hearn, CSA
333 Chatelaine Court
Willowbrook, IL 60527
630-654-8106
mohcsa@aol.com

AXA Advisors
John Passananti
1415 W. 22nd Street, Suite 330
Oak Brook, IL 60523
630-575-5000
john.passananti@axa-advisors.
   com

Porrey Leslie & Associates, LLC
Michael A. Porrey, Jr.
410 W. Grand Avenue
Chicago, IL 60610
312-923-8700
http://www.lpl.com/porrey.leslie
mike.porrey@lpl.com

JR Investment Group
John Russell
PO Box 1484
Decatur, IL 62525
217-877-4841
http://www.jrinvestmentgroup.
   com
5jer2@msn.com

AXA Advisors
Tom Wells, ChFC, CLU
1415 W. 22 Street, Suite 330
Oakbrook, IL 60523
630-954-6854
thomas.wells@axa-advisors.com

INDIANA

Hufford Financial Advisors, LLC
Roy C. Bodinus
10333 N. Meridian Street,
   Suite 475
Indianapolis, IN 46290
317-848-4987
http://www.huffordfinancial.com
rbodinus@huffordfinancial.com

American Express Financial
   Advisors
Thomas M. Calkusic, CFP®,
   CRPC
650 Morthland Drive, Suite D
Valparaiso, IN 46385
219-548-5969, ext. 24
http://advisors.americanexpress.
   com/thomas.x.calkusic
thomas.x.calkusic@aexp.com

Martin James, CPA, PC
Martin E. James, CPA
PO Box 503
410 N. Monroe Street #20
Mooresville, IN 46158
317-834-2276
http://www.mjamescpa.com
mjames@mjamescpa.com

Roy Keibler
4222 Grant Line Road
New Albany, IN 47150
812-948-9288
rlkeib@juno.com

Asset Preservation Group, LLC
Ronald D. Scherer
815 Airport North Office Park
Fort Wayne, IN 46825
800-505-9988
assetpg@csinet.net

Integrated Educators
Brian L. Smith
1316 Eagle Ridge Drive
Schererville, IN 46375
219-864-5050
http://www.integratededucators.
    com
bsmith@integratededucators.com

Asset Preservation Group, LLC
Patrick J. Steinke
815 Airport North Office Park
Fort Wayne, IN 46825
800-505-9988
assetpg@csinet.net

IOWA

Freeman Financial Services
Dennis L. Freeman, CLU, ChFC,
    CSA
2966 Monroe Drive
Ames, IA 50010
515-663-9600
dennis@freemanagency.net

Piper Jaffray
Richard Hinson
4150 Westown Parkway
West Des Moines, IA 50266
515-440-7655
http://www.pjc.com
richard.c.hinson@pjc.com

Tarkenton Financial, LLC
William H. Hurlin

375 Collins Road NE, Suite 108
Cedar Rapids, IA 52402
319-247-1200
http://www.tarkentonfinancial.
    com/start/whurlin
whurlin@tarkentonfinancial.com

NelsonCorp Wealth Management
David Nelson, CFP®, CLU,
    ChFC, CFS
4007 E. 53rd Street, Suite 300
Davenport, IA 52807
536-823-0532
http://www.nelsoncorp.com
david.nelson@lpl.com

CSB Advisors
Ken Wilson
817 N. Ankeny Boulevard
Ankeny, IA 50021
515-252-1278
http://www.bankcsb.com
kwilson@bankcsb.com

KANSAS

Professional Planning Services,
    Inc.
Scott A. Emley, CFP®, CLU
    ChFC
4809 Vue Du Lac Place,
    Suite 105
Manhattan, KS 66503
785-776-9118
http://www.4ppsinc.com
ppsscott@networksplus.net

Eagle Financial Group
Christopher M. Heller, CSA
12501 Antioch Road, Suite 102
Overland Park, KS 66213
913-851-1900
cheller@eaglefinancial1.com

Kramer Capital Management
Richard G. Kramer, CFP®
601 Leavenworth Street
Manhattan, KS 66502
785-539-0110
http://www.rickkramer.com

Logan & Kilp, Inc.
Ken Logan, CPA/PFS, CFP®, MS
12900 Metcalf Avenue, Suite 160
Overland Park, KS 66213
913-648-0330
ken@logan-kilp.com

Van Schaffer
3310 Mesa Way, Suite 101
Lawrence, KS 66049
785-843-7070
vschaffer@sunflower.com

Capital Enhancement Advisory
Ken E. Stowell, Jr., President,
  CLU, CFCA, CSA
9001 W. 110th Street, Suite 250
Overland Park, KS 66210
913-696-9800
kstowell@capitalenhancement
  advisory.com

LOUISIANA

Merrill Lynch Retirement Group
Michael Breyel, CRPC
372 Stonehaven Drive
Manderville, LA 70471
504-723-0870
michael_breyel@ml.com

Burke & Burke Insurance
  Marketing, Inc.
Chip Burke
8848 Youree Drive
Shreveport, LA 71115

318-798-7556
chip@burkeandburke
  insurance.com

Senior Health & Financial
  Group, LLC
Anthony Cangemi
1409 Hesper Drive
Metairie, LA 70005
800-830-0655
ajcangemi@cox.net

Raymond James Financial
  Services, Inc.
Linda Laborde Deane, CFP®,
  CRC, CEA, RFC
1100 Poydras Street, Suite 2065
New Orleans, LA 70163
504-582-2345
http://www.lindadeane.com
linda.deane@raymond
  james.com

SunAmerica Securities
Diana DeCharles, CFP®, MBA
2020 Line Avenue
Shreveport, LA 71104
318-221-7526
http://www.sunamericadirect.com
ddecharles@hotmail.com

Hotard Financial Services
M. Jeannette Hotard, CFP®
504 Wedgewood Drive
Bossier City, LA 71111
318-752-8981
hotard9760@bellsouth.net

Sun Life Financial
T.J. Semmes Hughs, CLU
212 Tchefuncte Parc Court
Madisonville, LA 70447
985-792-1318
hught@sunlife.com

Investment Professionals, Inc.
Sheila Maciasz
2002 False River Drive
New Roads, LA 70760
225-638-6051
http://www.invpro.com
sheilamaciasz@hotmail.com

McDaniel Financial
Ernest V. McDaniel
2001 E. 70th Street, Suite 407
Shreveport, LA 71105
318-798-9022
http://www.mcdaniel2004.com
emcdan9145@aol.com

JCN Retirement and Tax
   Advisory Group
John C. Neyland
13700 Coursey Boulevard,
   Building 4, Suite C
Baton Rouge, LA 70816
225-324-7722
jncgroup@cox.net

MetLife Financial Services
Frederick J. Yeager, CFP®, CLU,
   ChFC, CLTC
3838 N. Causeway Boulevard,
   Suite 3400
Metairie, LA 70002
504-613-2323
http://www.fredyeager.
   metlife.com
fyeager@metlife.com

MARYLAND

Mary K. Ameling, CSA, CLTC
11891 Lexington Drive
Dunkirk, MD 20754
410-257-6739
marlar20@juno.com

Ronald B. Caballero & Assoc.
Ronald B. Caballero, CLU
2100 Tanglewood Drive
Waldorf, MD 20601
888-775-3425
http://www.advtaxstrategies.com
rcaballero@advtaxstrategies.com

Jim Cantwell
1751 Elton Road, Suite 114
Silver Spring, MD 20903
301-408-2441
http://www.cantwellfinancial.com
taxsav2000@aol.com

Smith Barney
Tony Comer
7272 Wisconsin Avenue, Fourth
   Floor
Bethesda, MD 20814
301-657-6313
anthony.c.comer@smithbarney.
   com

Eagle Strategies Corp.
Brian L. Hardman, CLU
6901 Rockledge Drive, Suite 800
Bethesda, MD 20817
301-214-6672
blhtaxfree@aol.com

Wealth Management Strategies
Michael Lightfield
10480 Little Patuxent Parkway,
   Suite 400
Columbia, MD 21044
410-379-6611
http://www.mikelightfield.com
mike@mikelightfield.com

Middleton Gardiner Group, LLC
Jay Middleton, ChFC
570 Baltimore Annapolis
   Boulevard
Severna Park, MD 21446

410-647-7777
http://www.mggllc.com
jay@middletongardiner
  group.com

MASSACHUSETTS

Bradley Advisory Group, Inc.
John J. Bradley, CLU
Crown Colony
100 Congress Street
Quincy, MA 02169
617-774-1112
jack@bradadvgrp.com

Tom D. Fielding, CPA
46 Suffield Street
Agawam, MA 01001
413-786-5982
tdfcpapc@worldnet.att.net

UMassFive/CUSO Financial
  Services
Craig Layman
200 Westgate Center Drive
Hadley, MA 01035
413-256-5569
http://www.umassfive.org
clayman@umassfive.org

MICHIGAN

Fairhaven Financial Advisory
  Corp.
Joseph R. Brooks
1400 Abbott Road, Suite 330
East Lansing, MI 48823
517-332-2900
http://www.fairhavenfinancial.com
info@fairhavenfinancial.com

Lifetime Investment Mgmt., LLC
Ellie Deskin

363 W. Big Beaver Road,
  Suite 125
Troy, MI 48084
248-457-1215
http://lifetimeinvestment
  management.com
elliedeskin@prodigy.net

American Express Financial
Thomas Lampert, CFP®, CHFC
230 N. Second Street, Suite 100
Brighton, MI 48116
810-229-8700
http://www.americanexpress.com
thomas.a.lampert@aexp.com

Fiduciary Review Services
John E. Mayer, CFP®, MSFS,
  AIFA®
6815 Minnow Pond Drive
West Bloomfield, MI 48322
800-452-4983
http://www.fiduciaryreview.com
jemayer@fiduciaryreview.com

Hallbrook Asset Planning and
  Management
Lawrence M. McCoy, CSA
1992 Perry Street
Holland, MI 49424-2421
616-399-9757
lmmccoy@chartermi.net

Plan 4 Financial Design
Skip Nissen, MBA, CFP®, CSA
1803 Whites Road
Kalamazoo, MI 49008
800-600-2554
http://www.plan4fin.com
snissen@jasnetworks.net

Randy Redley & Associates
Randolph Redley, CSA, CEP
PO Box 672
Southfield, MI 48037-0672

248-352-1753
http://www.randyredley.com
rredleyandassoc@webtv.net

The Wellington Financial
   Strategies Corp.
Bryan Ulatowski
515 Clinton Avenue
St. Clair, MI 48079
810-329-5220
http://www.wellington
   investments.com
bryan@wellingtoninvestments.
   com

Strategic Financial Solutions,
   Inc.
Shawn Weera, President
7479 Old Lantern Drive
Caledonia, MI 49316
616-437-3412
weeralegal@aol.com

MINNESOTA

Springtime Associates
Mel Sommers, CSA
8680 Magnolia Trail, Suite 309
Eden Prairie, MN 55344
612-282-0200
msommersl@mn.rr.com

MISSOURI

Wendy W. Dietrich
7733 Forsyth Boulevard, Suite 600
St. Louis, MO 63105
314-889-9132
wendy.dietrich@sbcglobal.net

Financial Solutions & Assoicates.,
   Inc.
Michael Grimes, CRPC

12400 Olive Boulevard,
   Suite 202
St. Louis, MO 63141
877-212-1400
mgrimes@finsolinc.net

Financial Security Investment
   Advisors
Bud Kasper, CFP®
211A NW Executive Way
Lee's Summit, MO 64063
816-554-3736
http://www.retirement
   master.com
bud@retirementmaster.com

Logan & Kilp, Inc.
Mary Joe Kilp
14825 E. 42nd Street
Independence, MO 64055
816-373-7100
maryjoe@logan-kilp.com

C & M Financial Group, Inc.
Curtis D. Mase, CEPP, CEP,
   CSA
117 Main Street, Suite G
Festus, MO 63028
877-343-1878
mrfixit62034@yahoo.com

Berthel Fisher & Co. Financial
   Services, Inc.
Kerry J. Niece
4700 S. Cedar Crest Court,
   Suite 1100
Independence, MO 64055
816-478-9570
http://www.kansascity
   financialplanners.com
kjniece1@swbell.net

LTC Asset Management
   Consultants
Alan V. Niemi, CSA, GEPC

923 NE Woods Chapel Road,
Suite 143
Lee's Summit, MO 64064
816-373-6941
http://www.ltcassetmanagement.
com
aeniemi@msn.com

Strategic Financial Advisors
Robert S. Olsen, CPA, President
300 Chesterfield Center, Suite 100
Chesterfield, MO 63017
636-537-2506
rolsen@robertolsenonline.com

NEBRASKA

Boyle, Hess & Elliott, PC
Thomas Hosier
617 N. 90th Street
Omaha, NE 68114-2821
402-393-1850
http://www.bhecpa.com
tom@bhecpa.com

Benefit Planning Specialist, Inc.
Marvin R. Souchek
770 N. Cotner Boulevard,
Suite 100
Lincoln, NE 68505
402-434-5937
http://www.marvinsouchek.com
msouchek@mscmail.biz

NEVADA

Wealth Architects, LLC
Curtis W. Campbell
500 Damonte Ranch Parkway,
Suite 860
Reno, NV 89521
775-829-6800

http://www.wealth-architects.com
cwc@wealth-architects.com

Heritage Financial Place, Inc.
Darel T. Crosby, CSA
7251 Lake Mead Boulevard,
Suite 300
Las Vegas, NV 89128
800-867-2838
http://www.heritagefinancial
place.com

Wealth Architects, LLC
Gerald M. Dorn, Esq.
500 Damonte Ranch Parkway,
Suite 860
Reno, NV 89521
775-823-9455
jerry@wealth-counselors.com

Butterfield Financial Service, Inc.
Barry Lindsay
4335 Woodcrest Road
Las Vegas, NV 89121
888-668-2962
http://www.bfsi.org
barryl63@hotmail.com

Heritage Financial Place, Inc.
J. Blake Taylor, CFP®, ChFC,
RFC, CSA, LUTCF
7251 Lake Mead Boulevard,
Suite 300
Las Vegas, NV 89128
800-867-2838
http://www.heritagefinancial
place.com

NEW HAMPSHIRE

Equity Planning Partners, LLC
Ronald Lague
25 Warner Hill Road
Derry, NH 03038

603-898-1300
r.lague@comcast.net

NEW JERSEY

MetLife
Ash Ahluwalia
65 Jackson Drive, Third Floor
Cranford, NJ 07016
908-497-2601
http://www.wealthpg.com
aahluwalia@metlife.com

Bellmare Financial Group
Gary A. Borowiec, CLU, ChFC
21 Commerce Drive
Cranford, NJ 07016
908-272-8819
gborowiec@bellmarefg.com

Bellmare Financial Group
David Buckwald, CFP®
21 Commerce Drive
Cranford, NJ 07016
908-653-7292 or
   908-347-2707
http://www.davidbuckwald.
   com
dbuckwal@bellmarefg.com

The Legacy Group, Ltd.
Martin E. Ellner, CSA, CLU,
   ChFC
1 Greentree Centre, Suite 201
Marlton, NJ 8053
856-751-0373
lgcygroup@aol.com

Walter Golczewski
63 Butternut Drive
Wayne, NJ 07470
973-835-6255
walter@wjgenterprises.com

Couch Braunsdorf Senior
   Resources
Stephen B. Leitzell, CLU, ChFC,
   CFP®, CSA
701 Martinsville Road
PO Box 888
Liberty Corner, NJ 07938
800-223-5433, ext. 398
http://www.cbsenior.com
sleitzell@couchbraunsdorf.com

PFC Planned Financial Concepts,
   Inc.
Judith Panos, CLU/CEO
65 Willowbrook Boulevard,
   First Floor
Wayne, NJ 07470-7053
973-812-6933
jpanos@planningalliance.com

Senior Resources of New Jersey,
   Inc.
Lawrence D. Schuffman, CFP®,
   CFBS, CLTC, CLU
6 Timber Lane
Randolph, NJ 07869
973-366-8929
lschuffman@finsvcs.com

NEW MEXICO

Terri Berrenberg, CFP®
5801 Osuna Road NE,
   Suite A109
Albuquerque, NM 87109
505-797-3200
http://www.terriberrenberg.com
berrenbreg@qwest.net

Financial Blueprinting
Peggy Cook, VP
3200 Carlisle NE, Suite 224A
Albuquerque, NM 87110

505-980-8117
cfu@thuntek.net

Multi-financial Securities Corp.
Lee F. Courtright, CFP®
6121 Indian School Road, NE,
    Suite 101
Albuquerque, NM 87110
505-883-2600
lcourti@coredcs.com

Waddell & Reed
Fran McCarty, CFP®
6000 Uptown Boulevard,
    Suite 220
Albuquerque, NM 87110
505-888-7944, ext. 115
fmccarty@comcast.net

The Oxford Group, LLC
William Robertson, CSA
4200 Meadowlark Lane,
    Suite 1B
Rio Rancho, NM 87144
505-891-9800
wrobertson@srnm.net

The Stein Law Firm
Stuart L. Stein
City Place—Suite 2200
2155 Louisiana Boulevard NE
Albuquerque, NM 87110
505-889-0100
http://www.steinlawfirm.com
info@steinlawfirm.com

Zlotnick, Laws & Sandoval, PC
David Zlotnick, CPA
1 Calle Medico
Sante Fe, NM 87505
505-982-3894

NEW YORK

Eastern Planning, Inc.
Matt Blecker, CFP®
400 Rella Boulevard, Suite 175
Suffern, NY 10901-4249
845-369-0657
bleck319@aol.com

Retirement Planning Group
Daniel J. Bouchard, CLU, CHFC
24 Century Hills Boulevard
Latham, NY 12110
800-342-3867
dbouchard@metlife.com

Farm Family Insurance
Kevin J. Cantwell
356 Middle Country Road,
    Suite 206
Coram, NY 11727
631-696-7353
Kevin_cantwell@farmfamily.com

Quest Capital Management
S. Joseph DiSalvo, ChFC, CSA
58 North Country Road, Suite 2
Smithtown, NY 11787
631-724-3933
jdisalvo@optonline.net

Halliday Financial Group
Andrew W. Halliday
16 Corporate Woods Boulevard,
    Suite 203
Albany, NY 12211
518-463-2200
http://www.hallidayfinancial.com
ahalliday@hallidayfinancial.com

i Financial Plan, Inc.
Christopher Imerti
308 Grand Street
Croton-on-Hudson, NY 10520

646-261-1782
http://www.ifinancialplan.com
info@ifinancialplan.com

Dover Financial Group
Phillip Lubitz
300 Garden City Plaza
Garden City, NY 11530
516-747-4500, ext. 138
lillyfoo2@verizon.net

EBM Financial Services
Elke B. Mariotti, CFP®, CSA,
  CDFA, LUTCF
174 Corey Place
Huntington Station, NY 11746
631-367-9390
iraspecialist@hotmail.com

Resourceful Financial
  Management, Inc.
Robert F. Matt, CPA/PFS
421 New Karner Road,
  Suite 11
Albany, NY 12205
518-452-6950
rfmatt@rfm-inc.net

MetLife Rochester Financial
  Group
Paul Provenzano
400 Meridian Centre,
  Suite 101
Rochester, NY 14618
585-241-5240
http://www.rochester
  financialgroup.com
pprovenzano@metlife.com

Wilma Sheridan & Associates
Wilma Sheridan
8 Leroy Court
Commack, NY 11725-1703
631-543-4774
wilmasheridan@optonline.net

NORTH CAROLINA

Gerald B. Ahern, CFP®
Gerald B. Ahern
19209 Spring Lilly Court
Cornelius, NC 28031
704-896-8663
http://www.retincome.com
gerry.ahern@retincome.com

Cynthia Block-Taylor & Assoc.
Cynthia Block-Taylor, RFC,
  CSA
5605 Carnegie Boulevard,
  Suite 150
Charlotte, NC 28209
704-926-3424
cblocktaylor@mony.com

Jefferson Pilot Financial
Penni Foust, CLU, ChFC, RFC,
  LUTCF
100 N. Greene Street
Greensboro, NC 27401
336-691-3331
penni.foust@jpfinancial.com

Syndicated Capital, Inc.
Dan Gallagher, MBA, CLU,
  ChFC, CFP®, CBI
7124 Colleton Place
Charlotte, NC 28270
704-362-1001
http://www.dan-is-4u.com

The Estate Group
Morton P. Hansen
6015 Farrington Road,
  Suite 101
Chapel Hill, NC 27517
919-913-1140
mhansen@eg-dc.com

CGK Associates
C. Glenn Keller

79 Kuykendall Road
Alexander, NC 28701
828-658-3158
scatk@aol.com

Asset Protectors & Advisors
Tom McDermott
1130 Situs Court, Suite 200
Raleigh, NC 27606
919-851-0846
apa@guaranteedsafe.com

Carl B. Pitcock & Assoc.
Carl B. Pitcock, CSA
PO Box 814
Madison, NC 27025
336-548-3185
http://www.carl-pitcock-
    certifiedsenioradvisor.com
carlpcsa@aol.com

Dr. Richard Pucciarelli, CSA
9584 Blossom Hill Drive
Huntersville, NC 28078
704-453-6196
http://www.helpmeplan.com/csb
helpmeplan@bellsouth.net

Jefferson Pilot Financial
James Williams, Manager,
    Advanced Sales
100 N. Greene Street
Greensboro, NC 27401
336-691-3857
jim.williams@jpfinancial.com

OHIO

Senior Estate Advisors
Thomas Becker, CSA
7490 Bunker Ridge Court
Blacklick, OH 43004
614-863-0893
tbecker@insight.rr.com

American Express Financial
    Advisors
Robert R. Beckham, MBA, CPA,
    Registered Principal
5217 Monroe Street, Suite AAA
Toledo, OH 43623
419-882-1948
http://www.americanexpress.com/
    advisor
robert.r.beckham@aexp.com

Reliance Financial Services
David Bell, CRSP
401 Clinton Street
Defiance, OH 43512
419-783-8825
http://www.reliancefs.com
belld.rfs@rurban.net

Caes Financial Services
Timothy L. Caes, CLU, ChFC,
    CSA
77 W. Elmwood Drive, Suite 211
Dayton, OH 45459
937-886-0114

The Senior Connection, LLC
Martin W. Collins
7374 Reading Road, Suite 125
Cincinnati, OH 45237
513-631-0772

First Financial Resources, Inc.
Rao Garuda, CLU, ChFC
2 Summit Park Drive, Suite 350
Cleveland, OH 44131
800-255-6086
raogaruda@aol.com

Cynthia L. Hardman, CFP®
Cynthia L. Hardman
17800 Chillicothe Road,
    Suite 200
Chagrin Falls, OH 44023
440-543-0858

American Express Financial Advisors, Inc.
Deborah Linscott
655 Metro Place South, Suite 570
Dublin, OH 43017
800-770-7611
deborah.l.linscott@aexp.com

AXA Advisors, LLC
Andrew Maimona, CFP®
575 White Pond Drive, Suite A
Akron, OH 44320
330-865-0011, ext. 17
andrew.maimona@axa-advisors.com

Legend Financial Group
Lochlainn Ohaimhirgin, CSA,
  GEPC
2778 Som Center Road
Willoughby Hills, OH 44094
440-944-3600
http://www.legendfinancial.com
loh@legendfinancial.com

Michael Phillips & Associates
Michael Phillips, CLU, ChFC
2252 Ravine Woods Drive
Grove City, OH 43123
614-801-9006
michael.j.phillips@aexp.com

Capital Investment Advisors
Julia Sawyer, ChFC
8076 Beechmont Avenue
Cincinnati, OH 45255
513-231-7115
http://www.cialink.com
juliasawyer@fuse.net

Matoaka Money Management,
  Inc.
Edwin Paul Strickling
PO Box 9

Kings Mills, OH 45034-0009
513-677-6114
http://www.matoakamm.com
ed_strickling@earthlink.net

Pierce Financial Group/Legacy
  Financial Services
W. Scott Zerkle
2698 Sawbury Boulevard
Columbus, OH 43235
614-889-8761
szerkle1@hotmail.com

OKLAHOMA

Burns Advisory Group
John Burns
9401 Cedar Lake Avenue
Oklahoma City, OK 73114
405-478-1971
jburns@burnsag.com

Wachovia Securities
David K. Guier, CFP®
2431 E. 61st Street, Suite 400
Tulsa, OK 74136
918-742-8000
david.guier@wachoviasec.com

McAbee & Company, PC
Mitch McAbee, CPA
1000 Frisco Avenue
Clinton, OK 73601
580-323-5252
http://www.mcabeecompany.com
mitch@mcabeecompany.com

PENNSYLVANIA

Your Money Matters, Estate &
  Tax Advisory Group
Kellie Marie Dinich

301 W. Grove Street
Clarks Summit, PA 18411
800-729-1564
yourmoneymatters@epix.net

Your Money Matters, Estate &
Tax Advisory Group
Kellie Marie Dinich
830 N. Elmira Street
Sayre, PA 18840
800-729-1564
yourmoneymatters@epix.net

Your Money Matters, Estate &
Tax Advisory Group
Michael Andrew Dinich
301 W. Grove Street
Clarks Summit, PA 18411
800-729-1564
yourmoneymatters@epix.net

Your Money Matters, Estate &
Tax Advisory Group
Michael Andrew Dinich
830 N. Elmira Street
Sayre, PA 18840
800-729-1564
yourmoneymatters@epix.net

Your Money Matters, Estate &
Tax Advisory Group
Michael R. Dinich
301 W. Grove Street
Clarks Summit, PA 18411
800-729-1564
yourmoneymatters@epix.net

Your Money Matters, Estate &
Tax Advisory Group
Michael R. Dinich
830 N. Elmira Street
Sayre, PA 18840
800-729-1564
yourmoneymatters@epix.net

DiNuzzo Investment Advisors,
Inc.
Mark S. DiNuzzo, VP,
Financial Planning
1501 Third Street
Beaver, PA 15009
724-728-6564
http://www.dinuzzo.com
mdinuzzo@dinuzzo.com

DiNuzzo Investment Advisors,
Inc.
P. J. DiNuzzo, President
1501 Third Street
Beaver, PA 15009
724-728-6564
http://www.dinuzzo.com
mdinuzzo@dinuzzo.com

Legacy Retirement Services
Joy E. Fiester
151 John Brandy Drive, Suite 1
Muncy, PA 17756
570-546-6904
jfiester5@cs.com

Gollner & Associates, Inc.
David Gollner
490 N. Kerwood Drive, Suite 205
Hermitage, PA 16148-5202
800-264-4963
info@gollnerandassociates.com

Inevitable Wealth Consulting
Brendan Magee
8242 West Chester Pike
Upper Darby, PA 19082
610-446-4322
brendangee5@aol.com

McCann Financial Services
Pat McCann, CSA
1040-2 Benner Pike
State College, PA 16801

888-811-0841
http://www.mccannfinancial
  services.com
mccannp@adelphia.net

GDM Advisory Group, Ltd.
Glenn D. Meyer, President
123 Old York Road, Suite 200
Jenkintown, PA 19046
215-886-5800
http://www.gdmplan.com
glenn@gdmplan.com

Santori & Peters, Private Wealth
  Management
Maria E. Peters
3824 Northern Pike, Suite 330
Monroeville, PA 15146
412-373-6904
http://www.santoriandpeters.com
maria@santoriandpeters.com

Santori & Peters, Private Wealth
  Management
Norman J. Santori
3824 Northern Pike, Suite 330
Monroeville, PA 15146
412-373-6904
http://www.santoriandpeters.com
skip@santoriandpeters.com

Richard Thompson
210 Kerry Lane
Blue Bell, PA 19422
215-619-9988
http://www.positivewealth.com
richard@positivewealth.com

SOUTH CAROLINA

The Fields Law Firm, PA
Pete Fields
110 Liberty Drive, Suite 202
Clemson, SC 29631

864-877-8962
http://www.thefieldslawfirm.com
pete@thefieldslawfirm.com

The McDaniel Corporation
Craig M. McDaniel, CFP®
6156 Street Andrews Road,
  Suite 108
Columbia, SC 29212
803-750-4848
craigmcdaniel@bellsouth.net

Roy E. Miller
150 Spalding Circle
Goose Creek, SC 29445
843-824-9109
rmill3@comcast.net

Service Financial
Terry Lee Piper
4233 Ellis Drive
Little River, SC 29566
843-249-8083
terrypipr@yahoo.com

The Carolinas Planning Group,
  LLC
Dr. Kevin Skipper, ChFC, RFC
115 Atrium Way, Suite 102
Columbia, SC 29223
803-788-2030
http://www.carolinaplan.com
kskipper@carolinaplan.com

SOUTH DAKOTA

KT Investment Advisors, LLC
Jean Kostenbader, CPA
829 Quincy Street, Suite B
Rapid City, SD 57701
605-342-8840
http://www.ktllp.com
jeank@ktllp.com

TENNESSEE

Seniors Advisement Group
Carol Hawkins
821 Parksville Road
Benton, TN 37307
877-338-6710
http://www.carolhawkinsltc.com
info@ocoee-mist.com

Estate & Financial Strategies, Inc.
Hank Parrott
783 Old Hickory Boulevard,
    Suite 100
Brentwood, TN 37027
800-892-4102
http://www.seniorfinancialcoach.
    com
efsinc@bellsouth.net

TEXAS

Corpus Christi Financial Group
Deborah Anderson
555 N. Carancahua Street,
    Suite 790
Corpus Christi, TX 78478
361-882-8700
http://www.ccfinancialgroup.com
danderson@ccfinancialgroup.com

Barbara Barton
3416 Melanie Lane
Plano, TX 75023
972-208-1995
http://www.babarton.com
babarton@aol.com

Byron Boyd & Associates
Byron Boyd
8710 Ilona Road, Suite 3
Houston, TX 77025
832-778-1992
boyd2004@sbcglobal.net

Forrest and Manning Learning
Forrest Marshall Brown
3102 Oak Lawn Avenue,
    Suite 700
Dallas, TX 75219
214-560-2266
http://www.nesteggclass.com
marshall@nesteggclass.com

Rosenthal Retirement Planning
Jeff Carlton
100 W. 15th Street, Suite 100
Fort Worth, TX 76102
817-336-2000
http://www.rosenthalretirement.
    com
jeff@rosenthalretirement.com

BEH Advisory Group, Inc.
Donna L. Clark, CPA, CFP®,
    CSA
111 Soledad Street, Suite 830
San Antonio, TX 78205
210-226-8847
donna.clark@bexarenergy.com

Allen Cornwall
104 King Lance Street
Scroggins, TX 75480
903-860-3314
acorn@peoplescom.net

Financial & Retirement Planning
    Services of America
Richard S. Crabtree, CSA, RFA
3506 Vista Oaks Drive
Garland, TX 75043-6240
800-789-9442
http://www.financialplanning
    america.com
rcrabtree10@yahoo.com

Crouch Financial Services
Victoria Crouch
6859 Richwood Road

Houston, TX 77087
713-649-5014
vickic2881@sbcglobal.net

Crow, Mackey & Company
Richard Crow, CPA, CFP®
1516 E. Palm Valley Boulevard,
    Suite A2
Round Rock, TX 78664
512-255-7110
racrowcpa@swbell.net

Guy B. Garner, III, PC, Attorney
    at Law
Guy B. Garner, III
1101 W. Randol Mill Road
Arlington, TX 76012
817-261-5222
ggarner1@swbell.net

Carter & Gibson Tax Service
Richard L. Gibson, EA
1200 E. Collins Boulevard,
    Suite 114
Richardson, TX 75081
972-234-2212
http://www.cartergibson.com
rlgibson@cartergibson.com

Seniors First
Sue Grady
8903 Blankenship Drive
Houston, TX 77080
713-722-7777
sue@wordabuse.com

Strategic Advisory Services, LP
Dick Grbac, CFP®
5850 San Felipe Street,
    Suite 425
Houston, TX 77057
713-977-3800
http://www.askstrategicadvisory.
    com
dick@sasoffice.com

Action Advisors, Inc.
Emory Guest
5005 Mitchelldale Street,
    Suite 174
Houston, TX 77027
713-680-0509
http://www.actionadvisors.net
eguest@actionadvisors.net

Wylie Insurance Agency, Inc.
Donald G. Hallum, CLU, ChFC
PO Box 40
Wylie, TX 75098
972-442-3505
http://www.wylieinsurance.com
don@wylieinsurance.com

D. H. Hill Advisors, Inc.
Dan H. Hill, President
19747 Highway 59 North,
    Suite 101
Humble, TX 77338
281-446-0422
http://www.dhhillfinancial.com
dan@dhhill.com

Beneflex Financial Group
Jerry W. Hill
Atrium 10 Tower
11811 E. Freeway, Suite 410
Houston, TX 77029
713-455-7087
http://www.beneflexfinancial.com
jerry@beneflexfinancial.com

Merrill Lynch
Bobby W. Huff, CFP®
1221 McKinney Street,
    Suite 3900
Houston, TX 77010
713-658-1414
bobby_huff@ml.com

Security Financial Group
Greg Humphreys

1330 Post Oak Boulevard,
  Suite 1900
Houston, TX 77056
281-345-2502
http://www.gwhumphreys.
  nylagents.com
greghumphreys@sbcglobal.net

Wise$Counsel
Robert W. Huntley, CFP®, ChFC
5870 Highway 6 North,
  Suite 209
Houston, TX 77084
281-858-0000
http://www.wisecounsel-inc.com
wise.counsel@lpl.com

Advanced Financial Services
Jimmy Jeansonne, CFP®
797 W. Gibson Street
Jasper, TX 75951
409-384-5713
afsjimmy@sbcglobal.net

Frost Brokerage Services, Inc.
Steven G. Lea
1300 South Main Street
Boerne, TX 78006-2802
830-249-6609
http://www.frostbank.com
steve.lea@frostbank.com

ICS
Alisa LeSueur
800 NW Loop 410 at Blanco
  Road
North Tower, Suite 210
San Antonio, TX 78216
210-377-0623
txtophat@mail.com

New York Life
Rick Lucas
12201 Merit Drive, Suite 1000

Dallas, TX 75251
972-387-2929
rlucas29@sbcglobal.net

Jordan Financial Group, Inc.
Byron P. Jordan, MBA, CFP®
15303 Huebner Road, Building 7
San Antonio, TX 78248
210-692-8844
http://www.byronjordan.com
byron@byronjordan.com

Frost Bank
William C. Mays, Asst. VP,
  Investment Services
802 N. Carancahua Street
Corpus Christi, TX 78470
361-844-1136
william.mays@frostbank.com

Frost Brokerage Services
Urbin McKeever
777 Main Street
Fort Worth, TX 76102
817-420-5071
http://www.frostbank.com
urbin.mckeever@frostbank.com

William C. Quinton, CPA, CFP®,
  MPA
Bill Quinton
5934 S. Staples Street, Suite 203
Corpus Christi, TX 78413
361-992-8303
wquinton@wcquinton.com

Randy Redley & Associates
Randolph Redley, CSA, CEP
2500 Citywest Boulevard,
  Suite 300
Houston, TX 77042
713-267-2323
http://www.randyredley.com
rredleyandassoc@webtv.net

Legacy Private Asset Managers
Nathan Reneau, CPA, CFP®
186 S. Castell Avenue
New Braunfels, TX 78130
830-624-7265
nreneau@satx.com

Financial Distribution &
   Insurance Systems, Inc.
James Schmidt
3010 LBJ Freeway, Suite 1200
Dallas, TX 75234
800-281-9180
schmidt@sbcglobal.net

MCA Financial
Tim Starkey
4017 Edgehill Road
Fort Worth, TX 76116
817-313-8139
timstarkey@charter.net

Financial Vision Group
Robert Theisen
4704 Highway 377 South,
   Suite 300
Fort Worth, TX 76116
817-696-8400
http://www.financialvisiongroup.
   com
robb@financialvisiongroup.com

Puritan Financial Group, Inc.
Sam Thomas
16901 N. Dallas Parkway,
   Suite 214
Addison, TX 75001
972-380-1119
http://www.puritanfinancial
   group.com
sthomas@puritangroup.com

Frost Bank
Jerry Willborn, VP Investment
   Services

800 NW Loop 410, Suite 100N
San Antonio, TX 78216
210-220-6301
jwillborn@frostbank.com

Nationwide
Travis Wilson
811 Emerald Sound Boulevard
Oak Point, TX 75068
214-455-6785
http://www.bestofamerica.com
wilson3@nationwide.com

Corpus Christi Financial Group
W. Joe Wilson, CFP®
555 N. Carancahua Street,
   Suite 790
Corpus Christi, TX 78478
361-882-8700
http://www.wjoewilson.com
jwilson@wjoewilson.com

UTAH

Beneficial Financial Group
Gregory M. Butler, CSA
6985 Union Park Center,
   Suite 600
Midvale, UT 84047
800-251-4213
http://www.senior-resources.info
greg.butler@benfinancial.com

Heritage Financial Place, Inc.
Darel T. Crosby, CSA
9055 S. 1300 East, Suite 110
Sandy, UT 84094
800-867-2838
http://www.heritagefinancial
   place.com
heritage@aros.net

Gregson Tax Advisory Group, Inc.
Greg Gregson, CSA

3385 Harrison Boulevard, Suite 1
Ogden, UT 84403
801-621-5553
cplanner@relia.net

Beneficial Life
Gary R. Robinson, CLU
3549 N. University Avenue,
Suite 200
Provo, UT 84604
801-375-2266
robinson@networld.com

Mutual Service Corp.
Paul A. Smith
145 N. Main Street, Suite E
Bountiful, UT 84010
801-299-1600
plsmith@qwest.net

Heritage Financial Place, Inc.
J. Blake Taylor, CFP®, CHFC,
RFC, CSA, LUTCF
9055 S. 1300 East, Suite 110
Sandy, UT 84094
800-867-2838
http://www.heritage
financialplace.com
heritage@aros.net

State Farm Insurance
Justin Zlotnick
1444 N. Highway 89, Suite 240
Farmington, UT 84025
801-451-2997
justin.zlotnick.nyx7@
statefarm.com

VIRGINIA

Scott & Stringfellow, Inc.
Michael D. Ball
9113 Church Street
Manassas, VA 20110

703-368-4970
http://www.scottstringfellow.com
mball@scottstringfellow.com

Ronald B. Caballero & Associates
Ronald B. Caballero, CLU
5419 Governor Yeardley Drive
Fairfax, VA 22032
888-775-3425
http://www.advtaxstrategies.com
rcaballero@advtaxstrategies.com

Senior Strategies
Charles R. Cobb
1022 Court Street
Lynchburg, VA 24504
434-845-6655
ccobb@ntelos.net

Scott & Stringfellow, Inc.
Lee T. Hammack
909 E. Main Street
Richmond, VA 23219
478-329-0339
http://www.scottstringfellow.com
lhammack@scottstringfellow.com

Hartquist, Meisel & Noblet, Ltd.
Nora L. Hartquist
15 Francis Court
Stafford, VA 22554
540-659-0300
http://www.solution4you.com
nora@solution4you.com

Huff, Stuart & Carlton
Rick Huff, CPA
2107 Graves Mill Road, Suite C
Forest, VA 24551
434-316-9356
http://www.wealthmgt.net
rick@wealthmgt.net

Michael H. Spencer, CLU, ChFC,
CSA

4305 Bonney Road
Virginia Beach, VA 23452
757-498-3462
eligah57@cox.net

Douglas A. Stewart, CSA
Douglas A. Stewart, CSA
429 Saint Ivy Avenue
Troy, VA 22974
434-589-3138
http://www.stewartcsa.com
dstewartcsa@direcway.com

Zelman Tax Advisory Group, Inc.
Stanley S. Zelman, CFP®, CSA
4121 Plank Road, Suite 211
Fredericksburg, VA 22407
540-972-3630
financialplan@adelphi.net

WASHINGTON

Eads Financial, Inc.
Ray Eads, MFSF, MBA, CSA
19221 36th Avenue West,
    Suite 201
Lynnwood, WA 98036
800-296-9010
http://www.eadsfinancial.com
ray@eadsfinancial.com

Jang & Associates
Garold Jang
1529 240th Place SW
Bothell, WA 98021
425-483-5433
http://www.myfinancialarchitect.
    com
gary@myfinancialarchitect.com

Ragen MacKenzie Investment
    Services
Patrick J. McDevitt, CFP®

10740 Meridian Avenue North,
    Suite 107
Seattle, WA 98133
206-363-4355
pmcdevitt1@comcast.net

WEST VIRGINIA

JFP
Gary C. Thompson, CSA, RFP
PO Box 4324
2100 42nd Street
Parkersburg, WV 26104
304-422-7599
http://www.garythompson
    financialadvisors.com
gct@charter.net

WISCONSIN

Multi-Financial Securities Corp.
Lee F. Courtright, CFP®, ChFC,
    CSA
720 S. Maple Bluff Court
Stevens Point, WI 54481-9240
715-344-6300
http://www.courtrightadvisory.
    com

Crispigna Financial Services
Steve P. Crispigna
2131 S. Webster Avenue
Green Bay, WI 54301
920-435-4800
crispigna@itol.com

Daniel P. Hyland, LLC
Daniel P. Hyland, CFP®
49 Kessel Court, Suite 104
Madison, WI 53711
608-276-9691
dan.hyland@siionline.com

Extended Personal Services, Ltd.
Denise A. Jaenke, CSA, CLTC,
  CEPP
3000 North Highway BB
Columbus, WI 53925
800-296-2563, ext. IRAA (4722)
http://www.epsltc.com
jaehnke@internetwis.com

Kowal Investment Group/
  SunAmerica Securities
Jeffrey D. Kowal, CHFC, CLU,
  President
12700 W. Bluemound Road
Elm Grove, WI 53122
262-784-6240
http://www.kowalinvestment
  group.com
jkowal@kowalinvestmentgroup.
  com

Financial Independance Network
David M. Leist
15643 W. Brook Drive
New Berlin, WI 53151
262-796-0030
http://www.fin-moneycenter.com
dleist2@wi.rr.com

Winch Advisory Services
Christina V. Winch, CFP®,
  President
424 E. Wisconsin Avenue
Appleton, WI 54911
920-739-8577
http://www.winchadvisory
  services.com
info@winchadvisoryservices.com

Resources That Make for Top-Notch IRA Advisors

Expert IRA advisors need resources like anybody else to advance their knowledge in this highly specialized area. I use them all the time. These are the best and, I believe, *a minimum requirement for any IRA advisor you select* to help you parlay your IRA into a fortune.

Internet Resources

- www.leimbergservices.com. I rely on this site—LISI (Leimberg Information Services, Inc.)—from the brilliant Stephan Leimberg and his cadre of professional experts to keep me up-to-date on a daily basis on tax, retirement, and estate planning issues and rulings. So should your IRA advisor. Monthly fee: $19.95.

Newsletters

- *Ed Slott's IRA Advisor*™ newsletter. Any advisor will tell you that there is no other source of monthly IRA information and updates for advisors. IRA rules seem to change on almost a weekly basis; advisors can't keep up with them all, so I do it for them. If your advisor is not receiving this kind of timely IRA distribution planning information, you should not hand your IRA over to him or her. The newsletter can be ordered online at www.irahelp.com or by phone at 800-663-1340. Subscription cost: $125 a year.

Reference Guides

- *Life and Death Planning for Retirement Benefits* by attorney and IRA expert Natalie B. Choate, Esq., of Bingham McCutchen, LLP, Boston, Massachusetts. This is the bible on IRA distribution planning. Natalie is a brilliant colleague, and her book is a must for all advisors who wish to be seriously considered IRA experts. If your advisor does not have this book, find another advisor. (Ataxplan Publications, 2003; $89.95 plus $7 shipping); call 800-247-6553 or visit www.ataxplan.com.

Software

- NumberCruncher, an estate and financial planning program created by Stephan R. Leimberg and Robert T. LeClair that is essential for every financial advisor. I used this program for the estate, income tax, and compound interest computations in this book. NumberCruncher includes a financial planning module in addition to the estate planning module. It's the only program IRA advisors need to put real numbers on any type of planning situation. It includes every imaginable tax and financial planning calculation. It sells for $395 (plus shipping and handling) and can be ordered at www.leimberg.com.

- Pension & Roth IRA Analyzer by Brentmark Software. Any serious IRA expert should have some type of software. I use this because it's the best. Advisors who wish to offer expert IRA advice and counsel to their clients use this program. All the amazing (almost magical) exponential compounding opportunities of the stretch IRA illustrated in this book derive from projections made with this software. I cannot imagine helping clients parlay their IRAs without it. It provides a written goal—a long-term wealth-building plan in black and white—that IRA owners and beneficiaries can shoot for and stick with. Available from Brentmark Software, at www.brent mark.com, or call 800-879-6665. Cost: $395 for a single user license (includes six months of maintenance; thereafter annual maintenance is $129). One of Brentmark's most popular programs, the Pension & Roth IRA Analyzer helps you plan distributions from qualified pension plans. This program handles virtually all aspects of distribution planning: minimum distributions, pre-59½ distributions, splitting of inherited IRAs, Roth IRA conversions, spousal rollovers, income taxes, estate taxes, IRD calculations—even life insurance and donee-exclusion gifting. All results are presented in fully customizable color reports and 3-D graphs.

Uniform Lifetime Table

Age of IRA Owner or Plan Participant	Life Expectancy (in Years)	Age of IRA Owner or Plan Participant	Life Expectancy (in Years)
70	27.4	93	9.6
71	26.5	94	9.1
72	25.6	95	8.6
73	24.7	96	8.1
74	23.8	97	7.6
75	22.9	98	7.1
76	22.0	99	6.7
77	21.2	100	6.3
78	20.3	101	5.9
79	19.5	102	5.5
80	18.7	103	5.2
81	17.9	104	4.9
82	17.1	105	4.5
83	16.3	106	4.2
84	15.5	107	3.9
85	14.8	108	3.7
86	14.1	109	3.4
87	13.4	110	3.1
88	12.7	111	2.9
89	12.0	112	2.6
90	11.4	113	2.4
91	10.8	114	2.1
92	10.2	115+	1.9

IRS Joint Life Expectancy Tables

Joint Life and Last Survivor Expectancy
(For Use by Owners Whose Spouses Are
More Than 10 Years Younger)

Ages	0	1	2	3	4	5	6	7	8	9
0	90.0	89.5	89.0	88.6	88.2	87.8	87.4	87.1	86.8	86.5
1	89.5	89.0	88.5	88.1	87.6	87.2	86.8	86.5	86.1	85.8
2	89.0	88.5	88.0	87.5	87.1	86.6	86.2	85.8	85.5	85.1
3	88.6	88.1	87.5	87.0	86.5	86.1	85.6	85.2	84.8	84.5
4	88.2	87.6	87.1	86.5	86.0	85.5	85.1	84.6	84.2	83.8
5	87.8	87.2	86.6	86.1	85.5	85.0	84.5	84.1	83.6	83.2
6	87.4	86.8	86.2	85.6	85.1	84.5	84.0	83.5	83.1	82.6
7	87.1	86.5	85.8	85.2	84.6	84.1	83.5	83.0	82.5	82.1
8	86.8	86.1	85.5	84.8	84.2	83.6	83.1	82.5	82.0	81.6
9	86.5	85.8	85.1	84.5	83.8	83.2	82.6	82.1	81.6	81.0
10	86.2	85.5	84.8	84.1	83.5	82.8	82.2	81.6	81.1	80.6
11	85.9	85.2	84.5	83.8	83.1	82.5	81.8	81.2	80.7	80.1
12	85.7	84.9	84.2	83.5	82.8	82.1	81.5	80.8	80.2	79.7
13	85.4	84.7	84.0	83.2	82.5	81.8	81.1	80.5	79.9	79.2
14	85.2	84.5	83.7	83.0	82.2	81.5	80.8	80.1	79.5	78.9
15	85.0	84.3	83.5	82.7	82.0	81.2	80.5	79.8	79.1	78.5
16	84.9	84.1	83.3	82.5	81.7	81.0	80.2	79.5	78.8	78.1
17	84.7	83.9	83.1	82.3	81.5	80.7	80.0	79.2	78.5	77.8
18	84.5	83.7	82.9	82.1	81.3	80.5	79.7	79.0	78.2	77.5
19	84.4	83.6	82.7	81.9	81.1	80.3	79.5	78.7	78.0	77.3
20	84.3	83.4	82.6	81.8	80.9	80.1	79.3	78.5	77.7	77.0
21	84.1	83.3	82.4	81.6	80.8	79.9	79.1	78.3	77.5	76.8
22	84.0	83.2	82.3	81.5	80.6	79.8	78.9	78.1	77.3	76.5
23	83.9	83.1	82.2	81.3	80.5	79.6	78.8	77.9	77.1	76.3
24	83.8	83.0	82.1	81.2	80.3	79.5	78.6	77.8	76.9	76.1
25	83.7	82.9	82.0	81.1	80.2	79.3	78.5	77.6	76.8	75.9
26	83.6	82.8	81.9	81.0	80.1	79.2	78.3	77.5	76.6	75.8

Joint Life and Last Survivor Expectancy *(continued)*

Ages	0	1	2	3	4	5	6	7	8	9
27	83.6	82.7	81.8	80.9	80.0	79.1	78.2	77.4	76.5	75.6
28	83.5	82.6	81.7	80.8	79.9	79.0	78.1	77.2	76.4	75.5
29	83.4	82.6	81.6	80.7	79.8	78.9	78.0	77.1	76.2	75.4
30	83.4	82.5	81.6	80.7	79.7	78.8	77.9	77.0	76.1	75.2
31	83.3	82.4	81.5	80.6	79.7	78.8	77.8	76.9	76.0	75.1
32	83.3	82.4	81.5	80.5	79.6	78.7	77.8	76.8	75.9	75.0
33	83.2	82.3	81.4	80.5	79.5	78.6	77.7	76.8	75.9	74.9
34	83.2	82.3	81.3	80.4	79.5	78.5	77.6	76.7	75.8	74.9
35	83.1	82.2	81.3	80.4	79.4	78.5	77.6	76.6	75.7	74.8
36	83.1	82.2	81.3	80.3	79.4	78.4	77.5	76.6	75.6	74.7
37	83.0	82.2	81.2	80.3	79.3	78.4	77.4	76.5	75.6	74.6
38	83.0	82.1	81.2	80.2	79.3	78.3	77.4	76.4	75.5	74.6
39	83.0	82.1	81.1	80.2	79.2	78.3	77.3	76.4	75.5	74.5
40	82.9	82.1	81.1	80.2	79.2	78.3	77.3	76.4	75.4	74.5
41	82.9	82.0	81.1	80.1	79.2	78.2	77.3	76.3	75.4	74.4
42	82.9	82.0	81.1	80.1	79.1	78.2	77.2	76.3	75.3	74.4
43	82.9	82.0	81.0	80.1	79.1	78.2	77.2	76.2	75.3	74.3
44	82.8	81.9	81.0	80.0	79.1	78.1	77.2	76.2	75.2	74.3
45	82.8	81.9	81.0	80.0	79.1	78.1	77.1	76.2	75.2	74.3
46	82.8	81.9	81.0	80.0	79.0	78.1	77.1	76.1	75.2	74.2
47	82.8	81.9	80.9	80.0	79.0	78.0	77.1	76.1	75.2	74.2
48	82.8	81.9	80.9	80.0	79.0	78.0	77.1	76.1	75.1	74.2
49	82.7	81.8	80.9	79.9	79.0	78.0	77.0	76.1	75.1	74.1
50	82.7	81.8	80.9	79.9	79.0	78.0	77.0	76.0	75.1	74.1
51	82.7	81.8	80.9	79.9	78.9	78.0	77.0	76.0	75.1	74.1
52	82.7	81.8	80.9	79.9	78.9	78.0	77.0	76.0	75.0	74.1
53	82.7	81.8	80.8	79.9	78.9	77.9	77.0	76.0	75.0	74.0
54	82.7	81.8	80.8	79.9	78.9	77.9	76.9	76.0	75.0	74.0
55	82.6	81.8	80.8	79.8	78.9	77.9	76.9	76.0	75.0	74.0
56	82.6	81.7	80.8	79.8	78.9	77.9	76.9	75.9	75.0	74.0
57	82.6	81.7	80.8	79.8	78.9	77.9	76.9	75.9	75.0	74.0
58	82.6	81.7	80.8	79.8	78.8	77.9	76.9	75.9	74.9	74.0
59	82.6	81.7	80.8	79.8	78.8	77.9	76.9	75.9	74.9	74.0

Joint Life and Last Survivor Expectancy *(continued)*

Ages	0	1	2	3	4	5	6	7	8	9
60	82.6	81.7	80.8	79.8	78.8	77.8	76.9	75.9	74.9	73.9
61	82.6	81.7	80.8	79.8	78.8	77.8	76.9	75.9	74.9	73.9
62	82.6	81.7	80.7	79.8	78.8	77.8	76.9	75.9	74.9	73.9
63	82.6	81.7	80.7	79.8	78.8	77.8	76.8	75.9	74.9	73.9
64	82.5	81.7	80.7	79.8	78.8	77.8	76.8	75.9	74.9	73.9
65	82.5	81.7	80.7	79.8	78.8	77.8	76.8	75.8	74.9	73.9
66	82.5	81.7	80.7	79.7	78.8	77.8	76.8	75.8	74.9	73.9
67	82.5	81.7	80.7	79.7	78.8	77.8	76.8	75.8	74.9	73.9
68	82.5	81.6	80.7	79.7	78.8	77.8	76.8	75.8	74.8	73.9
69	82.5	81.6	80.7	79.7	78.8	77.8	76.8	75.8	74.8	73.9
70	82.5	81.6	80.7	79.7	78.8	77.8	76.8	75.8	74.8	73.9
71	82.5	81.6	80.7	79.7	78.7	77.8	76.8	75.8	74.8	73.8
72	82.5	81.6	80.7	79.7	78.7	77.8	76.8	75.8	74.8	73.8
73	82.5	81.6	80.7	79.7	78.7	77.8	76.8	75.8	74.8	73.8
74	82.5	81.6	80.7	79.7	78.7	77.8	76.8	75.8	74.8	73.8
75	82.5	81.6	80.7	79.7	78.7	77.8	76.8	75.8	74.8	73.8
76	82.5	81.6	80.7	79.7	78.7	77.8	76.8	75.8	74.8	73.8
77	82.5	81.6	80.7	79.7	78.7	77.7	76.8	75.8	74.8	73.8
78	82.5	81.6	80.7	79.7	78.7	77.7	76.8	75.8	74.8	73.8
79	82.5	81.6	80.7	79.7	78.7	77.7	76.8	75.8	74.8	73.8
80	82.5	81.6	80.7	79.7	78.7	77.7	76.8	75.8	74.8	73.8
81	82.4	81.6	80.7	79.7	78.7	77.7	76.8	75.8	74.8	73.8
82	82.4	81.6	80.7	79.7	78.7	77.7	76.8	75.8	74.8	73.8
83	82.4	81.6	80.7	79.7	78.7	77.7	76.8	75.8	74.8	73.8
84	82.4	81.6	80.7	79.7	78.7	77.7	76.8	75.8	74.8	73.8
85	82.4	81.6	80.6	79.7	78.7	77.7	76.8	75.8	74.8	73.8
86	82.4	81.6	80.6	79.7	78.7	77.7	76.7	75.8	74.8	73.8
87	82.4	81.6	80.6	79.7	78.7	77.7	76.7	75.8	74.8	73.8
88	82.4	81.6	80.6	79.7	78.7	77.7	76.7	75.8	74.8	73.8
89	82.4	81.6	80.6	79.7	78.7	77.7	76.7	75.8	74.8	73.8
90	82.4	81.6	80.6	79.7	78.7	77.7	76.7	75.8	74.8	73.8
91	82.4	81.6	80.6	79.7	78.7	77.7	76.7	75.8	74.8	73.8
92	82.4	81.6	80.6	79.7	78.7	77.7	76.7	75.8	74.8	73.8

Joint Life and Last Survivor Expectancy *(continued)*

Ages	0	1	2	3	4	5	6	7	8	9
93	82.4	81.6	80.6	79.7	78.7	77.7	76.7	75.8	74.8	73.8
94	82.4	81.6	80.6	79.7	78.7	77.7	76.7	75.8	74.8	73.8
95	82.4	81.6	80.6	79.7	78.7	77.7	76.7	75.8	74.8	73.8
96	82.4	81.6	80.6	79.7	78.7	77.7	76.7	75.8	74.8	73.8
97	82.4	81.6	80.6	79.7	78.7	77.7	76.7	75.8	74.8	73.8
98	82.4	81.6	80.6	79.7	78.7	77.7	76.7	75.8	74.8	73.8
99	82.4	81.6	80.6	79.7	78.7	77.7	76.7	75.8	74.8	73.8
100	82.4	81.6	80.6	79.7	78.7	77.7	76.7	75.8	74.8	73.8
101	82.4	81.6	80.6	79.7	78.7	77.7	76.7	75.8	74.8	73.8
102	82.4	81.6	80.6	79.7	78.7	77.7	76.7	75.8	74.8	73.8
103	82.4	81.6	80.6	79.7	78.7	77.7	76.7	75.8	74.8	73.8
104	82.4	81.6	80.6	79.7	78.7	77.7	76.7	75.8	74.8	73.8
105	82.4	81.6	80.6	79.7	78.7	77.7	76.7	75.8	74.8	73.8
106	82.4	81.6	80.6	79.7	78.7	77.7	76.7	75.8	74.8	73.8
107	82.4	81.6	80.6	79.7	78.7	77.7	76.7	75.8	74.8	73.8
108	82.4	81.6	80.6	79.7	78.7	77.7	76.7	75.8	74.8	73.8
109	82.4	81.6	80.6	79.7	78.7	77.7	76.7	75.8	74.8	73.8
110	82.4	81.6	80.6	79.7	78.7	77.7	76.7	75.8	74.8	73.8
111	82.4	81.6	80.6	79.7	78.7	77.7	76.7	75.8	74.8	73.8
112	82.4	81.6	80.6	79.7	78.7	77.7	76.7	75.8	74.8	73.8
113	82.4	81.6	80.6	79.7	78.7	77.7	76.7	75.8	74.8	73.8
114	82.4	81.6	80.6	79.7	78.7	77.7	76.7	75.8	74.8	73.8
115+	82.4	81.6	80.6	79.7	78.7	77.7	76.7	75.8	74.8	73.8

Joint Life and Last Survivor Expectancy
(For Use by Owners Whose Spouses Are
More Than 10 Years Younger)

Ages	10	11	12	13	14	15	16	17	18	19
10	80.0	79.6	79.1	78.7	78.2	77.9	77.5	77.2	76.8	76.5
11	79.6	79.0	78.6	78.1	77.7	77.3	76.9	76.5	76.2	75.8
12	79.1	78.6	78.1	77.6	77.1	76.7	76.3	75.9	75.5	75.2
13	78.7	78.1	77.6	77.1	76.6	76.1	75.7	75.3	74.9	74.5

Joint Life and Last Survivor Expectancy *(continued)*

Ages	10	11	12	13	14	15	16	17	18	19
14	78.2	77.7	77.1	76.6	76.1	75.6	75.1	74.7	74.3	73.9
15	77.9	77.3	76.7	76.1	75.6	75.1	74.6	74.1	73.7	73.3
16	77.5	76.9	76.3	75.7	75.1	74.6	74.1	73.6	73.1	72.7
17	77.2	76.5	75.9	75.3	74.7	74.1	73.6	73.1	72.6	72.1
18	76.8	76.2	75.5	74.9	74.3	73.7	73.1	72.6	72.1	71.6
19	76.5	75.8	75.2	74.5	73.9	73.3	72.7	72.1	71.6	71.1
20	76.3	75.5	74.8	74.2	73.5	72.9	72.3	71.7	71.1	70.6
21	76.0	75.3	74.5	73.8	73.2	72.5	71.9	71.3	70.7	70.1
22	75.8	75.0	74.3	73.5	72.9	72.2	71.5	70.9	70.3	69.7
23	75.5	74.8	74.0	73.3	72.6	71.9	71.2	70.5	69.9	69.3
24	75.3	74.5	73.8	73.0	72.3	71.6	70.9	70.2	69.5	68.9
25	75.1	74.3	73.5	72.8	72.0	71.3	70.6	69.9	69.2	68.5
26	75.0	74.1	73.3	72.5	71.8	71.0	70.3	69.6	68.9	68.2
27	74.8	74.0	73.1	72.3	71.6	70.8	70.0	69.3	68.6	67.9
28	74.6	73.8	73.0	72.2	71.3	70.6	69.8	69.0	68.3	67.6
29	74.5	73.6	72.8	72.0	71.2	70.4	69.6	68.8	68.0	67.3
30	74.4	73.5	72.7	71.8	71.0	70.2	69.4	68.6	67.8	67.1
31	74.3	73.4	72.5	71.7	70.8	70.0	69.2	68.4	67.6	66.8
32	74.1	73.3	72.4	71.5	70.7	69.8	69.0	68.2	67.4	66.6
33	74.0	73.2	72.3	71.4	70.5	69.7	68.8	68.0	67.2	66.4
34	73.9	73.0	72.2	71.3	70.4	69.5	68.7	67.8	67.0	66.2
35	73.9	73.0	72.1	71.2	70.3	69.4	68.5	67.7	66.8	66.0
36	73.8	72.9	72.0	71.1	70.2	69.3	68.4	67.6	66.7	65.9
37	73.7	72.8	71.9	71.0	70.1	69.2	68.3	67.4	66.6	65.7
38	73.6	72.7	71.8	70.9	70.0	69.1	68.2	67.3	66.4	65.6
39	73.6	72.7	71.7	70.8	69.9	69.0	68.1	67.2	66.3	65.4
40	73.5	72.6	71.7	70.7	69.8	68.9	68.0	67.1	66.2	65.3
41	73.5	72.5	71.6	70.7	69.7	68.8	67.9	67.0	66.1	65.2
42	73.4	72.5	71.5	70.6	69.7	68.8	67.8	66.9	66.0	65.1
43	73.4	72.4	71.5	70.6	69.6	68.7	67.8	66.8	65.9	65.0
44	73.3	72.4	71.4	70.5	69.6	68.6	67.7	66.8	65.9	64.9
45	73.3	72.3	71.4	70.5	69.5	68.6	67.6	66.7	65.8	64.9
46	73.3	72.3	71.4	70.4	69.5	68.5	67.6	66.6	65.7	64.8

Joint Life and Last Survivor Expectancy *(continued)*

Ages	10	11	12	13	14	15	16	17	18	19
47	73.2	72.3	71.3	70.4	69.4	68.5	67.5	66.6	65.7	64.7
48	73.2	72.2	71.3	70.3	69.4	68.4	67.5	66.5	65.6	64.7
49	73.2	72.2	71.2	70.3	69.3	68.4	67.4	66.5	65.6	64.6
50	73.1	72.2	71.2	70.3	69.3	68.4	67.4	66.5	65.5	64.6
51	73.1	72.2	71.2	70.2	69.3	68.3	67.4	66.4	65.5	64.5
52	73.1	72.1	71.2	70.2	69.2	68.3	67.3	66.4	65.4	64.5
53	73.1	72.1	71.1	70.2	69.2	68.3	67.3	66.3	65.4	64.4
54	73.1	72.1	71.1	70.2	69.2	68.2	67.3	66.3	65.4	64.4
55	73.0	72.1	71.1	70.1	69.2	68.2	67.2	66.3	65.3	64.4
56	73.0	72.1	71.1	70.1	69.1	68.2	67.2	66.3	65.3	64.3
57	73.0	72.0	71.1	70.1	69.1	68.2	67.2	66.2	65.3	64.3
58	73.0	72.0	71.0	70.1	69.1	68.1	67.2	66.2	65.2	64.3
59	73.0	72.0	71.0	70.1	69.1	68.1	67.2	66.2	65.2	64.3
60	73.0	72.0	71.0	70.0	69.1	68.1	67.1	66.2	65.2	64.2
61	73.0	72.0	71.0	70.0	69.1	68.1	67.1	66.2	65.2	64.2
62	72.9	72.0	71.0	70.0	69.0	68.1	67.1	66.1	65.2	64.2
63	72.9	72.0	71.0	70.0	69.0	68.1	67.1	66.1	65.2	64.2
64	72.9	71.9	71.0	70.0	69.0	68.0	67.1	66.1	65.1	64.2
65	72.9	71.9	71.0	70.0	69.0	68.0	67.1	66.1	65.1	64.2
66	72.9	71.9	70.9	70.0	69.0	68.0	67.1	66.1	65.1	64.1
67	72.9	71.9	70.9	70.0	69.0	68.0	67.0	66.1	65.1	64.1
68	72.9	71.9	70.9	70.0	69.0	68.0	67.0	66.1	65.1	64.1
69	72.9	71.9	70.9	69.9	69.0	68.0	67.0	66.1	65.1	64.1
70	72.9	71.9	70.9	69.9	69.0	68.0	67.0	66.0	65.1	64.1
71	72.9	71.9	70.9	69.9	69.0	68.0	67.0	66.0	65.1	64.1
72	72.9	71.9	70.9	69.9	69.0	68.0	67.0	66.0	65.1	64.1
73	72.9	71.9	70.9	69.9	68.9	68.0	67.0	66.0	65.0	64.1
74	72.9	71.9	70.9	69.9	68.9	68.0	67.0	66.0	65.0	64.1
75	72.8	71.9	70.9	69.9	68.9	68.0	67.0	66.0	65.0	64.1
76	72.8	71.9	70.9	69.9	68.9	68.0	67.0	66.0	65.0	64.1
77	72.8	71.9	70.9	69.9	68.9	68.0	67.0	66.0	65.0	64.1
78	72.8	71.9	70.9	69.9	68.9	67.9	67.0	66.0	65.0	64.0
79	72.8	71.9	70.9	69.9	68.9	67.9	67.0	66.0	65.0	64.0

Joint Life and Last Survivor Expectancy *(continued)*

Ages	10	11	12	13	14	15	16	17	18	19
80	72.8	71.9	70.9	69.9	68.9	67.9	67.0	66.0	65.0	64.0
81	72.8	71.8	70.9	69.9	68.9	67.9	67.0	66.0	65.0	64.0
82	72.8	71.8	70.9	69.9	68.9	67.9	67.0	66.0	65.0	64.0
83	72.8	71.8	70.9	69.9	68.9	67.9	67.0	66.0	65.0	64.0
84	72.8	71.8	70.9	69.9	68.9	67.9	67.0	66.0	65.0	64.0
85	72.8	71.8	70.9	69.9	68.9	67.9	66.9	66.0	65.0	64.0
86	72.8	71.8	70.9	69.9	68.9	67.9	66.9	66.0	65.0	64.0
87	72.8	71.8	70.9	69.9	68.9	67.9	66.9	66.0	65.0	64.0
88	72.8	71.8	70.9	69.9	68.9	67.9	66.9	66.0	65.0	64.0
89	72.8	71.8	70.9	69.9	68.9	67.9	66.9	66.0	65.0	64.0
90	72.8	71.8	70.9	69.9	68.9	67.9	66.9	66.0	65.0	64.0
91	72.8	71.8	70.9	69.9	68.9	67.9	66.9	66.0	65.0	64.0
92	72.8	71.8	70.9	69.9	68.9	67.9	66.9	66.0	65.0	64.0
93	72.8	71.8	70.9	69.9	68.9	67.9	66.9	66.0	65.0	64.0
94	72.8	71.8	70.8	69.9	68.9	67.9	66.9	66.0	65.0	64.0
95	72.8	71.8	70.8	69.9	68.9	67.9	66.9	66.0	65.0	64.0
96	72.8	71.8	70.8	69.9	68.9	67.9	66.9	66.0	65.0	64.0
97	72.8	71.8	70.8	69.9	68.9	67.9	66.9	66.0	65.0	64.0
98	72.8	71.8	70.8	69.9	68.9	67.9	66.9	66.0	65.0	64.0
99	72.8	71.8	70.8	69.9	68.9	67.9	66.9	66.0	65.0	64.0
100	72.8	71.8	70.8	69.9	68.9	67.9	66.9	66.0	65.0	64.0
101	72.8	71.8	70.8	69.9	68.9	67.9	66.9	66.0	65.0	64.0
102	72.8	71.8	70.8	69.9	68.9	67.9	66.9	66.0	65.0	64.0
103	72.8	71.8	70.8	69.9	68.9	67.9	66.9	66.0	65.0	64.0
104	72.8	71.8	70.8	69.9	68.9	67.9	66.9	66.0	65.0	64.0
105	72.8	71.8	70.8	69.9	68.9	67.9	66.9	66.0	65.0	64.0
106	72.8	71.8	70.8	69.9	68.9	67.9	66.9	66.0	65.0	64.0
107	72.8	71.8	70.8	69.9	68.9	67.9	66.9	66.0	65.0	64.0
108	72.8	71.8	70.8	69.9	68.9	67.9	66.9	66.0	65.0	64.0
109	72.8	71.8	70.8	69.9	68.9	67.9	66.9	66.0	65.0	64.0
110	72.8	71.8	70.8	69.9	68.9	67.9	66.9	66.0	65.0	64.0
111	72.8	71.8	70.8	69.9	68.9	67.9	66.9	66.0	65.0	64.0
112	72.8	71.8	70.8	69.9	68.9	67.9	66.9	66.0	65.0	64.0

Joint Life and Last Survivor Expectancy *(continued)*

Ages	10	11	12	13	14	15	16	17	18	19
113	72.8	71.8	70.8	69.9	68.9	67.9	66.9	66.0	65.0	64.0
114	72.8	71.8	70.8	69.9	68.9	67.9	66.9	66.0	65.0	64.0
115+	72.8	71.8	70.8	69.9	68.9	67.9	66.9	66.0	65.0	64.0

Joint Life and Last Survivor Expectancy
(For Use by Owners Whose Spouses Are
More Than 10 Years Younger)

Ages	20	21	22	23	24	25	26	27	28	29
20	70.1	69.6	69.1	68.7	68.3	67.9	67.5	67.2	66.9	66.6
21	69.6	69.1	68.6	68.2	67.7	67.3	66.9	66.6	66.2	65.9
22	69.1	68.6	68.1	67.6	67.2	66.7	66.3	65.9	65.6	65.2
23	68.7	68.2	67.6	67.1	66.6	66.2	65.7	65.3	64.9	64.6
24	68.3	67.7	67.2	66.6	66.1	65.6	65.2	64.7	64.3	63.9
25	67.9	67.3	66.7	66.2	65.6	65.1	64.6	64.2	63.7	63.3
26	67.5	66.9	66.3	65.7	65.2	64.6	64.1	63.6	63.2	62.8
27	67.2	66.6	65.9	65.3	64.7	64.2	63.6	63.1	62.7	62.2
28	66.9	66.2	65.6	64.9	64.3	63.7	63.2	62.7	62.1	61.7
29	66.6	65.9	65.2	64.6	63.9	63.3	62.8	62.2	61.7	61.2
30	66.3	65.6	64.9	64.2	63.6	62.9	62.3	61.8	61.2	60.7
31	66.1	65.3	64.6	63.9	63.2	62.6	62.0	61.4	60.8	60.2
32	65.8	65.1	64.3	63.6	62.9	62.2	61.6	61.0	60.4	59.8
33	65.6	64.8	64.1	63.3	62.6	61.9	61.3	60.6	60.0	59.4
34	65.4	64.6	63.8	63.1	62.3	61.6	60.9	60.3	59.6	59.0
35	65.2	64.4	63.6	62.8	62.1	61.4	60.6	59.9	59.3	58.6
36	65.0	64.2	63.4	62.6	61.9	61.1	60.4	59.6	59.0	58.3
37	64.9	64.0	63.2	62.4	61.6	60.9	60.1	59.4	58.7	58.0
38	64.7	63.9	63.0	62.2	61.4	60.6	59.9	59.1	58.4	57.7
39	64.6	63.7	62.9	62.1	61.2	60.4	59.6	58.9	58.1	57.4
40	64.4	63.6	62.7	61.9	61.1	60.2	59.4	58.7	57.9	57.1
41	64.3	63.5	62.6	61.7	60.9	60.1	59.3	58.5	57.7	56.9
42	64.2	63.3	62.5	61.6	60.8	59.9	59.1	58.3	57.5	56.7
43	64.1	63.2	62.4	61.5	60.6	59.8	58.9	58.1	57.3	56.5

Joint Life and Last Survivor Expectancy *(continued)*

Ages	20	21	22	23	24	25	26	27	28	29
44	64.0	63.1	62.2	61.4	60.5	59.6	58.8	57.9	57.1	56.3
45	64.0	63.0	62.2	61.3	60.4	59.5	58.6	57.8	56.9	56.1
46	63.9	63.0	62.1	61.2	60.3	59.4	58.5	57.7	56.8	56.0
47	63.8	62.9	62.0	61.1	60.2	59.3	58.4	57.5	56.7	55.8
48	63.7	62.8	61.9	61.0	60.1	59.2	58.3	57.4	56.5	55.7
49	63.7	62.8	61.8	60.9	60.0	59.1	58.2	57.3	56.4	55.6
50	63.6	62.7	61.8	60.8	59.9	59.0	58.1	57.2	56.3	55.4
51	63.6	62.6	61.7	60.8	59.9	58.9	58.0	57.1	56.2	55.3
52	63.5	62.6	61.7	60.7	59.8	58.9	58.0	57.1	56.1	55.2
53	63.5	62.5	61.6	60.7	59.7	58.8	57.9	57.0	56.1	55.2
54	63.5	62.5	61.6	60.6	59.7	58.8	57.8	56.9	56.0	55.1
55	63.4	62.5	61.5	60.6	59.6	58.7	57.8	56.8	55.9	55.0
56	63.4	62.4	61.5	60.5	59.6	58.7	57.7	56.8	55.9	54.9
57	63.4	62.4	61.5	60.5	59.6	58.6	57.7	56.7	55.8	54.9
58	63.3	62.4	61.4	60.5	59.5	58.6	57.6	56.7	55.8	54.8
59	63.3	62.3	61.4	60.4	59.5	58.5	57.6	56.7	55.7	54.8
60	63.3	62.3	61.4	60.4	59.5	58.5	57.6	56.6	55.7	54.7
61	63.3	62.3	61.3	60.4	59.4	58.5	57.5	56.6	55.6	54.7
62	63.2	62.3	61.3	60.4	59.4	58.4	57.5	56.5	55.6	54.7
63	63.2	62.3	61.3	60.3	59.4	58.4	57.5	56.5	55.6	54.6
64	63.2	62.2	61.3	60.3	59.4	58.4	57.4	56.5	55.5	54.6
65	63.2	62.2	61.3	60.3	59.3	58.4	57.4	56.5	55.5	54.6
66	63.2	62.2	61.2	60.3	59.3	58.4	57.4	56.4	55.5	54.5
67	63.2	62.2	61.2	60.3	59.3	58.3	57.4	56.4	55.5	54.5
68	63.1	62.2	61.2	60.2	59.3	58.3	57.4	56.4	55.4	54.5
69	63.1	62.2	61.2	60.2	59.3	58.3	57.3	56.4	55.4	54.5
70	63.1	62.2	61.2	60.2	59.3	58.3	57.3	56.4	55.4	54.4
71	63.1	62.1	61.2	60.2	59.2	58.3	57.3	56.4	55.4	54.4
72	63.1	62.1	61.2	60.2	59.2	58.3	57.3	56.3	55.4	54.4
73	63.1	62.1	61.2	60.2	59.2	58.3	57.3	56.3	55.4	54.4
74	63.1	62.1	61.2	60.2	59.2	58.2	57.3	56.3	55.4	54.4
75	63.1	62.1	61.1	60.2	59.2	58.2	57.3	56.3	55.3	54.4
76	63.1	62.1	61.1	60.2	59.2	58.2	57.3	56.3	55.3	54.4

Joint Life and Last Survivor Expectancy *(continued)*

Ages	20	21	22	23	24	25	26	27	28	29
77	63.1	62.1	61.1	60.2	59.2	58.2	57.3	56.3	55.3	54.4
78	63.1	62.1	61.1	60.2	59.2	58.2	57.3	56.3	55.3	54.4
79	63.1	62.1	61.1	60.2	59.2	58.2	57.2	56.3	55.3	54.3
80	63.1	62.1	61.1	60.1	59.2	58.2	57.2	56.3	55.3	54.3
81	63.1	62.1	61.1	60.1	59.2	58.2	57.2	56.3	55.3	54.3
82	63.1	62.1	61.1	60.1	59.2	58.2	57.2	56.3	55.3	54.3
83	63.1	62.1	61.1	60.1	59.2	58.2	57.2	56.3	55.3	54.3
84	63.0	62.1	61.1	60.1	59.2	58.2	57.2	56.3	55.3	54.3
85	63.0	62.1	61.1	60.1	59.2	58.2	57.2	56.3	55.3	54.3
86	63.0	62.1	61.1	60.1	59.2	58.2	57.2	56.2	55.3	54.3
87	63.0	62.1	61.1	60.1	59.2	58.2	57.2	56.2	55.3	54.3
88	63.0	62.1	61.1	60.1	59.2	58.2	57.2	56.2	55.3	54.3
89	63.0	62.1	61.1	60.1	59.1	58.2	57.2	56.2	55.3	54.3
90	63.0	62.1	61.1	60.1	59.1	58.2	57.2	56.2	55.3	54.3
91	63.0	62.1	61.1	60.1	59.1	58.2	57.2	56.2	55.3	54.3
92	63.0	62.1	61.1	60.1	59.1	58.2	57.2	56.2	55.3	54.3
93	63.0	62.1	61.1	60.1	59.1	58.2	57.2	56.2	55.3	54.3
94	63.0	62.1	61.1	60.1	59.1	58.2	57.2	56.2	55.3	54.3
95	63.0	62.1	61.1	60.1	59.1	58.2	57.2	56.2	55.3	54.3
96	63.0	62.1	61.1	60.1	59.1	58.2	57.2	56.2	55.3	54.3
97	63.0	62.1	61.1	60.1	59.1	58.2	57.2	56.2	55.3	54.3
98	63.0	62.1	61.1	60.1	59.1	58.2	57.2	56.2	55.3	54.3
99	63.0	62.1	61.1	60.1	59.1	58.2	57.2	56.2	55.3	54.3
100	63.0	62.1	61.1	60.1	59.1	58.2	57.2	56.2	55.3	54.3
101	63.0	62.1	61.1	60.1	59.1	58.2	57.2	56.2	55.3	54.3
102	63.0	62.1	61.1	60.1	59.1	58.2	57.2	56.2	55.3	54.3
103	63.0	62.1	61.1	60.1	59.1	58.2	57.2	56.2	55.3	54.3
104	63.0	62.1	61.1	60.1	59.1	58.2	57.2	56.2	55.3	54.3
105	63.0	62.1	61.1	60.1	59.1	58.2	57.2	56.2	55.3	54.3
106	63.0	62.1	61.1	60.1	59.1	58.2	57.2	56.2	55.3	54.3
107	63.0	62.1	61.1	60.1	59.1	58.2	57.2	56.2	55.3	54.3
108	63.0	62.1	61.1	60.1	59.1	58.2	57.2	56.2	55.3	54.3
109	63.0	62.1	61.1	60.1	59.1	58.2	57.2	56.2	55.3	54.3

Joint Life and Last Survivor Expectancy *(continued)*

Ages	20	21	22	23	24	25	26	27	28	29
110	63.0	62.1	61.1	60.1	59.1	58.2	57.2	56.2	55.3	54.3
111	63.0	62.1	61.1	60.1	59.1	58.2	57.2	56.2	55.3	54.3
112	63.0	62.1	61.1	60.1	59.1	58.2	57.2	56.2	55.3	54.3
113	63.0	62.1	61.1	60.1	59.1	58.2	57.2	56.2	55.3	54.3
114	63.0	62.1	61.1	60.1	59.1	58.2	57.2	56.2	55.3	54.3
115+	63.0	62.1	61.1	60.1	59.1	58.2	57.2	56.2	55.3	54.3

Joint Life and Last Survivor Expectancy
(For Use by Owners Whose Spouses Are More Than 10 Years Younger)

Ages	30	31	32	33	34	35	36	37	38	39
30	60.2	59.7	59.2	58.8	58.4	58.0	57.6	57.3	57.0	56.7
31	59.7	59.2	58.7	58.2	57.8	57.4	57.0	56.6	56.3	56.0
32	59.2	58.7	58.2	57.7	57.2	56.8	56.4	56.0	55.6	55.3
33	58.8	58.2	57.7	57.2	56.7	56.2	55.8	55.4	55.0	54.7
34	58.4	57.8	57.2	56.7	56.2	55.7	55.3	54.8	54.4	54.0
35	58.0	57.4	56.8	56.2	55.7	55.2	54.7	54.3	53.8	53.4
36	57.6	57.0	56.4	55.8	55.3	54.7	54.2	53.7	53.3	52.8
37	57.3	56.6	56.0	55.4	54.8	54.3	53.7	53.2	52.7	52.3
38	57.0	56.3	55.6	55.0	54.4	53.8	53.3	52.7	52.2	51.7
39	56.7	56.0	55.3	54.7	54.0	53.4	52.8	52.3	51.7	51.2
40	56.4	55.7	55.0	54.3	53.7	53.0	52.4	51.8	51.3	50.8
41	56.1	55.4	54.7	54.0	53.3	52.7	52.0	51.4	50.9	50.3
42	55.9	55.2	54.4	53.7	53.0	52.3	51.7	51.1	50.4	49.9
43	55.7	54.9	54.2	53.4	52.7	52.0	51.3	50.7	50.1	49.5
44	55.5	54.7	53.9	53.2	52.4	51.7	51.0	50.4	49.7	49.1
45	55.3	54.5	53.7	52.9	52.2	51.5	50.7	50.0	49.4	48.7
46	55.1	54.3	53.5	52.7	52.0	51.2	50.5	49.8	49.1	48.4
47	55.0	54.1	53.3	52.5	51.7	51.0	50.2	49.5	48.8	48.1
48	54.8	54.0	53.2	52.3	51.5	50.8	50.0	49.2	48.5	47.8
49	54.7	53.8	53.0	52.2	51.4	50.6	49.8	49.0	48.2	47.5
50	54.6	53.7	52.9	52.0	51.2	50.4	49.6	48.8	48.0	47.3

Joint Life and Last Survivor Expectancy *(continued)*

Ages	30	31	32	33	34	35	36	37	38	39
51	54.5	53.6	52.7	51.9	51.0	50.2	49.4	48.6	47.8	47.0
52	54.4	53.5	52.6	51.7	50.9	50.0	49.2	48.4	47.6	46.8
53	54.3	53.4	52.5	51.6	50.8	49.9	49.1	48.2	47.4	46.6
54	54.2	53.3	52.4	51.5	50.6	49.8	48.9	48.1	47.2	46.4
55	54.1	53.2	52.3	51.4	50.5	49.7	48.8	47.9	47.1	46.3
56	54.0	53.1	52.2	51.3	50.4	49.5	48.7	47.8	47.0	46.1
57	54.0	53.0	52.1	51.2	50.3	49.4	48.6	47.7	46.8	46.0
58	53.9	53.0	52.1	51.2	50.3	49.4	48.5	47.6	46.7	45.8
59	53.8	52.9	52.0	51.1	50.2	49.3	48.4	47.5	46.6	45.7
60	53.8	52.9	51.9	51.0	50.1	49.2	48.3	47.4	46.5	45.6
61	53.8	52.8	51.9	51.0	50.0	49.1	48.2	47.3	46.4	45.5
62	53.7	52.8	51.8	50.9	50.0	49.1	48.1	47.2	46.3	45.4
63	53.7	52.7	51.8	50.9	49.9	49.0	48.1	47.2	46.3	45.3
64	53.6	52.7	51.8	50.8	49.9	48.9	48.0	47.1	46.2	45.3
65	53.6	52.7	51.7	50.8	49.8	48.9	48.0	47.0	46.1	45.2
66	53.6	52.6	51.7	50.7	49.8	48.9	47.9	47.0	46.1	45.1
67	53.6	52.6	51.7	50.7	49.8	48.8	47.9	46.9	46.0	45.1
68	53.5	52.6	51.6	50.7	49.7	48.8	47.8	46.9	46.0	45.0
69	53.5	52.6	51.6	50.6	49.7	48.7	47.8	46.9	45.9	45.0
70	53.5	52.5	51.6	50.6	49.7	48.7	47.8	46.8	45.9	44.9
71	53.5	52.5	51.6	50.6	49.6	48.7	47.7	46.8	45.9	44.9
72	53.5	52.5	51.5	50.6	49.6	48.7	47.7	46.8	45.8	44.9
73	53.4	52.5	51.5	50.6	49.6	48.6	47.7	46.7	45.8	44.8
74	53.4	52.5	51.5	50.5	49.6	48.6	47.7	46.7	45.8	44.8
75	53.4	52.5	51.5	50.5	49.6	48.6	47.7	46.7	45.7	44.8
76	53.4	52.4	51.5	50.5	49.6	48.6	47.6	46.7	45.7	44.8
77	53.4	52.4	51.5	50.5	49.5	48.6	47.6	46.7	45.7	44.8
78	53.4	52.4	51.5	50.5	49.5	48.6	47.6	46.6	45.7	44.7
79	53.4	52.4	51.5	50.5	49.5	48.6	47.6	46.6	45.7	44.7
80	53.4	52.4	51.4	50.5	49.5	48.5	47.6	46.6	45.7	44.7
81	53.4	52.4	51.4	50.5	49.5	48.5	47.6	46.6	45.7	44.7
82	53.4	52.4	51.4	50.5	49.5	48.5	47.6	46.6	45.6	44.7

Joint Life and Last Survivor Expectancy *(continued)*

Ages	30	31	32	33	34	35	36	37	38	39
83	53.4	52.4	51.4	50.5	49.5	48.5	47.6	46.6	45.6	44.7
84	53.4	52.4	51.4	50.5	49.5	48.5	47.6	46.6	45.6	44.7
85	53.3	52.4	51.4	50.4	49.5	48.5	47.5	46.6	45.6	44.7
86	53.3	52.4	51.4	50.4	49.5	48.5	47.5	46.6	45.6	44.6
87	53.3	52.4	51.4	50.4	49.5	48.5	47.5	46.6	45.6	44.6
88	53.3	52.4	51.4	50.4	49.5	48.5	47.5	46.6	45.6	44.6
89	53.3	52.4	51.4	50.4	49.5	48.5	47.5	46.6	45.6	44.6
90	53.3	52.4	51.4	50.4	49.5	48.5	47.5	46.6	45.6	44.6
91	53.3	52.4	51.4	50.4	49.5	48.5	47.5	46.6	45.6	44.6
92	53.3	52.4	51.4	50.4	49.5	48.5	47.5	46.6	45.6	44.6
93	53.3	52.4	51.4	50.4	49.5	48.5	47.5	46.6	45.6	44.6
94	53.3	52.4	51.4	50.4	49.5	48.5	47.5	46.6	45.6	44.6
95	53.3	52.4	51.4	50.4	49.5	48.5	47.5	46.5	45.6	44.6
96	53.3	52.4	51.4	50.4	49.5	48.5	47.5	46.5	45.6	44.6
97	53.3	52.4	51.4	50.4	49.5	48.5	47.5	46.5	45.6	44.6
98	53.3	52.4	51.4	50.4	49.5	48.5	47.5	46.5	45.6	44.6
99	53.3	52.4	51.4	50.4	49.5	48.5	47.5	46.5	45.6	44.6
100	53.3	52.4	51.4	50.4	49.5	48.5	47.5	46.5	45.6	44.6
101	53.3	52.4	51.4	50.4	49.5	48.5	47.5	46.5	45.6	44.6
102	53.3	52.4	51.4	50.4	49.5	48.5	47.5	46.5	45.6	44.6
103	53.3	52.4	51.4	50.4	49.5	48.5	47.5	46.5	45.6	44.6
104	53.3	52.4	51.4	50.4	49.5	48.5	47.5	46.5	45.6	44.6
105	53.3	52.4	51.4	50.4	49.4	48.5	47.5	46.5	45.6	44.6
106	53.3	52.4	51.4	50.4	49.4	48.5	47.5	46.5	45.6	44.6
107	53.3	52.4	51.4	50.4	49.4	48.5	47.5	46.5	45.6	44.6
108	53.3	52.4	51.4	50.4	49.4	48.5	47.5	46.5	45.6	44.6
109	53.3	52.4	51.4	50.4	49.4	48.5	47.5	46.5	45.6	44.6
110	53.3	52.4	51.4	50.4	49.4	48.5	47.5	46.5	45.6	44.6
111	53.3	52.4	51.4	50.4	49.4	48.5	47.5	46.5	45.6	44.6
112	53.3	52.4	51.4	50.4	49.4	48.5	47.5	46.5	45.6	44.6
113	53.3	52.4	51.4	50.4	49.4	48.5	47.5	46.5	45.6	44.6
114	53.3	52.4	51.4	50.4	49.4	48.5	47.5	46.5	45.6	44.6
115+	53.3	52.4	51.4	50.4	49.4	48.5	47.5	46.5	45.6	44.6

Joint Life and Last Survivor Expectancy *(continued)*

Joint Life and Last Survivor Expectancy
(For Use by Owners Whose Spouses Are
More Than 10 Years Younger)

Ages	40	41	42	43	44	45	46	47	48	49
40	50.2	49.8	49.3	48.9	48.5	48.1	47.7	47.4	47.1	46.8
41	49.8	49.3	48.8	48.3	47.9	47.5	47.1	46.7	46.4	46.1
42	49.3	48.8	48.3	47.8	47.3	46.9	46.5	46.1	45.8	45.4
43	48.9	48.3	47.8	47.3	46.8	46.3	45.9	45.5	45.1	44.8
44	48.5	47.9	47.3	46.8	46.3	45.8	45.4	44.9	44.5	44.2
45	48.1	47.5	46.9	46.3	45.8	45.3	44.8	44.4	44.0	43.6
46	47.7	47.1	46.5	45.9	45.4	44.8	44.3	43.9	43.4	43.0
47	47.4	46.7	46.1	45.5	44.9	44.4	43.9	43.4	42.9	42.4
48	47.1	46.4	45.8	45.1	44.5	44.0	43.4	42.9	42.4	41.9
49	46.8	46.1	45.4	44.8	44.2	43.6	43.0	42.4	41.9	41.4
50	46.5	45.8	45.1	44.4	43.8	43.2	42.6	42.0	41.5	40.9
51	46.3	45.5	44.8	44.1	43.5	42.8	42.2	41.6	41.0	40.5
52	46.0	45.3	44.6	43.8	43.2	42.5	41.8	41.2	40.6	40.1
53	45.8	45.1	44.3	43.6	42.9	42.2	41.5	40.9	40.3	39.7
54	45.6	44.8	44.1	43.3	42.6	41.9	41.2	40.5	39.9	39.3
55	45.5	44.7	43.9	43.1	42.4	41.6	40.9	40.2	39.6	38.9
56	45.3	44.5	43.7	42.9	42.1	41.4	40.7	40.0	39.3	38.6
57	45.1	44.3	43.5	42.7	41.9	41.2	40.4	39.7	39.0	38.3
58	45.0	44.2	43.3	42.5	41.7	40.9	40.2	39.4	38.7	38.0
59	44.9	44.0	43.2	42.4	41.5	40.7	40.0	39.2	38.5	37.8
60	44.7	43.9	43.0	42.2	41.4	40.6	39.8	39.0	38.2	37.5
61	44.6	43.8	42.9	42.1	41.2	40.4	39.6	38.8	38.0	37.3
62	44.5	43.7	42.8	41.9	41.1	40.3	39.4	38.6	37.8	37.1
63	44.5	43.6	42.7	41.8	41.0	40.1	39.3	38.5	37.7	36.9
64	44.4	43.5	42.6	41.7	40.8	40.0	39.2	38.3	37.5	36.7
65	44.3	43.4	42.5	41.6	40.7	39.9	39.0	38.2	37.4	36.6
66	44.2	43.3	42.4	41.5	40.6	39.8	38.9	38.1	37.2	36.4
67	44.2	43.3	42.3	41.4	40.6	39.7	38.8	38.0	37.1	36.3

Joint Life and Last Survivor Expectancy *(continued)*

Ages	40	41	42	43	44	45	46	47	48	49
68	44.1	43.2	42.3	41.4	40.5	39.6	38.7	37.9	37.0	36.2
69	44.1	43.1	42.2	41.3	40.4	39.5	38.6	37.8	36.9	36.0
70	44.0	43.1	42.2	41.3	40.3	39.4	38.6	37.7	36.8	35.9
71	44.0	43.0	42.1	41.2	40.3	39.4	38.5	37.6	36.7	35.9
72	43.9	43.0	42.1	41.1	40.2	39.3	38.4	37.5	36.6	35.8
73	43.9	43.0	42.0	41.1	40.2	39.3	38.4	37.5	36.6	35.7
74	43.9	42.9	42.0	41.1	40.1	39.2	38.3	37.4	36.5	35.6
75	43.8	42.9	42.0	41.0	40.1	39.2	38.3	37.4	36.5	35.6
76	43.8	42.9	41.9	41.0	40.1	39.1	38.2	37.3	36.4	35.5
77	43.8	42.9	41.9	41.0	40.0	39.1	38.2	37.3	36.4	35.5
78	43.8	42.8	41.9	40.9	40.0	39.1	38.2	37.2	36.3	35.4
79	43.8	42.8	41.9	40.9	40.0	39.1	38.1	37.2	36.3	35.4
80	43.7	42.8	41.8	40.9	40.0	39.0	38.1	37.2	36.3	35.4
81	43.7	42.8	41.8	40.9	39.9	39.0	38.1	37.2	36.2	35.3
82	43.7	42.8	41.8	40.9	39.9	39.0	38.1	37.1	36.2	35.3
83	43.7	42.8	41.8	40.9	39.9	39.0	38.0	37.1	36.2	35.3
84	43.7	42.7	41.8	40.8	39.9	39.0	38.0	37.1	36.2	35.3
85	43.7	42.7	41.8	40.8	39.9	38.9	38.0	37.1	36.2	35.2
86	43.7	42.7	41.8	40.8	39.9	38.9	38.0	37.1	36.1	35.2
87	43.7	42.7	41.8	40.8	39.9	38.9	38.0	37.0	36.1	35.2
88	43.7	42.7	41.8	40.8	39.9	38.9	38.0	37.0	36.1	35.2
89	43.7	42.7	41.7	40.8	39.8	38.9	38.0	37.0	36.1	35.2
90	43.7	42.7	41.7	40.8	39.8	38.9	38.0	37.0	36.1	35.2
91	43.7	42.7	41.7	40.8	39.8	38.9	37.9	37.0	36.1	35.2
92	43.7	42.7	41.7	40.8	39.8	38.9	37.9	37.0	36.1	35.1
93	43.7	42.7	41.7	40.8	39.8	38.9	37.9	37.0	36.1	35.1
94	43.7	42.7	41.7	40.8	39.8	38.9	37.9	37.0	36.1	35.1
95	43.6	42.7	41.7	40.8	39.8	38.9	37.9	37.0	36.1	35.1
96	43.6	42.7	41.7	40.8	39.8	38.9	37.9	37.0	36.1	35.1
97	43.6	42.7	41.7	40.8	39.8	38.9	37.9	37.0	36.1	35.1
98	43.6	42.7	41.7	40.8	39.8	38.9	37.9	37.0	36.0	35.1
99	43.6	42.7	41.7	40.8	39.8	38.9	37.9	37.0	36.0	35.1

Joint Life and Last Survivor Expectancy *(continued)*

Ages	40	41	42	43	44	45	46	47	48	49
100	43.6	42.7	41.7	40.8	39.8	38.9	37.9	37.0	36.0	35.1
101	43.6	42.7	41.7	40.8	39.8	38.9	37.9	37.0	36.0	35.1
102	43.6	42.7	41.7	40.8	39.8	38.9	37.9	37.0	36.0	35.1
103	43.6	42.7	41.7	40.8	39.8	38.9	37.9	37.0	36.0	35.1
104	43.6	42.7	41.7	40.8	39.8	38.8	37.9	37.0	36.0	35.1
105	43.6	42.7	41.7	40.8	39.8	38.8	37.9	37.0	36.0	35.1
106	43.6	42.7	41.7	40.8	39.8	38.8	37.9	37.0	36.0	35.1
107	43.6	42.7	41.7	40.8	39.8	38.8	37.9	37.0	36.0	35.1
108	43.6	42.7	41.7	40.8	39.8	38.8	37.9	37.0	36.0	35.1
109	43.6	42.7	41.7	40.7	39.8	38.8	37.9	37.0	36.0	35.1
110	43.6	42.7	41.7	40.7	39.8	38.8	37.9	37.0	36.0	35.1
111	43.6	42.7	41.7	40.7	39.8	38.8	37.9	37.0	36.0	35.1
112	43.6	42.7	41.7	40.7	39.8	38.8	37.9	37.0	36.0	35.1
113	43.6	42.7	41.7	40.7	39.8	38.8	37.9	37.0	36.0	35.1
114	43.6	42.7	41.7	40.7	39.8	38.8	37.9	37.0	36.0	35.1
115+	43.6	42.7	41.7	40.7	39.8	38.8	37.9	37.0	36.0	35.1

Joint Life and Last Survivor Expectancy
(For Use by Owners Whose Spouses Are More Than 10 Years Younger)

Ages	50	51	52	53	54	55	56	57	58	59
50	40.4	40.0	39.5	39.1	38.7	38.3	38.0	37.6	37.3	37.1
51	40.0	39.5	39.0	38.5	38.1	37.7	37.4	37.0	36.7	36.4
52	39.5	39.0	38.5	38.0	37.6	37.2	36.8	36.4	36.0	35.7
53	39.1	38.5	38.0	37.5	37.1	36.6	36.2	35.8	35.4	35.1
54	38.7	38.1	37.6	37.1	36.6	36.1	35.7	35.2	34.8	34.5
55	38.3	37.7	37.2	36.6	36.1	35.6	35.1	34.7	34.3	33.9
56	38.0	37.4	36.8	36.2	35.7	35.1	34.7	34.2	33.7	33.3
57	37.6	37.0	36.4	35.8	35.2	34.7	34.2	33.7	33.2	32.8
58	37.3	36.7	36.0	35.4	34.8	34.3	33.7	33.2	32.8	32.3
59	37.1	36.4	35.7	35.1	34.5	33.9	33.3	32.8	32.3	31.8
60	36.8	36.1	35.4	34.8	34.1	33.5	32.9	32.4	31.9	31.3

Joint Life and Last Survivor Expectancy *(continued)*

Ages	50	51	52	53	54	55	56	57	58	59
61	36.6	35.8	35.1	34.5	33.8	33.2	32.6	32.0	31.4	30.9
62	36.3	35.6	34.9	34.2	33.5	32.9	32.2	31.6	31.1	30.5
63	36.1	35.4	34.6	33.9	33.2	32.6	31.9	31.3	30.7	30.1
64	35.9	35.2	34.4	33.7	33.0	32.3	31.6	31.0	30.4	29.8
65	35.8	35.0	34.2	33.5	32.7	32.0	31.4	30.7	30.0	29.4
66	35.6	34.8	34.0	33.3	32.5	31.8	31.1	30.4	29.8	29.1
67	35.5	34.7	33.9	33.1	32.3	31.6	30.9	30.2	29.5	28.8
68	35.3	34.5	33.7	32.9	32.1	31.4	30.7	29.9	29.2	28.6
69	35.2	34.4	33.6	32.8	32.0	31.2	30.5	29.7	29.0	28.3
70	35.1	34.3	33.4	32.6	31.8	31.1	30.3	29.5	28.8	28.1
71	35.0	34.2	33.3	32.5	31.7	30.9	30.1	29.4	28.6	27.9
72	34.9	34.1	33.2	32.4	31.6	30.8	30.0	29.2	28.4	27.7
73	34.8	34.0	33.1	32.3	31.5	30.6	29.8	29.1	28.3	27.5
74	34.8	33.9	33.0	32.2	31.4	30.5	29.7	28.9	28.1	27.4
75	34.7	33.8	33.0	32.1	31.3	30.4	29.6	28.8	28.0	27.2
76	34.6	33.8	32.9	32.0	31.2	30.3	29.5	28.7	27.9	27.1
77	34.6	33.7	32.8	32.0	31.1	30.3	29.4	28.6	27.8	27.0
78	34.5	33.6	32.8	31.9	31.0	30.2	29.3	28.5	27.7	26.9
79	34.5	33.6	32.7	31.8	31.0	30.1	29.3	28.4	27.6	26.8
80	34.5	33.6	32.7	31.8	30.9	30.1	29.2	28.4	27.5	26.7
81	34.4	33.5	32.6	31.8	30.9	30.0	29.2	28.3	27.5	26.6
82	34.4	33.5	32.6	31.7	30.8	30.0	29.1	28.3	27.4	26.6
83	34.4	33.5	32.6	31.7	30.8	29.9	29.1	28.2	27.4	26.5
84	34.3	33.4	32.5	31.7	30.8	29.9	29.0	28.2	27.3	26.5
85	34.3	33.4	32.5	31.6	30.7	29.9	29.0	28.1	27.3	26.4
86	34.3	33.4	32.5	31.6	30.7	29.8	29.0	28.1	27.2	26.4
87	34.3	33.4	32.5	31.6	30.7	29.8	28.9	28.1	27.2	26.4
88	34.3	33.4	32.5	31.6	30.7	29.8	28.9	28.0	27.2	26.3
89	34.3	33.3	32.4	31.5	30.7	29.8	28.9	28.0	27.2	26.3
90	34.2	33.3	32.4	31.5	30.6	29.8	28.9	28.0	27.1	26.3
91	34.2	33.3	32.4	31.5	30.6	29.7	28.9	28.0	27.1	26.3
92	34.2	33.3	32.4	31.5	30.6	29.7	28.8	28.0	27.1	26.2
93	34.2	33.3	32.4	31.5	30.6	29.7	28.8	28.0	27.1	26.2

Joint Life and Last Survivor Expectancy *(continued)*

Ages	50	51	52	53	54	55	56	57	58	59
94	34.2	33.3	32.4	31.5	30.6	29.7	28.8	27.9	27.1	26.2
95	34.2	33.3	32.4	31.5	30.6	29.7	28.8	27.9	27.1	26.2
96	34.2	33.3	32.4	31.5	30.6	29.7	28.8	27.9	27.0	26.2
97	34.2	33.3	32.4	31.5	30.6	29.7	28.8	27.9	27.0	26.2
98	34.2	33.3	32.4	31.5	30.6	29.7	28.8	27.9	27.0	26.2
99	34.2	33.3	32.4	31.5	30.6	29.7	28.8	27.9	27.0	26.2
100	34.2	33.3	32.4	31.5	30.6	29.7	28.8	27.9	27.0	26.1
101	34.2	33.3	32.4	31.5	30.6	29.7	28.8	27.9	27.0	26.1
102	34.2	33.3	32.4	31.4	30.5	29.7	28.8	27.9	27.0	26.1
103	34.2	33.3	32.4	31.4	30.5	29.7	28.8	27.9	27.0	26.1
104	34.2	33.3	32.4	31.4	30.5	29.6	28.8	27.9	27.0	26.1
105	34.2	33.3	32.3	31.4	30.5	29.6	28.8	27.9	27.0	26.1
106	34.2	33.3	32.3	31.4	30.5	29.6	28.8	27.9	27.0	26.1
107	34.2	33.3	32.3	31.4	30.5	29.6	28.8	27.9	27.0	26.1
108	34.2	33.3	32.3	31.4	30.5	29.6	28.8	27.9	27.0	26.1
109	34.2	33.3	32.3	31.4	30.5	29.6	28.7	27.9	27.0	26.1
110	34.2	33.3	32.3	31.4	30.5	29.6	28.7	27.9	27.0	26.1
111	34.2	33.3	32.3	31.4	30.5	29.6	28.7	27.9	27.0	26.1
112	34.2	33.3	32.3	31.4	30.5	29.6	28.7	27.9	27.0	26.1
113	34.2	33.3	32.3	31.4	30.5	29.6	28.7	27.9	27.0	26.1
114	34.2	33.3	32.3	31.4	30.5	29.6	28.7	27.9	27.0	26.1
115+	34.2	33.3	32.3	31.4	30.5	29.6	28.7	27.9	27.0	26.1

Joint Life and Last Survivor Expectancy
(For Use by Owners Whose Spouses Are
More Than 10 Years Younger)

Ages	60	61	62	63	64	65	66	67	68	69
60	30.9	30.4	30.0	29.6	29.2	28.8	28.5	28.2	27.9	27.6
61	30.4	29.9	29.5	29.0	28.6	28.3	27.9	27.6	27.3	27.0
62	30.0	29.5	29.0	28.5	28.1	27.7	27.3	27.0	26.7	26.4
63	29.6	29.0	28.5	28.1	27.6	27.2	26.8	26.4	26.1	25.7

Joint Life and Last Survivor Expectancy *(continued)*

Ages	60	61	62	63	64	65	66	67	68	69
64	29.2	28.6	28.1	27.6	27.1	26.7	26.3	25.9	25.5	25.2
65	28.8	28.3	27.7	27.2	26.7	26.2	25.8	25.4	25.0	24.6
66	28.5	27.9	27.3	26.8	26.3	25.8	25.3	24.9	24.5	24.1
67	28.2	27.6	27.0	26.4	25.9	25.4	24.9	24.4	24.0	23.6
68	27.9	27.3	26.7	26.1	25.5	25.0	24.5	24.0	23.5	23.1
69	27.6	27.0	26.4	25.7	25.2	24.6	24.1	23.6	23.1	22.6
70	27.4	26.7	26.1	25.4	24.8	24.3	23.7	23.2	22.7	22.2
71	27.2	26.5	25.8	25.2	24.5	23.9	23.4	22.8	22.3	21.8
72	27.0	26.3	25.6	24.9	24.3	23.7	23.1	22.5	22.0	21.4
73	26.8	26.1	25.4	24.7	24.0	23.4	22.8	22.2	21.6	21.1
74	26.6	25.9	25.2	24.5	23.8	23.1	22.5	21.9	21.3	20.8
75	26.5	25.7	25.0	24.3	23.6	22.9	22.3	21.6	21.0	20.5
76	26.3	25.6	24.8	24.1	23.4	22.7	22.0	21.4	20.8	20.2
77	26.2	25.4	24.7	23.9	23.2	22.5	21.8	21.2	20.6	19.9
78	26.1	25.3	24.6	23.8	23.1	22.4	21.7	21.0	20.3	19.7
79	26.0	25.2	24.4	23.7	22.9	22.2	21.5	20.8	20.1	19.5
80	25.9	25.1	24.3	23.6	22.8	22.1	21.3	20.6	20.0	19.3
81	25.8	25.0	24.2	23.4	22.7	21.9	21.2	20.5	19.8	19.1
82	25.8	24.9	24.1	23.4	22.6	21.8	21.1	20.4	19.7	19.0
83	25.7	24.9	24.1	23.3	22.5	21.7	21.0	20.2	19.5	18.8
84	25.6	24.8	24.0	23.2	22.4	21.6	20.9	20.1	19.4	18.7
85	25.6	24.8	23.9	23.1	22.3	21.6	20.8	20.1	19.3	18.6
86	25.5	24.7	23.9	23.1	22.3	21.5	20.7	20.0	19.2	18.5
87	25.5	24.7	23.8	23.0	22.2	21.4	20.7	19.9	19.2	18.4
88	25.5	24.6	23.8	23.0	22.2	21.4	20.6	19.8	19.1	18.3
89	25.4	24.6	23.8	22.9	22.1	21.3	20.5	19.8	19.0	18.3
90	25.4	24.6	23.7	22.9	22.1	21.3	20.5	19.7	19.0	18.2
91	25.4	24.5	23.7	22.9	22.1	21.3	20.5	19.7	18.9	18.2
92	25.4	24.5	23.7	22.9	22.0	21.2	20.4	19.6	18.9	18.1
93	25.4	24.5	23.7	22.8	22.0	21.2	20.4	19.6	18.8	18.1
94	25.3	24.5	23.6	22.8	22.0	21.2	20.4	19.6	18.8	18.0
95	25.3	24.5	23.6	22.8	22.0	21.1	20.3	19.6	18.8	18.0

(Joint Life and Last Survivor Expectancy) (*continued*)

Ages	60	61	62	63	64	65	66	67	68	69
96	25.3	24.5	23.6	22.8	21.9	21.1	20.3	19.5	18.8	18.0
97	25.3	24.5	23.6	22.8	21.9	21.1	20.3	19.5	18.7	18.0
98	25.3	24.4	23.6	22.8	21.9	21.1	20.3	19.5	18.7	17.9
99	25.3	24.4	23.6	22.7	21.9	21.1	20.3	19.5	18.7	17.9
100	25.3	24.4	23.6	22.7	21.9	21.1	20.3	19.5	18.7	17.9
101	25.3	24.4	23.6	22.7	21.9	21.1	20.2	19.4	18.7	17.9
102	25.3	24.4	23.6	22.7	21.9	21.1	20.2	19.4	18.6	17.9
103	25.3	24.4	23.6	22.7	21.9	21.0	20.2	19.4	18.6	17.9
104	25.3	24.4	23.5	22.7	21.9	21.0	20.2	19.4	18.6	17.8
105	25.3	24.4	23.5	22.7	21.9	21.0	20.2	19.4	18.6	17.8
106	25.3	24.4	23.5	22.7	21.9	21.0	20.2	19.4	18.6	17.8
107	25.2	24.4	23.5	22.7	21.8	21.0	20.2	19.4	18.6	17.8
108	25.2	24.4	23.5	22.7	21.8	21.0	20.2	19.4	18.6	17.8
109	25.2	24.4	23.5	22.7	21.8	21.0	20.2	19.4	18.6	17.8
110	25.2	24.4	23.5	22.7	21.8	21.0	20.2	19.4	18.6	17.8
111	25.2	24.4	23.5	22.7	21.8	21.0	20.2	19.4	18.6	17.8
112	25.2	24.4	23.5	22.7	21.8	21.0	20.2	19.4	18.6	17.8
113	25.2	24.4	23.5	22.7	21.8	21.0	20.2	19.4	18.6	17.8
114	25.2	24.4	23.5	22.7	21.8	21.0	20.2	19.4	18.6	17.8
115+	25.2	24.4	23.5	22.7	21.8	21.0	20.2	19.4	18.6	17.8

Joint Life and Last Survivor Expectancy
(For Use by Owners Whose Spouses Are
More Than 10 Years Younger)

Ages	70	71	72	73	74	75	76	77	78	79
70	21.8	21.3	20.9	20.6	20.2	19.9	19.6	19.4	19.1	18.9
71	21.3	20.9	20.5	20.1	19.7	19.4	19.1	18.8	18.5	18.3
72	20.9	20.5	20.0	19.6	19.3	18.9	18.6	18.3	18.0	17.7
73	20.6	20.1	19.6	19.2	18.8	18.4	18.1	17.8	17.5	17.2
74	20.2	19.7	19.3	18.8	18.4	18.0	17.6	17.3	17.0	16.7
75	19.9	19.4	18.9	18.4	18.0	17.6	17.2	16.8	16.5	16.2

(Joint Life and Last Survivor Expectancy) (*continued*)

Ages	70	71	72	73	74	75	76	77	78	79
76	19.6	19.1	18.6	18.1	17.6	17.2	16.8	16.4	16.0	15.7
77	19.4	18.8	18.3	17.8	17.3	16.8	16.4	16.0	15.6	15.3
78	19.1	18.5	18.0	17.5	17.0	16.5	16.0	15.6	15.2	14.9
79	18.9	18.3	17.7	17.2	16.7	16.2	15.7	15.3	14.9	14.5
80	18.7	18.1	17.5	16.9	16.4	15.9	15.4	15.0	14.5	14.1
81	18.5	17.9	17.3	16.7	16.2	15.6	15.1	14.7	14.2	13.8
82	18.3	17.7	17.1	16.5	15.9	15.4	14.9	14.4	13.9	13.5
83	18.2	17.5	16.9	16.3	15.7	15.2	14.7	14.2	13.7	13.2
84	18.0	17.4	16.7	16.1	15.5	15.0	14.4	13.9	13.4	13.0
85	17.9	17.3	16.6	16.0	15.4	14.8	14.3	13.7	13.2	12.8
86	17.8	17.1	16.5	15.8	15.2	14.6	14.1	13.5	13.0	12.5
87	17.7	17.0	16.4	15.7	15.1	14.5	13.9	13.4	12.9	12.4
88	17.6	16.9	16.3	15.6	15.0	14.4	13.8	13.2	12.7	12.2
89	17.6	16.9	16.2	15.5	14.9	14.3	13.7	13.1	12.6	12.0
90	17.5	16.8	16.1	15.4	14.8	14.2	13.6	13.0	12.4	11.9
91	17.4	16.7	16.0	15.4	14.7	14.1	13.5	12.9	12.3	11.8
92	17.4	16.7	16.0	15.3	14.6	14.0	13.4	12.8	12.2	11.7
93	17.3	16.6	15.9	15.2	14.6	13.9	13.3	12.7	12.1	11.6
94	17.3	16.6	15.9	15.2	14.5	13.9	13.2	12.6	12.0	11.5
95	17.3	16.5	15.8	15.1	14.5	13.8	13.2	12.6	12.0	11.4
96	17.2	16.5	15.8	15.1	14.4	13.8	13.1	12.5	11.9	11.3
97	17.2	16.5	15.8	15.1	14.4	13.7	13.1	12.5	11.9	11.3
98	17.2	16.4	15.7	15.0	14.3	13.7	13.0	12.4	11.8	11.2
99	17.2	16.4	15.7	15.0	14.3	13.6	13.0	12.4	11.8	11.2
100	17.1	16.4	15.7	15.0	14.3	13.6	12.9	12.3	11.7	11.1
101	17.1	16.4	15.6	14.9	14.2	13.6	12.9	12.3	11.7	11.1
102	17.1	16.4	15.6	14.9	14.2	13.5	12.9	12.2	11.6	11.0
103	17.1	16.3	15.6	14.9	14.2	13.5	12.9	12.2	11.6	11.0
104	17.1	16.3	15.6	14.9	14.2	13.5	12.8	12.2	11.6	11.0
105	17.1	16.3	15.6	14.9	14.2	13.5	12.8	12.2	11.5	10.9
106	17.1	16.3	15.6	14.8	14.1	13.5	12.8	12.2	11.5	10.9
107	17.0	16.3	15.6	14.8	14.1	13.4	12.8	12.1	11.5	10.9

Joint Life and Last Survivor Expectancy *(continued)*

Ages	70	71	72	73	74	75	76	77	78	79
108	17.0	16.3	15.5	14.8	14.1	13.4	12.8	12.1	11.5	10.9
109	17.0	16.3	15.5	14.8	14.1	13.4	12.8	12.1	11.5	10.9
110	17.0	16.3	15.5	14.8	14.1	13.4	12.7	12.1	11.5	10.9
111	17.0	16.3	15.5	14.8	14.1	13.4	12.7	12.1	11.5	10.8
112	17.0	16.3	15.5	14.8	14.1	13.4	12.7	12.1	11.5	10.8
113	17.0	16.3	15.5	14.8	14.1	13.4	12.7	12.1	11.4	10.8
114	17.0	16.3	15.5	14.8	14.1	13.4	12.7	12.1	11.4	10.8
115+	17.0	16.3	15.5	14.8	14.1	13.4	12.7	12.1	11.4	10.8

Joint Life and Last Survivor Expectancy
(For Use by Owners Whose Spouses Are More Than 10 Years Younger)

Ages	80	81	82	83	84	85	86	87	88	89
80	13.8	13.4	13.1	12.8	12.6	12.3	12.1	11.9	11.7	11.5
81	13.4	13.1	12.7	12.4	12.2	11.9	11.7	11.4	11.3	11.1
82	13.1	12.7	12.4	12.1	11.8	11.5	11.3	11.0	10.8	10.6
83	12.8	12.4	12.1	11.7	11.4	11.1	10.9	10.6	10.4	10.2
84	12.6	12.2	11.8	11.4	11.1	10.8	10.5	10.3	10.1	9.9
85	12.3	11.9	11.5	11.1	10.8	10.5	10.2	9.9	9.7	9.5
86	12.1	11.7	11.3	10.9	10.5	10.2	9.9	9.6	9.4	9.2
87	11.9	11.4	11.0	10.6	10.3	9.9	9.6	9.4	9.1	8.9
88	11.7	11.3	10.8	10.4	10.1	9.7	9.4	9.1	8.8	8.6
89	11.5	11.1	10.6	10.2	9.9	9.5	9.2	8.9	8.6	8.3
90	11.4	10.9	10.5	10.1	9.7	9.3	9.0	8.6	8.3	8.1
91	11.3	10.8	10.3	9.9	9.5	9.1	8.8	8.4	8.1	7.9
92	11.2	10.7	10.2	9.8	9.3	9.0	8.6	8.3	8.0	7.7
93	11.1	10.6	10.1	9.6	9.2	8.8	8.5	8.1	7.8	7.5
94	11.0	10.5	10.0	9.5	9.1	8.7	8.3	8.0	7.6	7.3
95	10.9	10.4	9.9	9.4	9.0	8.6	8.2	7.8	7.5	7.2
96	10.8	10.3	9.8	9.3	8.9	8.5	8.1	7.7	7.4	7.1
97	10.7	10.2	9.7	9.2	8.8	8.4	8.0	7.6	7.3	6.9
98	10.7	10.1	9.6	9.2	8.7	8.3	7.9	7.5	7.1	6.8

Joint Life and Last Survivor Expectancy *(continued)*

Ages	80	81	82	83	84	85	86	87	88	89
99	10.6	10.1	9.6	9.1	8.6	8.2	7.8	7.4	7.0	6.7
100	10.6	10.0	9.5	9.0	8.5	8.1	7.7	7.3	6.9	6.6
101	10.5	10.0	9.4	9.0	8.5	8.0	7.6	7.2	6.9	6.5
102	10.5	9.9	9.4	8.9	8.4	8.0	7.5	7.1	6.8	6.4
103	10.4	9.9	9.4	8.8	8.4	7.9	7.5	7.1	6.7	6.3
104	10.4	9.8	9.3	8.8	8.3	7.9	7.4	7.0	6.6	6.3
105	10.4	9.8	9.3	8.8	8.3	7.8	7.4	7.0	6.6	6.2
106	10.3	9.8	9.2	8.7	8.2	7.8	7.3	6.9	6.5	6.2
107	10.3	9.8	9.2	8.7	8.2	7.7	7.3	6.9	6.5	6.1
108	10.3	9.7	9.2	8.7	8.2	7.7	7.3	6.8	6.4	6.1
109	10.3	9.7	9.2	8.7	8.2	7.7	7.2	6.8	6.4	6.0
110	10.3	9.7	9.2	8.6	8.1	7.7	7.2	6.8	6.4	6.0
111	10.3	9.7	9.1	8.6	8.1	7.6	7.2	6.8	6.3	6.0
112	10.2	9.7	9.1	8.6	8.1	7.6	7.2	6.7	6.3	5.9
113	10.2	9.7	9.1	8.6	8.1	7.6	7.2	6.7	6.3	5.9
114	10.2	9.7	9.1	8.6	8.1	7.6	7.1	6.7	6.3	5.9
115+	10.2	9.7	9.1	8.6	8.1	7.6	7.1	6.7	6.3	5.9

Joint Life and Last Survivor Expectancy
(For Use by Owners Whose Spouses Are
More Than 10 Years Younger)

Ages	90	91	92	93	94	95	96	97	98	99
90	7.8	7.6	7.4	7.2	7.1	6.9	6.8	6.6	6.5	6.4
91	7.6	7.4	7.2	7.0	6.8	6.7	6.5	6.4	6.3	6.1
92	7.4	7.2	7.0	6.8	6.6	6.4	6.3	6.1	6.0	5.9
93	7.2	7.0	6.8	6.6	6.4	6.2	6.1	5.9	5.8	5.6
94	7.1	6.8	6.6	6.4	6.2	6.0	5.9	5.7	5.6	5.4
95	6.9	6.7	6.4	6.2	6.0	5.8	5.7	5.5	5.4	5.2
96	6.8	6.5	6.3	6.1	5.9	5.7	5.5	5.3	5.2	5.0
97	6.6	6.4	6.1	5.9	5.7	5.5	5.3	5.2	5.0	4.9
98	6.5	6.3	6.0	5.8	5.6	5.4	5.2	5.0	4.8	4.7

Joint Life and Last Survivor Expectancy *(continued)*

Ages	90	91	92	93	94	95	96	97	98	99
99	6.4	6.1	5.9	5.6	5.4	5.2	5.0	4.9	4.7	4.5
100	6.3	6.0	5.8	5.5	5.3	5.1	4.9	4.7	4.5	4.4
101	6.2	5.9	5.6	5.4	5.2	5.0	4.8	4.6	4.4	4.2
102	6.1	5.8	5.5	5.3	5.1	4.8	4.6	4.4	4.3	4.1
103	6.0	5.7	5.4	5.2	5.0	4.7	4.5	4.3	4.1	4.0
104	5.9	5.6	5.4	5.1	4.9	4.6	4.4	4.2	4.0	3.8
105	5.9	5.6	5.3	5.0	4.8	4.5	4.3	4.1	3.9	3.7
106	5.8	5.5	5.2	4.9	4.7	4.5	4.2	4.0	3.8	3.6
107	5.8	5.4	5.1	4.9	4.6	4.4	4.2	3.9	3.7	3.5
108	5.7	5.4	5.1	4.8	4.6	4.3	4.1	3.9	3.7	3.5
109	5.7	5.3	5.0	4.8	4.5	4.3	4.0	3.8	3.6	3.4
110	5.6	5.3	5.0	4.7	4.5	4.2	4.0	3.8	3.5	3.3
111	5.6	5.3	5.0	4.7	4.4	4.2	3.9	3.7	3.5	3.3
112	5.6	5.3	4.9	4.7	4.4	4.1	3.9	3.7	3.5	3.2
113	5.6	5.2	4.9	4.6	4.4	4.1	3.9	3.6	3.4	3.2
114	5.6	5.2	4.9	4.6	4.3	4.1	3.9	3.6	3.4	3.2
115+	5.5	5.2	4.9	4.6	4.3	4.1	3.8	3.6	3.4	3.1

Joint Life and Last Survivor Expectancy
(For Use by Owners Whose Spouses Are
More Than 10 Years Younger)

Ages	100	101	102	103	104	105	106	107	108	109
100	4.2	4.1	3.9	3.8	3.7	3.5	3.4	3.3	3.3	3.2
101	4.1	3.9	3.7	3.6	3.5	3.4	3.2	3.1	3.1	3.0
102	3.9	3.7	3.6	3.4	3.3	3.2	3.1	3.0	2.9	2.8
103	3.8	3.6	3.4	3.3	3.2	3.0	2.9	2.8	2.7	2.6
104	3.7	3.5	3.3	3.2	3.0	2.9	2.7	2.6	2.5	2.4
105	3.5	3.4	3.2	3.0	2.9	2.7	2.6	2.5	2.4	2.3
106	3.4	3.2	3.1	2.9	2.7	2.6	2.4	2.3	2.2	2.1
107	3.3	3.1	3.0	2.8	2.6	2.5	2.3	2.2	2.1	2.0
108	3.3	3.1	2.9	2.7	2.5	2.4	2.2	2.1	1.9	1.8

Joint Life and Last Survivor Expectancy *(continued)*

Ages	100	101	102	103	104	105	106	107	108	109
109	3.2	3.0	2.8	2.6	2.4	2.3	2.1	2.0	1.8	1.7
110	3.1	2.9	2.7	2.5	2.3	2.2	2.0	1.9	1.7	1.6
111	3.1	2.9	2.7	2.5	2.3	2.1	1.9	1.8	1.6	1.5
112	3.0	2.8	2.6	2.4	2.2	2.0	1.9	1.7	1.5	1.4
113	3.0	2.8	2.6	2.4	2.2	2.0	1.8	1.6	1.5	1.3
114	3.0	2.7	2.5	2.3	2.1	1.9	1.8	1.6	1.4	1.3
115+	2.9	2.7	2.5	2.3	2.1	1.9	1.7	1.5	1.4	1.2

Joint Life and Last Survivor Expectancy
(For Use by Owners Whose Spouses Are More Than 10 Years Younger)

Ages	110	111	112	113	114	115+
110	1.5	1.4	1.3	1.2	1.1	1.1
111	1.4	1.2	1.1	1.1	1.0	1.0
112	1.3	1.1	1.0	1.0	1.0	1.0
113	1.2	1.1	1.0	1.0	1.0	1.0
114	1.1	1.0	1.0	1.0	1.0	1.0
115+	1.1	1.0	1.0	1.0	1.0	1.0

ACKNOWLEDGMENTS

My dad would have loved to see this book and show it to everyone he knows. I wish he could have. He's gone now, but I continue to thank him as I reach each successful milestone in my career. It is his inherent goodness, integrity, and principled life that inspire me, always.

Thank you to my wife, Linda, for supporting all that I do. She does an amazing job taking care of the home front while I'm away spreading my IRA message, so that I always have a warm home and a loving family to come back to. I also want to thank my children, Ilana and Rachel, for being great kids and for their patience with and understanding of the work I do.

I would like to thank all the financial advisors, insurance professionals, CPAs, and attorneys who understand the importance of this field and have attended my IRA training sessions to show their support. Thanks also to the fund and insurance companies, broker firms, banks, and all the other sponsoring organizations that make these sessions possible. These are the people and firms that bring this knowledge to you and your family and help you take advantage of it.

My thanks to the wonderful people and members of the Million Dollar Round Table and Top of the Table for consistently inviting me to speak and for supporting my ideas among their members. MDRT is the elite of worldwide insurance professionals and financial advisors. They really make a difference in people's lives, including mine.

Thanks once again to Seymour "Sy" Goldberg, Esq., CPA, a friend, Long Island neighbor, and IRA guru. Sy, you are a genius for seeing the trillion-dollar IRA market potential at least a decade before anyone else even dreamed about it. This book and much of my IRA career would not have been possible without you.

Thank you to my IRA maven colleague Natalie B. Choate, Esq., for consistently supporting my efforts to train financial advisors to be IRA experts and help their clients. Natalie, like me, is an IRA road warrior and a member of the IRA Experts Speakers Union, Local 401(a)(9). Not really. There is no such group. We just call it that because we are the only members!

I must thank my friend, IRA expert, and still-loyal Met fan, Barry C. Picker, CPA/PFS, CFP®, who is the technical editor of my IRA monthly newsletter, *Ed Slott's IRA Advisor*. Barry has been helping me with the newsletter since the very first issue was published years ago.

Thank you to the folks at Bank of America who help edit my IRA newsletter. This group includes Marvin R. Rotenberg, national director of retirement services, The Private Bank, Bank of America, and his expert IRA team members, Beverly DeVeny, Mark LaVangie, and Richard B. James. Beverly DeVeny and Mark LaVangie have also given their time to help edit this book for technical accuracy. I cannot possibly thank Beverly and Mark enough for all the time they generously lend helping me make sure my books, newsletters, and other IRA information are reliably accurate.

Thank you to Denise Appleby for giving her time to help with the technical editing of this book. Denise also helps me out with the editing of my newsletter and is active on the discussion forum of our Web site (www.irahelp.com), answering IRA questions for our visitors. These are just *some* of Denise Appleby's credentials: Accredited Pension Administrator (APA) from the National Institute of Pension Administrators; the Certified IRA Services Professional (CISP) designation from the Institute of Certified Bankers; the Chartered Retirement Plans Specialist (CRPS) designation from the College for Financial Planning; the Certified Retirement Services Professional (CRSP) designation from the Institute of Certified Bankers—OK, I think you get the point. She knows her stuff.

Thanks also to John Ferguson of Baron Consulting (www.bizhub.com), our Webmaster, who created and maintains my Web site.

Thank you to Dan Sullivan and Dan Taylor at The Strategic

Coach. The "Coach" program has helped me to hone my creativity and channel my efforts in a focused direction that enables me to work on projects I believe in and love, such as this book.

Thanks to John Whelan and the rest of the crew at Thomson Media who publish and distribute my newsletter and promote me in their publications. Richard Koreto is the editor of my newsletter and works closely with me each month getting my IRA message out to our subscribers. Thomson also publishes *Financial Planning* magazine where I want to acknowledge the terrific work of Jennifer Liptow.

Without publicity you might never be reading this; so, a big thanks goes to Brian Feinblum at PTA (Planned Television Arts). PTA has directed several of my national radio tours for this book and others over the years, and has always done so professionally, making these events an enjoyable experience for me and, I hope, my audiences as well.

John McCarty is the person you and I must thank for making this book readable, interesting, and meaningful to you. He worked closely with me, and with my hectic schedule, as both collaborator and coach to get this book done not just on time, but even a few days early! Thank you, John, for the stellar job you did. Next time I'll give you more time—maybe even another whole week.

Thank you to Joy Tutela, my literary agent at the David Black Agency, for your quick reaction time and your attention to important details. Joy inherited me as a client and I'm happy it worked out that way. It is comforting to know that you are there to help me communicate my ideas. And what a perfect name you have—since you are indeed a Joy to work with.

Thank you to Jane von Mehren, associate publisher of Viking Penguin and my editor, for once again believing in me and the meaningful message of this book, and for making it become a reality. Thank you to Clare Ferraro, Nancy Sheppard, Carolyn Coleburn and Jennifer Ehmann for being supportive of this work. Thanks also to Brett Kelly, who never seems to take a day off. Whenever I call, she's there.

Thank you to Gregory Kolojeski, president of Brentmark Software, for granting me permission to reproduce the stretch IRA compounding projections created for this book with Brentmark software programs. Thanks also to Jane Schuck, Brentmark's field representative. I owe

Jane a debt of gratitude for making me an expert Brentmark user and for always being on call to help me make the examples in this book more meaningful for you, the reader. She has the patience of a saint.

Sandeep Varma is one of the world's leading insurance professionals and financial advisors. Sandeep and his San Diego financial planning firm, Advanced Trustee Strategies Inc., have been very helpful to me in promoting my IRA message and for assisting me in developing creative financial plans for my clients that offered solutions to problems that appeared to have no solution. Sandeep, you are a model of excellence for all financial advisors to follow, and I value both our business and personal friendship.

Part Three of this book shows you how to find the right financial advisor. I have taken my own advice here and would like to thank my own professional advisor, Alan J. Kahn, CPA, MBA, CLU, ChFC, of the AJK Financial Group, in Syosset, New York, and my attorney, Mark I. Rozell, Esq., CPA.

Thanks also to the wonderful team of people I work with: Margot Reilly and Michael Lichter, our office's tax pros—they make it possible for me to be out on the road spreading the word—and to our newest team member, Susan Mark, who with her great people skills makes sure our office runs smoothly. Laurin Levine is technically my assistant, but really more my partner and friend. Laurin manages everything I do and has a brilliant mind for business and making the right decisions. Laurin has an incredible natural talent for creating long-lasting relationships instantly with everyone she meets because she loves people and they love her. If you have ever spoken with her or met her, you know exactly what I mean. Give her a call and you'll see. Thank you, Laurin, for your part in every one of our successes.

My mom is an amazing person. Along with my dad, she has always supported and taken pride in all my endeavors. It was my mom's idea that I go into the accounting field when I was in high school and considering my future as a rock star. Thanks, Mom, for helping me to choose more wisely.

Ed Slott is a nationally recognized IRA expert and a highly sought-after professional speaker and consultant. He regularly educates financial professionals of all kinds—financial advisor firms, mutual fund companies, brokerage firms, insurance professionals, financial planners, trust companies, banks, CPAs, and attorneys—on IRA distribution planning and estate planning issues at seminars and workshops that he hosts at major financial industry conferences year-round all across the country. The author of the top-selling *The Retirement Savings Time Bomb . . . and How to Defuse It* (Viking Penguin, 2003), Mr. Slott hosts the Web site **www.irahelp.com,** which contains extensive IRA information for advisors and consumers. He is also the creator of The IRA Leadership Program™ (**www.iraleadership.com**), developed specifically to help financial institutions, financial advisor firms, and insurance companies become recognized leaders in the IRA marketplace. Mr. Slott writes and edits *Ed Slott's IRA Advisor™,* a monthly newsletter to help financial advisors keep current on all major IRA distribution tax strategies, laws, and IRS rulings.

Mr. Slott was dubbed "America's IRA Expert" by *Mutual Funds* magazine, was recognized by the *Wall Street Journal* for "the best advice for questions about IRAs," and was referred to as "one of the country's leading IRA experts" by *Reader's Digest.* Often quoted in *The New York Times, Newsday, The Wall Street Journal, The Washington Post, The Los Angeles Times, The Boston Globe, Time, Newsweek, Reader's Digest, Fortune, Forbes, Money, Kiplinger's Personal Finance, Kiplinger's Retirement Report, USA Today, Trusts & Estates, Research Magazine, Bloomberg Wealth Manager, Bloomberg*

Personal, Medical Economics, Investor's Business Daily, SmartMoney, and a host of additional national magazines and financial publications, Mr. Slott also appears frequently as an expert on IRA and retirement planning and distribution matters on NBC, ABC, CBS, CNBC, MSNBC, CNN, CNNfn, FOX, PBS, National Public Radio, and Bloomberg TV and radio. Mr. Slott is also a columnist and consultant for *Financial Planning, On Wall Street, Tax Hotline, Bottom Line Personal, Tax Savings Report, The Practical Accountant,* and other financial and trade publications.

Mr. Slott presents approximately 150 IRA distribution training programs and workshops nationwide each year, reaching a combined audience of more than 50,000 people (financial advisors and the general public). A partial list of Mr. Slott's clients includes: Fidelity Investments; American Express; Merrill Lynch; Nationwide Insurance; Oppenheimer Funds; Mainstay Funds; Pacific Life; AXA Advisors; Northwestern Mutual; Pioneer Funds; Jefferson Pilot; New York Life; MFS; AGN International; MetLife; John Hancock; Signator Investors, Inc.; The Principal Financial Group; Lincoln Financial; American Funds; Beneficial Life; Mass Mutual; Prudential; Royal Alliance; Sun America; Cadaret Grant; LPL; CUSO; Wachovia Securities; Morgan Stanley; Mutual Service Corp.; Main Street Management; Schwab Institutional; PNC Bank; Sun Trust; Quick & Reilly; Securities America; Security Service Network; Jackson Life National Distributors.

He addresses these professional organizations on retirement distribution issues: The New York State Society of CPAs; AICPA; National Conference of CPA Practitioners; The New York State Bar Association; Financial Planning Association; Society of Financial Service Professionals; Million Dollar Round Table; Top of the Table; NAIFA; NAPFA; and Estate Planning Councils.

"Ed, I just received flowers from Commonwealth thanking me for recommending you as a speaker and telling me what a success you were!! They said you were the best, but I expected nothing else, having heard you several times. Thanks again."
   —Marie Coyle, Commonwealth Financial Network,
   Waltham, MA

For more information on Ed Slott, *Ed Slott's IRA Advisor* newsletter or information on booking Ed Slott as a keynote speaker for your next conference or meeting, please contact:

Laurin Levine,
Event Coordinator

E. Slott & Company
100 Merrick Road
Suite 200 East
Rockville Centre, NY 11570

Toll-free: 1-800-663-1340
E-mail: laurin@irahelp.com

Or visit our Web site at www.irahelp.com. (Go to Speaker Inquiry Section.)

Now that you know how to grow your IRA into a fortune, find out how to *protect that growth*! Save your retirement plan from excessive and needless taxation with Ed Slott's *The Retirement Savings Time Bomb . . . and How To Defuse It*

Order Ed Slott's top selling *The Retirement Savings Time Bomb . . . and How To Defuse It* now at www.irahelp.com or through your local or any online bookstore.

For volume discounts for your group or organization, contact Penguin Group (USA) Inc. at (212) 366-2034.